CU00820717

St Antony's/Macmillan series

General editors Archie Brown (1978–85) and Rosema[...]
St Antony's College, Oxford

Series Standing Order

If you would like to receive future titles in this series as they
are published, you can make use of our standing order
facility. To place a standing order please contact your
bookseller or, in case of difficulty, write to us at the address
below with your name and address and the name of the
series. Please state with which title you wish to begin your
standing order. (If you live outside the UK we may not have
the rights for your area, in which case we will forward your
order to the publisher concerned.)

Standing Order Service, Macmillan Distribution Ltd,
Houndmills, Basingstoke, Hampshire, RG21 2XS, England.

Gender, Culture and Empire

European Women in Colonial Nigeria

Helen Callaway

M

MACMILLAN in association with
PRESS ST ANTONY'S COLLEGE, OXFORD

First published 1987

Published by
THE MACMILLAN PRESS LTD
Houndmills, Basingstoke, Hampshire RG21 2XS
and London
Companies and representatives
throughout the world

Typeset by Wessex Typesetters
(Division of The Eastern Press Ltd)
Frome, Somerset

**Printed and bound in Great Britain by
Anchor Brendon Ltd, Tiptree, Essex**

British Library Cataloguing in Publication Data
Callaway, Helen
Gender, culture and empire: European women in colonial Nigeria.
1. Nigeria—Politics and government—
To 1960   2. Women colonial administrators—
Nigeria—History
I. Title
325'.341'09669   JQ3092.Z13W6
ISBN 0-333-43641-5

For my mother
and in memory of my father

Hertha and George N. Lund

Contents

List of Illustrations

List of Abbreviations

ADC	Aide-de-camp
ADO	Assistant District Officer
AS	Assistant Secretary
CBE	Commander of the Order of the British Empire
CNA	Colonial Nursing Association
CDWA	Colonial Development and Welfare Act
CWEO	Chief Woman Education Officer
DC	District Commissioner
DO	District Officer
EO	Education Officer
IWM	Imperial War Museum
KCMG	Knight Commander of St. Michael and St. George
LMO	Lady Medical Officer
MBE	Member of the Order of the British Empire
MO	Medical Officer
NA	Native Authority
OBE	Officer of the Order of the British Empire
ODRP	Oxford Development Records Project
ONA	Overseas Nursing Association
PEO	Provincial Education Officer
PGS	Provincial Girls' School
PMO	Principal Medical Officer
PRO	Public Records Office
PWEO	Provincial Woman Education Officer
PWD	Public Works Department
RWAFF	Royal West African Frontier Force
REO	Rural Education Officer
RH	Rhodes House
SMO	Senior Medical Officer
WAAF	Women's Auxiliary Air Force
WAFF	West African Frontier Force
WANS	West African Nursing Staff
WAS	Woman Assistant Secretary
WEO	Woman Education Officer
WRNS	Women's Royal Naval Service
WTC	Women's Training Centre

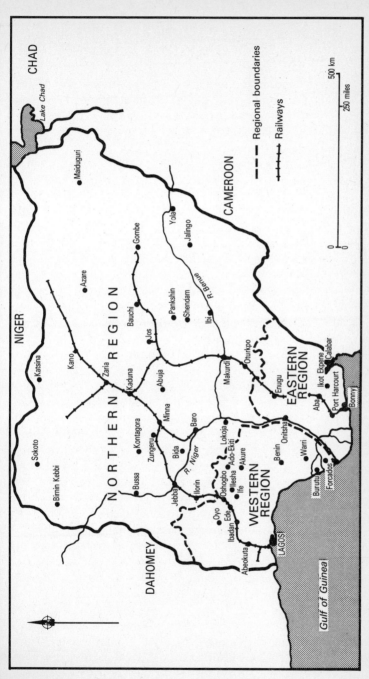

Map of Nigeria c.1955, showing principal places named

Acknowledgements

This book has evolved indirectly from the span of eleven years I spent in Nigeria, from the end of 1959 until September 1970, and the reflection this engendered on the colonial situation and on my own position as a privileged guest in a foreign land. Only recently has the notion gained currency of anthropological study directed towards the ruling group of a colonial territory rather than its indigenous peoples. While my project started with the idea of an ethnography of the European women in the historical setting of colonial Nigeria, I soon recognised that an examination of the gender roles of such a society first requires an analysis of the symbolic dimensions of power created by the specific culture of imperialism. The study thus found its direction and scope.

My first thanks are due to the many Nigerian friends who welcomed me into their midst during that splendidly flourishing period of the arts – painting, poetry, novels and plays – at the time of Independence and who entertained my numerous queries about their languages, cultures and history.

Without the memoirs and letters of many British women and men on their experiences in colonial Nigeria, this book could not have been written. I have tried to present their accounts with accuracy and fairness, although I am aware that some may hesitate to accept my interpretations. The women who agreed to be interviewed not only generously gave their time but 'colonial hospitality' as well; I am most grateful to them. In particular, I would like to thank Dr. Greta Lowe-Jellicoe, Lady Alexander, Freda Gwilliam, the Hon. Nancy Dickinson, Joy Bourdillon, Irene Fatayi-Williams, Mary Elisabeth Oake, Elizabeth Purdy, Cecily Swaisland, Joan Allen and Angela Aitchison.

To those who have given permission for quotations from unpublished (and, in some cases, restricted) material, my thanks are due: Eleanor G. Antrobus (for the use of a photograph and records from the Overseas Nursing Association), M. C. Atkinson, H. T. Bourdillon (for the late Lady Bourdillon), Margaret Burness, Evelyn Clark, John Clayton (for the late Aileen Clayton), Morag Corrie, Margery Daniels, Carol Davies, Henrietta Davies, Marjorie Davies, Mary Hargreave, Muriel Holmes, Marion Hooley, Phillis James, Carolyn Jenkins, Jeanne

Keene, Mary King, Janet Longden, Patricia MacDermot, Anne Macdonald, Masry MacGregor, Marjorie Pears, Christine Prince, Lady Sharwood Smith, Phyllis Treitel, A. H. T. Trevor (for the late Jean Trevor), Pat Walters, Jill Whitfield, Anne Wren and Sheelagh Wrench. I would also like to thank the few others who could not be reached whose permission I sought for the use of quotations and the many whose records proved enriching but were not cited in these pages for lack of space. Rhodes House, with the facilities of the Bodleian Library, supplied the illustrations for the use of which Elizabeth Paterson and Kathleen Player have kindly given their permission.

The Oxford Development Records Project provided central documentation for this work; my thanks to its Director, Anthony Kirk-Greene, and also to Ingrid Thomas, Alison Smith and Mary Bull for their friendly co-operation. The Librarian of Rhodes House, Alan Bell, and the staff have been invariably helpful. I am also much indebted to Bob Townsend, Librarian of the Institute of Commonwealth Studies, for assistance on many obscure details as well as routine matters. June Anderson, Librarian of the Institute of Social Anthropology, has supplied many books at opportune moments. Charles Allen offered the use of the tapes and transcripts of his interviews for his BBC programme and book, *Tales from the Dark Continent*. I am grateful to him and to the staff of the Imperial War Museum for making these available. Kenneth Robinson kindly sent me an unpublished lecture and made useful critical notes on part of a chapter.

My intellectual and institutional debts stretch over many years: to mentors and colleagues at the Institute of Social Anthropology, Somerville College, St. Antony's College and Queen Elizabeth House. The Oxford University seminar on African affairs, convened by Professor Kenneth Kirkwood and Anthony Kirk-Greene, has been important in sustaining links with those who come from Africa as well as those with scholarly interests there. Since its initial meeting in 1973, the Thursday seminar on the social anthropology of women has provided a lively forum. In more recent years, I have benefited from the intellectual resources and support of the Centre for Cross-Cultural Research on Women, Queen Elizabeth House; my thanks to its Director, Shirley Ardener, Members and Visiting Fellows. In particular, the workship convened by Hilary Callan and Shirley Ardener resulting in their collection, *The Incorporated Wife* (1984), gave insights and stimulus for my study.

Numerous friends and colleagues, too many to name, have given encouragement and ideas for this book. With Janice Brownfoot, whose paper on European women in colonial Malaya sparked my interest in this topic, I have enjoyed many hours of fruitful talk on problems and sources. Hilary Callan, Julie Marcus and Lidia Sciama each gave critical advice on specific chapters. Alison Callaway, Tom Forrest, Renée Hirschon, Patricia Knapp, and Constance Sutton have all given significant help in various ways. Valuable suggestions for turning the thesis into a book were made by Sally Chilver and Elizabeth Tonkin. The successive editors of the St. Antony's/Macmillan Series, Archie Brown and Rosemary Thorp, have given their time and support to this publication. Susan Dickinson at Macmillan eased the production process with her flexibility and efficiency. And during a crowded Christmas season, Stephen and Matthew Callaway diligently read proofs and helped with the index.

My greatest debt, and most abundant gratitude, I owe to the supervisors of the thesis on which this book is based: Anthony Kirk-Greene has drawn from his immense historical and personal understanding of colonial Nigeria to give direction and generous help at every stage of this project; Edwin Ardener has continued to guide my anthropological analysis in this as well as previous work.

My husband and family shared the rich experience of living in Nigeria and, in the background, the making of this book. I warmly encourage their innovative ideas and varied enterprises, as they have so strongly supported mine. My dedication is for my parents, whose caring generosity has been with me all these years.

Part One

Imperial Culture in Nigeria

The meaning of history, at least such as it is deciphered by the actors themselves, comes through the important events and men. The 'least' are those who are not captured within this meaning of history. But there is another meaning that reassembles all the minute encounters left unaccounted for by the history of the greats; there is another history, a history of acts, events, personal compassions, woven into the history of structures, advents, and institutions. But this meaning and this history are hidden.

(Paul Ricoeur, *History and Truth*, 1965, p. 100)

1 Women in 'A Man's Country'

It's a well-known saying that the women lost us the Empire. It's true.

(Sir David Lean, 1985)[1]

BLAMING THE WOMEN

Although today our post-colonial generation condemns the Empire as a particularly aggressive and exploitative phase of Western expansion, successive rewritings have hardly diminished the 'history of the greats' and its male figures are still on occasion called forth to personify an intensified masculine image of courage, fortitude and heroic action. Women of the Empire, in contrast, are all too often reincarnated as representations of the worst side of the ruling group – its racism, petty snobbishness and pervading aura of superiority. In men's memoirs of the colonial period European women appear, if at all, as nameless figures in the background, while in widely-read anti-colonial novels (those of E. M. Forster and George Orwell, for example) women in the colonies are shown as shallow, self-centred and preoccupied with maintaining the hierarchy of their narrow social worlds. Popular lore as well portrays these women in sordid competition over trivial signs of social status; sociological studies cite them as the cause of deteriorating race relations between the rulers and their subject peoples.

In such ways, then, the successive reconstructions of the colonial record have either left women out altogether or presented them in a negative role. Yet when women's documents – memoirs, letters and professional reports – of their daily lives and work in a colony are searched for, collected and read as a corpus, they reveal complexity and personal compassions, the stories of women attempting to give meaning and connection to their lives in a foreign world where they often felt themselves to be doubly alien.[2] These documents tell of their involvement in various ways with indigenous women; in particular, the reports of women education officers show strong commitment to the educational advancement of Nigerian girls and women in the face of general bureaucratic neglect.

As an anthropologist, my concern has been not with the history of a colonial group or subgroup as such, but with the relatively new field of imperial culture (for example, Beidelman, 1982; Hobsbawm and Ranger, 1983; Ranger, 1980). My study takes up the problem of this discrepancy between the dominant culture's images of colonial women and women's presentation of their own reality by examining their diverse perceptions and encounters in the specific context of colonial Nigeria. The analysis of gender relations within this imperial culture shows the restrictions on women's lives, as wives dependent on their husbands' rank, as professional women in subordinate positions. At the same time, the study brings out women's initiatives in going beyond the constraints of the colonial hierarchy to reach across racial boundaries in their professional and voluntary work and in social life. In this particular case, at least, women of the Empire appear in a different light.

But why then have these women's lives so often been distorted, misrepresented, seen as caricature? Why has the blame for the arrogance and excesses of Empire fallen so heavily on European women? This project, which begins with the study of women's 'real' lives within a particular social formation, must be extended to an examination of the historical processes and cultural productions which invent and reinvent the images of these women through time.

'NO PLACE FOR A WHITE WOMAN'

Nigeria represented for British colonial officers in Africa an example, perhaps the prime example, of 'a man's country'.[3] This concept had meanings at different levels, the most obvious being the 'man's job' to be done. At the turn of the century, the conquering soldiers and visionary empire-builders of these vast, roadless, not yet fully mapped territories had to be men, not boys, and certainly not women. Living conditions were rough, extreme physical exertion was called for. Besides the fighting still going on, risks to health from tropical diseases were high. One in five of the

European population in Northern Nigeria either died or was invalided home every year.[4] Conditions for living remained generally difficult, with the qualified exception of a few main cities, until after the Second World War. Even at the end of the colonial period in 1960, officers in many posts had no electricity, no running water, no access to medical care, no telephone and infrequent mail service.

From a woman's perspective, Mrs Horace Tremlett, who accompanied her mining engineer husband to Nigeria before the First World War, describes her situation:

> I often found myself reflecting rather bitterly on the insignificant position of a woman in what is practically a man's country . . . If there is one spot on earth where a woman feels of no importance whatever, it is in Nigeria at the present day. She is frankly there on sufferance.   (1915, p. 280)

Sir Rex Niven writes that when he brought his bride to Nigeria in 1925 the Resident in Lokoja greeted her, 'Mrs. Niven, this is no place for a white woman' (1982, p. 62). In the eleven months she stayed in Kabba, he relates, she met only seven white people and none of them a woman. In 1928, Mary Elisabeth Oake went with her husband to the British Cameroons, then administered as an extension of Nigeria, and found herself the only European woman in the station. She writes, 'My host, one of the kindest I have ever known, confessed to me that he considered women out of place in West Africa' (1933, p. 11). The sense of alienation never really left her in Buea; she entitled her memoirs *No Place for a White Woman* (1933). Noël Rowling, in turn, took up this title for the first chapter of her recollections of twenty-one years in Nigeria (1982).

These writers indirectly point to the ambivalence of this phrase. Its literal meaning is clear enough: the tough conditions of colonial life in Nigeria during the early years. But it also suggests tacit knowledge of the Colonial Service marking European women as 'out of place' in men's exclusive territory. In her well-known analysis of social structure and the fear of disorder, Mary Douglas (1966) shows how this classification – 'out of place' – takes on strong symbolic overtones of pollution and danger.

Formed for the purpose of governing subject peoples, the Colonial Service was a male institution in all its aspects: its 'masculine' ideology, its military organisation and processes, its rituals of power and hierarchy, its strong boundaries between the sexes. It would have been 'unthinkable' in the belief system of the time even to consider the part women might play, other than as nursing sisters, who had earlier become recognised for their important 'feminine' work overseas under the direction of Florence Nightingale. At a more submerged level, the Nigerian hinterland was projected as an area of 'men's wilds' (see E. Ardener, 1972). Here young men went through ordeals (real enough) carrying out the archetypal mission, in this way achieving full masculinity – as in the schoolboy novels of Thomas Hughes – by separation from women.

British women, however, did take part in this scene, a very few at first in relation to the male population, later proportionately more. They were seen not so much as subordinates, a situation taken for granted, but (in the beginning, at least) as unwelcome appendages. They came in various capacities: as nursing sisters and dependent wives (the largest number), then as education officers, doctors, secretaries, welfare workers and, in the last stage of colonial rule, as junior administrative officers. These women took on new roles for themselves and, as a group, supported the colonial enterprise with their various services, both to the colonial group itself and (of greater significance) to the wider Nigerian society.

Some of these European women spent many years in Nigeria, Sylvia Leith-Ross being the foremost example; she returned many times over the sixty years from her first journey in 1907 to her last visit in 1968. During the early period, only a few wives had the opportunity to go to Nigeria, although their husbands were away for a year or more at a time. The required permission was granted only in special circumstances, for wives of high-ranking officials or those in stations where housing was available for married officers. Joyce Cary's wife, for example, was not allowed to join him in Borgu; their long separations provided the impetus for his daily letters which give an intimate and witty account of his duties as a colonial officer at the time of the First World War.[5]

Here a linguistic note might be inserted. These women in their talk and writings refer to themselves mainly as 'Europeans', a self-designation which entered the British colonial lexicon at an earlier stage in India (King, 1976, p. 63) and continued in Nigeria where it was used in opposition to 'African' or 'Native'. As is common practice in ethnographies, I shall use the self-defining terms of the group under study. Near the end of colonial rule, it should be added, the terms appropriately changed their primacy of reference to 'Nigerian' and 'expatriate'.

In the colonial record itself, Nigeria has remained 'a man's country'. Such exceptional European women as Mary Slessor and Mary Kingsley have been cited, but they have featured as outstanding individuals, even as heroines in a symbolic inversion of the prescribed place of women elevating them to 'honorary men'. Through their travels and their unusual self-appointed tasks, they claimed autonomy for themselves, rather than remaining 'relative creatures' (Basch, 1974) identified through men as daughters, wives, or mothers. They stepped outside the category of 'women' as this was defined in the Victorian system of ideas and retained in that predominantly Victorian institution, the Colonial Service.

Two other women held prominent positions in relation to colonial Nigeria: Flora Shaw (Lady Lugard), who coined the name of this future nation, and Margery Perham, 'the *guru* of colonial administrators' (Kirk-Greene, 1982, p. 129). Flora Shaw became the foremost writer on colonial affairs during the 1890s as Colonial Editor of *The Times*; the proposal for the name 'Nigeria' appeared in 1897 in an unsigned article in that newspaper attributed to her (Kirk-Greene, 1956, p. 1035; Perham, 1960, p. 11). Later, as Lady Lugard, she became an influential figure behind the scenes of Nigerian colonial rule during her husband's terms of high office. In her turn, Margery Perham travelled throughout Nigeria during 1931–2 to examine the structures and processes of colonial governing. As a result, she published her first academic book (1937), which launched her career as 'an authority on colonial administration in general and Nigeria's administrative history in particular' (Kirk-Greene, 1983, p. 7). Both women gained high honours: Lady Lugard the title of Dame of the British Empire and Margery Perham recognition as Dame in the 'predominantly Colonial Service order of chivalry' (p. 12), that of St. Michael and St. George.[6]

Other European women who came to Nigeria have remained nameless and unrecorded, 'left unaccounted for by the history of the greats'. For a wider social history of imperial rule, some recognition of these women is clearly necessary.[7] Yet, from the anthropologist's view, it is not merely an extra chapter that is required, providing additional 'data', as it were; rather, different theoretical aims are called for, ones which examine women's experience and their self-definitions within the context of the power relations and gender constructions of imperial culture.

THE ETHNOGRAPHY OF A COLONIAL GROUP

The specific group of women in my study are those associated with the Colonial Service, either as officers or dependent wives. Other European women came to Nigeria as missionaries or as wives of missionaries, as explorer-travellers and anthropologists, as wives of miners and men in commerce, and in the late stage of colonial rule as wives of Nigerians who had been students in Britain. While all were 'European women in Nigeria', there were clearly wide variations among them in their objectives, their material circumstances, their personal experience, as well as the ways their social relations with other Europeans and Nigerians were structured. These other groups will be cited for comparative purposes, but my focus remains on the European women incorporated within the institution of the Colonial Service.

For the anthropology of women, this study presents an unusual case. The Colonial Service in Nigeria (as in other colonial areas) engendered a particular culture shaped by imperial purpose and male prestige structures. This was a society formed by a select group of men – young adults and those in their prime. Although European women were allowed to join this society, they were not involved in its formation nor were they – and this is a crucial factor – essential to its structure: the physiological and social reproduction of the society took place in the homeland; in Nigeria, male clerks carried out the office and secretarial duties, male servants did the domestic work for colonial officers, and indigenous women were available as sexual partners.

Important, then, to the self-definitions of these colonial women, as well as the images of them in the writings of others, was the fact that they were explicitly and implicitly placed in a separate, marginal sphere: devalued as a category, although exceptions were made for individuals. The women who served as officers (nursing, education, medical, social welfare) belonged to subsidiary branches or had jobs in the lower ranks; at no time were they perceived as other than assistants. For professional women, it seemed a compliment to be seen as *not* a woman. Mary King (née Beaton) writes of her reception in Lagos in 1953 as one of the first women administrative officers, 'After the initial stage when some of my colleagues were surprised, amused, even disconcerted to find a female in their midst, I felt accepted and treated on merit as an "assistant secretary", not as "a woman" ' (King, Ms., p. 7). The two categories were assumed to be incompatible. The Colonial Service in Nigeria considered itself to be a men's institution, doing a job requiring 'masculine' capacities. Women were perceived as an addition – in some ways helpful, perhaps an unnecessary luxury and distraction, often a burden, possibly a danger.

The time period of this ethnography is not that of the usual anthropological fieldwork, the familiar 'ethnographic present' (often presented as timeless), but rather a fixed period of historically-structured time, from 1900 to 1960. This is significant: women's experience is woven into the texture of more general historical change. The early years of conquest and 'pacification' were followed by a period of colonial enterprise establishing the structures of government, building the railway line of communication from Lagos to Kano, and exploiting agricultural and mineral resources; the interwar years reflected the worldwide depression in a general slowing down. The Second World War ruptured this more or less continuous change. Before that, colonial rule operated on the assumption that it would extend indefinitely, as Sir Kenneth Blackburne writes of the attitude of the 1930s, 'The Empire would go on for ever' (1976, p. xiv); this was based on the idea of benefiting both the homeland and the colony – Lugard's famous 'dual mandate' (Lugard, 1922). After the Second World War, this premise was questioned on numerous fronts and a series of negotiations led to the 'transfer of power' and Nigerian Independence. Imperial culture went through a sudden transformation; its rules changed. Two separate periods might thus be discerned, as two 'more or less disconnected, discontinuous and yet overlapping semantic spaces', as Kirsten Hastrup has perceptively set out in another context (1982, p. 155).

In terms of geographical space, as well, this ethnography does not match the classic anthropological model of a face-to-face group. These women lived and worked in different areas of Nigeria. They found themselves in the traditional cities of Kano or Ibadan, or the bustling commercial ports of Lagos or Port Harcourt, or the newly established administrative centres of

Kaduna and Enugu. Others spent their entire time in rural outposts. They lived among different ethnic groups in Nigeria with varying degrees of interaction with local people. Some women learned local languages, sympathetically observed and recorded local ceremonies and customs, started baby clinics or initiated other voluntary ways to be of service to the wider community. At the other extreme were those who turned inward to the European society, engaging their energies in reproducing the social milieu of the homeland. These are the ones, it would seem, who have provided the negative stereotypes of the 'memsahib' (see Brownfoot, 1984).

Given such diversity of activities and experience, how can these European women in colonial Nigeria be designated as a social group? They shared the 'signifying system' of their home culture and social class – its language, values, symbolic structures, sacred and secular rituals, hidden meanings, reference points. And in Nigeria they learned the new social prescriptions that upheld the power relations of this specific imperial culture. Although they were separated from each other in both time and space, and present a polyphony of voices, they all took part in a continuing moral pageant with its implicit ordering of the social world.

Mary Douglas discusses the complex relations of unwritten social rules, individual consciousness, and the construction of social reality:

> How the moral order is known – how the inner experience of morality is related to the moral order without – this depends on hidden processes. Each person confronted with a system of ends and means (not necessarily a tidy and coherent system) seems to face the order of nature, objective and independent of human wishes. But the moral order and the knowledge which sustains it are created by social conventions. If their man-made origins were not hidden, they would be stripped of some of their authority. Therefore the conventions are not merely tacit, but extremely inaccessible to investigation.   (1973, p. 15)

It is unlikely that Douglas used 'man-made origins' to mean male origins, but this would be particularly apt in relation to the structures of power and communication of the imperial ruling group.

The question might be asked whether professional women of the Colonial Service should be considered in the same study as dependent wives, since they held different positions in the colonial social structure. My reason for bringing both groups into this analysis is that in 'real life' career women often married colonial officers, sometimes continuing their work on a contract basis; in at least one case a colonial wife, whose husband died, subsequently took up varied work with the Colonial Service in Nigeria. While the two categories are distinct, individual women often belonged to one and then the other, or both at the same time. Moreover, both groups were committed to the same social order and held the same set of generative principles for dealing with daily living.

In the classification system of the Colonial Service, the boundaries were more strongly drawn between male and female than between officers and dependants. The Corona Club typifies the exclusion of women (both women officers and wives) from the male domain, from men's recreation as well as from men's work. Founded in 1901 by Joseph Chamberlain when he was Colonial Secretary, this club organised an annual dinner in London for the 300 or 400 men of the Colonial Service on leave or retired. Kirk-Greene describes, 'The head table on those dining evenings was indeed a sight to behold, a night to remember. Begartered and bemedaled, festooned with colorful decorations, here were the British colonial governors in all their dazzling splendor' (1978, p. 240).

In 1937, the Women's Corona Club was established for women members of the Service and wives (Macdonald, Ms. [b]). Besides its own annual dinner in London, this second club set up local branches in many countries and developed various lines of welfare work. In Nigeria this became an active multiracial group, its work to be noted later. The point here is that the dividing line of the Corona Club was sustained between male and female spheres even when professional women were admitted as administrative officers in the Colonial Service. While the joining of the two groups for the annual dinner was considered at various times, the tradition continued of the separation between the sexes. Only recently, wives and daughters of male officers have been invited for drinks before dinner, but invitations were not extended to women officers (Elizabeth O'Kelly, personal communication, 1984). The Victorian principles of the male Corona Club's foundation have thus been reinforced, giving priority to women as 'relative creatures' and excluding the autonomous women officers.

THE COLONIAL SERVICE: A MALE ELITE

In answer to the question, 'Why study the Colonial Service?', Heussler argued that the colonial mode of government was, during the first half of the twentieth century, 'one of the most significant systems whereby power was exercised by men over men'. He continues:

> Colonial administrators have not been civil servants in the usual sense, that is servants of elected or appointed Governments whose higher officers hold the lion's share of whatever power there is to be exercised. They themselves *were* the Government. Spread thinly over the ground, relying on their wits, personalities and physical stamina, they have embodied in their own persons virtually all the stuff and substance of rule.   (1961, pp. 165–6)

This quotation presents clearly the idea of the *embodiment* of power and responsibility in the male administrative cadres.

Particularly during the early years, the colonial literature sets out the vision of the young administrator in the colonies with the power to take decisive action for bringing dramatic improvements. Even as late as 1940, Lord Lloyd, then Colonial Secretary, had this to say to a group of young officers about to take up appointments in various colonies:

> You are not going to have a soft job. You will indeed have plenty of hard work and not too many of the comforts of life, and quite possibly no lack of danger, but I know you would not have it otherwise . . . In what other task can you have so much power so early? You can at the age of twenty-five be the father of your people: you can drive the road, bridge the river, and water the desert; you can be the arm of justice and hand of mercy to millions. You can, in fact, serve England.   (quoted in Jeffries, 1949, p. 19)

This talk, given during the dark months of the Second World War, echoes Kipling in its emphasis on 'power' and 'service'. The concept of 'service', central to the belief system of the Colonial Service, usually relates to the particular colony; here, at a time of national emergency, the note of patriotism became dominant.

The Colonial Service as a bureaucracy must be separated from the wider question of the economic exploitation of the colonies. In certain cases, colonial officers opposed the commercial interests of their own countrymen, although in the main the administrative and the commercial were seen as parallel lines of development. Its purpose in the official discourse was seen as a 'mission' – in the beginning for pacification, the end of internal slavery and the bringing of civilisation; later for development and social welfare. The Colonial Service consisted of 'men who regarded colonialism as a venture in applied philanthropy – not as an enterprise designed to maximise metropolitan profits' (Gann and Duignan, 1978, p. 51).

Writing of his experience as a district officer, Kenneth Bradley tells of his ancestry for 400 years of 'dons, parsons or schoolmasters' and considers this typical of most of his colleagues (1966, p. 6). Rewards for those in the Colonial Service came in terms of the prestige structures of the British middle class: duties requiring initiative and leadership at a young age, the opportunity to take part in what was seen as a beneficial (even altruistic) enterprise abroad, the possibility of reaching positions of high responsibility and status and, for the few, the recognition of a knighthood. Those who were ambitious predicted the timing of their accolades. For example, when awarded the honour of KCMG, Sir Hesketh Bell (Governor of Northern Nigeria from 1909 to 1912) wrote in his diary: 'I am, of course, very pleased, but in the "forecast" of my official career which I made in this diary in 1896, I put down 1905 as the year in which I would get my K. I am therefore three years late' (1946, p. 182).

In the analysis of how the Colonial Service patterned the gender relations between men and women who were attached to it, the details of administration and the political aspects of colonial rule are not relevant, other than to note that through the system known as 'indirect rule',[8] only a few hundred colonial officers supervised the governing of millions of Africans. Kirk-Greene (1980) provides data on the number of administrators in Nigeria (Table 1.1).

This tabulation does not include those officers in the specialised branches of medicine, education, agriculture, public works and the like, nor does it include officers of the police and the military. The distribution of Colonial Service posts in Nigeria in 1926 shows a total of 2226 European staff. In his discussion of the relatively small size of the Colonial Service in British Africa, Kirk-Greene attributes the strength of what he has called this

Table 1.1   Colonial officers in Nigeria, 1920–50

	1920	*1925*	*1930*	*1935*	*1940*	*1945*	*1950*
Senior Residents	10	10	10	9	10	11	10
Residents	30	29	29	21	21	28	24
Senior DOs	—	—	—	—	18	25	53
DOs/ADOs	291	294	392	333	364	337	448
Total	331	333	431	363	413	421	515

Source: Kirk-Greene, 'The Thin White Line: The Size of the British Civil Service in Africa', *African Affairs*, vol 79 (1980), no. 314, pp. 25–44.

'thin white line' to the assistance of subordinate African staff, as well as to the confidence and competence of these administrators.

This male ruling group was assumed to be superior, in India known as the 'heaven born', its officers being specially selected for their leadership qualities ideally developed (though not always in practice) through education in favoured public schools, followed by military training or university education at Oxford or Cambridge. The Colonial Service can be viewed as another male institution in the separate sex arrangements of the British middle class of that time – beginning with preparatory schools, continuing through public schools, and then in military establishments or the men's colleges of Oxford and Cambridge, and extending through adulthood (even to senility) in the London clubs.

But women did join the specialised branches and, eventually, the administrative cadre of the Colonial Service. Jeffries provides the statistics on women with appointments in the Colonial Service during the years 1922 to 1943: 'In this period 83 women were recruited for educational posts, 72 for medical posts, and 8 for "miscellaneous" posts, but no fewer than 2189 were recruited as nursing sisters' (1949, p. 152). Throughout the colonial period women were a 'marked' category in the sense that they were officially designated in the interwar years by the terms 'Lady Superintendent of Education', 'Mistress' and 'Lady Medical Officer'; after the war (less chivalrously) as 'Woman Education Officer' and 'Woman Assistant Secretary'.

Women were excluded for many years from the administrative branch of the Colonial Service. As a result of the Sex

Disqualification (Removal) Act in 1919, women became eligible for employment in the administrative grades of the home Civil Service and were appointed on the basis of open examinations. In 1921, however, an Order in Council was passed 'to reserve to men any branch of or posts in the Civil Service in any of His Majesty's possessions overseas or in any foreign country' (Adam, 1975, pp. 99–100). It was only in 1944, with the extreme shortage of 'manpower' during the war, that women were offered administrative posts in the Colonial Service; these appointments were explicitly stated to be 'experimental' with employment by temporary contract.

The first two women administrative officers went to The Gambia in 1944. During the years between 1953 and 1957, about 25 women were recruited to serve in this capacity in Nigeria, mainly in Lagos and Kaduna. While men administrative officers were taken on as cadets and then (after passing law and language examinations and with approval) confirmed in the permanent and pensionable establishment of the Colonial Service, women were appointed on contract for an initial tour lasting from 18 to 24 months, with renewal on the same short-term basis. Their official documents referred to them as 'temporary Woman Assistant Secretary'. While their male cohorts were sent to the districts, they served in junior positions in the offices of the Secretariats (again, 'women's work'); they had to resign on marriage; and in only a few cases were European women in a superordinate position to European men.

It is not surprising that these women administrative officers did not perceive themselves to be full members of the Colonial Service, nor that scholars such as Heussler in his well-known study of *Yesterday's Rulers* (1963) should overlook these junior women administrators who appeared on the scene towards the end of the colonial rule. Although the Colonial Service did take women in its specialised branches and eventually as junior administrative officers, it established and sustains its identity as male. Strong ideological boundaries protect its 'masculinity', more so in that it represents a 'lost masculine world' similar to the frontier experience of Australia, New Zealand and America. Its nostalgic celebration of masculine ethos recurs in individual memoirs and in cultural myths.

IMPERIAL RULE AS 'TOTAL INSTITUTION'

Besides its entrenched ideas on 'women's work' and its incompatibility with family life, the British Colonial Service had other features which contributed to constraints on women, and men as well, not experienced by those who stayed at home. With its origins in military experience overseas, the Colonial Service retained this disciplined authoritarian organisation as the means for its rule over large populations and vast territories. Although not made explicit in those terms, the Colonial Service had developed over a long professional tradition both formal regulations and unwritten conventions which in its own belief system upheld its prestige in relation to the subordinate group.

The frequent production of ceremonial displays of power and authority made visible not only the pre-eminence of colonial rulers but served as well to reinforce the positions of traditional emirs and chiefs. If 'indirect rule' provided the main administrative device for gaining the assent of the Nigerian peoples, this was augmented by powerful symbolic pageantry – the daily official rituals such as flag-raising, the welcomes and farewells of dignitaries, gun salutes for high-ranking officers, Empire Day parades, colourful mass performances in durbars – as a means of incorporating the indigenous peoples of Nigeria into the British Empire.

For colonial officers, all aspects of work and living in Nigeria were conducted under the authority of the Colonial Service, a characteristic noted by Goffman (1968, pp. 13–116) as central to a 'total institution'.[9] In a 'normal' bureaucracy, Goffman notes, only the specific work duties of the employee come under the authority of the employer, leisure and private life being carried out in the company of different groups of people and in separate domains. But when they were in Nigeria, colonial officers had all their arrangements – work schedules, postings (both location and frequency of change), travel within the country, timing for leave, accommodation and furnishings, ceremonial duties, requirements for uniform, entertaining and hospitality obligations – under the authority of the Colonial Service. In actual practice, of course, individual officers had a great deal of leeway and personal responsibility, but nevertheless for the whole of each tour in Nigeria they were identified at all times as colonial officers, not as private persons.

Work and life as a colonial officer were inseparable. In the words of Richard Oakley, who went to Northern Nigeria in 1921:

> The plain truth is that a Political Officer's job is his life in whatever country it may be his good fortune to be placed, and his life is his work. . . . From the moment that he lands from his ship to the moment when he goes aboard again to proceed on leave, he is on duty all the time. (1938, p. 8)

John Smith, serving during the last decade of colonial rule, writes in the same vein, 'The job, which we lived for twenty-four hours in every day and never tired of talking about' (1968, p. 107).

Work thus tended to carry over into sports and other leisure activities with no clear lines of demarcation. Colleagues at work became fellow players at polo or tennis, fellow guests at a formal dinner party, and convivial company for 'shop talk' at the club. Often there was little spatial separation between professional and private life, the European cantonment or 'reservation' enclosing both offices and housing and set in an area apart from African habitations. This aspect called not only for the officer's public commitment to his work, common after all in most professional life, but in this case a greater degree of conformity in private life.

Both work and social life were conducted according to the formal procedures of the imperial tradition. These written regulations and tacit conventions carried over from professional duties into the etiquette of social life, forming a continuum. Thus dinner parties were usually formal occasions with entry into the dining room and seating arrangements carried out according to strict precedence. For certain reasons (to be more fully analysed later), the formalities and subtle distinctions of social life were not only more intricate and inflexible than in social circles back in the homeland but they were also carried on in a kind of time warp long after they had gone out of date in England.[10]

Similar to military institutions, orders were sent down from above with no consultation of the officers concerned and little consideration given to personal inconvenience. The sudden change of postings was perhaps the most irksome feature; officers could not make plans in advance with any certainty. The most outspoken criticism of this 'capricious system of postings', as well as many other aspects of colonial administration, comes in the published diary of the years 1933–4 kept by W. R. Crocker in Northern Nigeria,

Through this chopping and changing, I had only just got settled down in Abinsi and was just learning enough of the Area to become useful when I was sent off to Katsina Ala, to be relieved in less than two months by the very man who relieved me at Abinsi.   (1936, p. 63)

He adds, 'If questioned, of course, such inefficient posting would as usual be ascribed to the "exigencies of the service" (a hallowed phrase in the mouth of our seniors).'

Another institutional procedure was that all officers were subjected to confidential reports by superiors on their general conduct as well as their professional work. Crocker writes of the secret personal report as 'the most vicious single factor behind the demoralisation of the Service' (p. 244). Senior officers had the power of making accusations, of which the accused would never be told, let alone be given an opportunity to defend himself. Mercedes Mackay, wife of a geologist with the Mines Department, tells of an instance that could have had a damaging effect on her husband's career. By accident they found out that the former head of the department had written a report 'not only untrue, but absolutely scurrilous ' (Ms. p. 31).

WOMEN AS 'INTRUDERS'

At the beginning of the colonial period only very senior officials brought their wives to Nigeria, and then with deep concern about their health. A letter in 1899 from Sir William MacGregor, Governor of Lagos, tells of his worry:

I am very solitary, tristissimo, alone. My wife and daughter came out here for about three months, but the risk was too great, and I felt immense relief when I got them both away alive. They left nearly a month ago, and I have heard nothing of them since, so that I am not yet free of anxiety for our fever frequently kills between Lagos and Liverpool. (quoted in Joyce, 1971, p. 226)

While in the neighbouring French and German colonies relatively more officers brought their wives during these early years with their fares defrayed by their governments (see Talbot, 1968, pp. 240–1), the British Colonial Office did not encourage the presence of wives. Confidential correspondence between Lugard and the Colonial Office in 1904 shows its objections on several grounds: the fact that most officers were required to travel extensively, the cost of building suitable accommodations and the unsatisfactory health conditions (PRO/CO 446/39).

In the semi-mythical beginnings of colonial rule in Nigeria, according to the 'folk model', the hardened 'Old Coaster' often objected to white women as such. 'He regarded them as intruders into what had been essentially a bachelor's paradise, where a man could dress as he pleased, drink as much as he liked, and be easy in his morals without causing scandal,' writes Sir Alan Burns (1949, p. 42), who came to Nigeria in 1912 and later served as Governor of the Gold Coast. But there were other reasons as well, in his account: wives were often considered a 'nuisance' in West Africa because husbands were reluctant to take them travelling in difficult country and equally reluctant to leave them behind; a wife's illness upset her husband; and sometimes a wife quarrelled with officers or their wives, a disastrous situation in a small community. Burns concludes, however, that even with these difficulties the official view (at a later date) considered it desirable that married officers should be accompanied by their wives.

> The officer who has his wife with him (unless she is entirely unsuitable as a wife) lives a better and happier life, and eats better food, than he can possibly do as a grass-widower. I attribute my own good health, after so many years' service in West Africa, to the fact that my wife was with me nearly every tour.

The presence of wives was thus justified as *instrumental* to the better health of men.[11]

By 1920 the Colonial Office held that married life should be the rule rather than the exception in the Crown colonies and Protectorates (Lugard, 1922, p. 142). But difficulties apparently were still discerned in Nigeria, as a brief article in *West Africa* brings out after posing the question: 'When an advertisement appears calling for men for appointment to West Africa, it is often announced that "preference will be given to unmarried candidates". Why?' (26 December 1925, p. 1737). This and the ensuing correspondence (2 January 1926, p. 1775) emphasise the improved domestic standards and the congenial companionship of white women, while noting the disadvantages of the

unfavourable climate, the sudden transfers, and the lack of things
for the wife to do while the officer carried out his duties. Even in
1939, when M. C. Atkinson arrived in Western Nigeria, the
situation had not changed very much:

> White society was almost exclusively male. The only white
> women were Nursing Sisters and a small number of wives. My
> guess is that fewer than a third of married men had their wives
> with them at any given time and it was still necessary for junior
> officers to obtain permission to bring out their wives.   (Ms.,
> p. 108)

An old British Army adage states, 'Lieutenants can't marry,
captains may marry, majors should marry, colonels must marry'
(Gann and Duignan, 1978, p. 113). These unwritten regulations
were transferred to the Colonial Service at roughly the same
grades: 'ADOs must not marry, DOs are better unmarried, a
Resident   is   better   married'   (Kirk-Greene,   personal
communication). Cadets were not allowed to marry, as Stanhope
White explains, 'We had signed contracts as cadets which bound
us not to get married for three years, so that we could serve in
stations where no white woman could live' (White, 1966, p. 14).
This regulation was relaxed only after the Second World War
when a number of married officers were recruited.

The administration of Nigeria was carried out on a stringent
allocation of funds based on revenues. After the First World War,
Sir Hugh Clifford (who replaced Lord Lugard) found on his first
tour of the country that problems had been mounting up, as I. F.
Nicolson writes:

> the main, insistent grouse of the disgruntled service – placed
> ahead of the shocking housing conditions, the frequent
> postings, the under-staffing and overwork, the stagnant
> promotion, the prolonged tours, and all the rest – was the fact
> that few married officers could live on their pay, even with the
> most stringent economy'.   (1969, p. 224)

Despite myths of luxurious living in the tropics, the Colonial
Service offered little monetary incentive for its lower ranks. Only
in the very top positions were salaries comparatively high.

Passages to Nigeria for wives were not paid until 1919,
following Clifford's review, when tours were lengthened from
twelve to eighteen months. Between the wars, some wives joined

their husbands for six months or so, but no children were allowed to come to Nigeria. Pregnant women were sent home well in advance of their expected delivery. In his memoirs Sir Rex Niven tells the story of one woman in 1928 who gained fame through what he calls her 'maternal indiscretion':

> She kept her pregnancy very secret and in the end even the doctor was taken by surprise. The story was that the baby was delivered on the doctor's breakfast table. There was only a tiny African hospital in Bauchi and no nursing sister, and the M.O. had to do all the work: he was not pleased. She was sent home as soon as she could move.   (1982, p. 84)

Under such circumstances, wives in Nigeria had to be childless or separated from their children.

Only after the Second World War were children permitted to come to Nigeria, and even then the attitude of the senior generation was grudging. Ian Brook tells that a Resident upbraided him as a junior officer because he had not provided the information that his wife, soon to arrive with their two children, was pregnant. When she went into the tiny station hospital for the birth, the Resident phoned Brook to inquire about her. He concluded. 'Good, I hope it is clearly understood that her condition is not allowed to interfere with your duties' (1966, p. 95). No concessions were made to families in regard to accommodation. On another tour, when his children were still very young, Brook was assigned to a bungalow which stood at the edge of an escarpment. He notes, 'The children were, in any case, in Nigeria only on sufferance. No consideration was given to them; the service had to come first' (1966, p. 152). Officials in Northern Nigeria appear to have been even less hospitable to wives and children. John Smith writes of 1950:

> I was told the story of the cadet who had been unwise enough to arrive the previous year with a wife, and worse still, two children. When sent on tour he inquired about his family, because cadets in Kano were not given houses. 'Buy a horse for your wife and a donkey for your children,' was the reply.   (1968, p. 12)

Few provisions were made available for children's education even at the primary levels, and this meant that mothers had to return home with their schoolchildren or send them to boarding schools at a young age. Near the end of the colonial period, financial help was provided for children's passages to Nigeria and they become at least an accepted part of the social scene. But as Heussler so aptly summed up, 'Apart from the question of pay (the Colonial Service has never been well paid), no military or civil service could possibly have been less conducive to normal married life than the Colonial Service' (1963, p. 23).

NAMELESS FIGURES IN MEN'S MEMOIRS

The typical memoirs of male colonial officers who served in Nigeria provide only rare glimpses of European women (and even fewer of African women). In the early days, the nursing sisters at remote stations are most often cited, but seldom named. Even the wives accompanying these officers are sometimes left without a name for an entire book, being referred to only in the possessive as 'my wife' or, in one case, by her initial. Other married women are identified as 'the wife of' (placing them in the category of 'relative creatures').

This absence of women, or the anonymity of those present, is understandable within the conventions of this literary genre, a type which gives little attention to the domestic scene, other than comic accounts of failed communication with the cook or grateful remarks about faithful servants, and draws a strong boundary line excluding the private world. These memoirs stand as individual reports within a cumulative colonial record. They necessarily focus on the public domain and the problems of governing, of collecting taxes from recalcitrant groups and building roads through uncharted territory, of listening to complaints and settling disputes, of political turbulence and administrative response. This is where history was generated, where decisive action took place, in that ideational field designated as 'a man's country'.

These memoirs are written in what Bourdieu terms 'official language', not I should hasten to add in the turgid vocabulary and leaden syntax of office papers (indeed, many of these authors show subtle literary skills), but rather in the wider sense of a semantic field invested with authority by an official group:

Official language, particularly the system of concepts by means of which the members of a given group provide themselves with a representation of their social relations (e.g. the lineage model or the vocabulary of honour), sanctions and imposes what it states, tacitly laying down the dividing line between the thinkable and the unthinkable, thereby contributing towards the maintenance of the symbolic order from which it draws its authority. (1977, p. 23)

Sometimes in these writings women, as a category, are rewarded with the verbal equivalent of a pat on the back. Sir George Beresford-Stooke writes of the colonial servants 'who put service before self' and took their brides to remote places where there were no shops, no water supplies, no theatres and no newspapers. He goes on, 'The girls submitted cheerfully to their exile and made homes for their men, and when the time came had to make that most difficult of decisions – husband or child' (1959, p. 9). Although conveying a subtly different tone of patronising affection, this linguistic asymmetry between men and 'girls' follows the same pattern of diminution and devaluation as that of calling household male servants 'boys', no matter what their maturity.

In rare instances, a particular woman is cited, almost the exception that proves the rule of 'the anonymity of women'. Serving in Bornu before the First World War, Langa Langa (pseudonym for the Hon. Harry Baldwin Hermon-Hodge) tells about his severe illness:

> And so to Maiduguri once more, where Mrs. Ruxton insisted on providing me with every meal for a fortnight of my convalescence. What a difference a woman can make to a station, for better – or *for worse*. The trim little earthenware jugs and bowls, spotless serviettes, appetising little dishes, and good red wine would have reconciled me to a perpetual period of convalescence. (Langa Langa, 1922, p. 149; his italics)

In this case, praise for a specific woman clearly does not mean acclaim for women in general.

A reference to women's expected 'cattishness' comes through in the comments of Richard Oakley about station life at Yola in 1921:

> This station, on the face of it, was no place for a woman. . . . Yet in spite of the sand-flies, in spite of the mosquitoes and other

poochies, the two women, who were there during my sojourn, liked it, and vied with a friendly rivalry in entertaining the less fortunate men. Contrary to what is generally supposed under such circumstances, there was no 'cattishness', but just good-fellowship. Both were interested in the life of the country and in their men's work, and one paid the supreme sacrifice through her devotion.　(1938, p. 45)

This brief epitaph for an unnamed woman carries messages on several levels: the assumptions at that time about women's feline propensities; praise awarded in the abstract rhetoric of interest in 'the life of the country' and 'their men's work'; death distanced and made heroic by euphemism, 'the supreme sacrifice'.

The difficulties of intense social competition within the colonial group are commented on by A. F. B. Bridges in 1926:

In July I had to go to Enugu to help Lawton, the DO, over the Governor's visit, to find him almost tearing his hair with exasperation as first one European and then another rang him up to complain that he or she (usually she) was more entitled to be asked to dinner than someone else, or that she appeared to be only invited to one of the less august occasions. It is hard to believe that people could be so childish and yet it was common then. One saw it on the boats too, where there was always a lot of jockeying for invitations to sit at the Captain's table.　(1980, p. 26)

Here the hint appears of women being more anxious, more 'childish', about the signs of social status.

Again, the argument emerges that European women figured as an obstacle to better relations between Africans and Europeans. Burns came to Nigeria in 1912, bringing his wife three years later. He compares the 'Old Coasters' with his own generation:

Perhaps for the very reason that they had not to consider the comfort or the prejudices of white women they were always on better terms with the Africans than we are. They travelled more and saw more of the people in their villages; they visited and were visited by Africans more freely than is the case today.　(1949, p. 41)

Two points here are open to question: whether relations between Europeans and Africans *were* better in the early days (perhaps a myth of 'the Golden Age') and what prejudices women actually held.

In similar vein, Brook remarks on social life in Warri after the Second World War:

In Lagos and more sophisticated centres, Africans had for some time joined in social life in a limited way with Europeans. In the Provinces, it was less common except on official occasions, *particularly in stations where there were European women.* In Warri, there was little mixing although the African judge was a member of the club.   (1966, p. 90; my italics)

This question of the part of European women in maintaining social distance between two races, not only established as popular wisdom but in sociological theory, will also be taken up later.

While comments on women in the memoirs of male colonial officers are seldom overtly critical, 'the Resident's wife' appears with regularity in the negative, as a category or a particular individual. In his recollections of Western Nigeria during the 1920s, J. W. A. Thorburn sets out his views on women: 'Some Residents' wives were rather terrifying, and used ADOs as their personal ADCs. At that time no European wife ever had a job, and wives spent their time playing bridge or talking scandal' (1958, p. 88). Writing of a period thirty years later, John Smith observes that one of the problems of working for the Resident in Zaria was the possibility of being drafted for extra jobs by the Resident's wife. 'She was a rather status-conscious Bostonian, the only hostess I ever knew who produced a table plan when there were only six of us dining' (1968, p. 58). At one stage, he found himself every morning for a week selling raffle tickets in the markets to raise money for the Red Cross – the favoured charity of the Resident's wife.

Brook writes, 'I had met Mrs. Pender some time previously and she had told me peremptorily that she didn't approve of men who brought their children out to the Coast. Resident's wives are important in the station and they can crack a whip as lethal as a pistol shot if they are women of character' (1966, p. 121). Then a new generation took over, marking the transition both to family life and more genial relations within the community:

The Province was a friendly place under John Hamilton and the Residency at Akure, with the two young children in it, very different from the Residencies in my first tour, where visitors had to tread with respectful circumspection. The Hamiltons made their Residency a centre for Europeans and Africans in the Province.   (p. 311)

It is important to note that even this brief survey shows evidence of social change from the earlier to the later stages of colonial rule, in the more relaxed social life during the phase of decolonisation, the literary genre itself becoming less reserved about private life, and also the increasing recognition of women as named persons rather than as 'relative creatures' or anonymous beings.

REPRESENTATIONS OF COLONIAL WOMEN

The negative images in fiction of European women in the colonies have been widely attested (for example, Brownfoot, 1984; Gartrell, 1984; Pearce, 1983), the familiar stereotype being that of the 'memsahib', so vividly portrayed in *A Passage to India*. At the beginning Forster establishes the views of two Indian men: 'Granted the exceptions, he agreed that all Englishwomen are haughty and venal' (1979, p. 36). First published in 1924, this widely-read anti-imperialist novel depicts colonial men, the Turtons and the Burtons, as racist, ignorant and insensitive, but their wives appear even more bigoted and crude in their insistence on their social and racial superiority. George Orwell's portrayal of colonial women in *Burmese Days* (1967), a decade later, follows the same pattern.

Turning to Nigeria, we find the wives of colonial officers in Joyce Cary's novels hardly less unsympathetic. At the end of *The American Visitor*, published in 1933, Marie Bewsher (as an American anthropologist, admittedly an atypical colonial wife) directly causes her husband's death. *Mister Johnson*, published in 1939, shows the neurotic calculations of Celia Rudbeck setting in motion the series of events which finally place her husband in the disquieting position of having to preside over the execution of an inventive African for whom he feels responsibility and common humanity.

In this range of anti-colonial novels, the non-productive, 'parasitic' European woman, so eager to display signs of her derived rank, has become in a sense the key symbol of colonial exploitation. The moral evils attributed to imperialism find their most concentrated fictional embodiment not in the active imperialist men who fought the military battles and imposed their administration but in their dependent women. The 'oral tradition' as well presents women in an unfavourable light. 'It has often been said that all the worst faults of the Raj – its petty intolerance, its prejudices and snobberies, its cold-hearted arrogance – stemmed from the memsahib', notes Charles Allen (1977, p. 18).

Not only in fiction and the popular media, but in scholarly writings as well, the arrival of European women in a colonial territory has generally been seen as the cause for the deterioration of race relations, or at least for a widening of social distance between the rulers and the ruled (for example, Ballhatchet, 1980; Banton, 1971; Henriques, 1974). Again, as already noted, women are widely seen as more concerned about protocol and status, more keenly competitive in matters of invitations for special social occasions. These views have been challenged and placed within a wider sociological framework (by, among others, Brownfoot, 1984; Gartrell, 1984; Kuklick, 1979). The evidence from Nigeria similarly suggests the need for 'rethinking' the question of gender roles in colonial situations both in regard to race relations and social practice.

On the basis of evidence from Uganda, Beverley Gartrell (1984) cogently argues that the label of 'villains' applies only to a few colonial wives actively disliked within their own circles while most wives might better be characterised as 'victims' – oppressed by stressful demands of frequent moves, difficult living conditions, and the restricting conformity of colonial social structures. She concludes that, nevertheless, many colonial wives found strategies for coping and lived relatively 'successful' lives mainly within the privileged white enclave, itself marking the greater oppression of the colonised society.

Gartrell's study, however, lacks historical foundation and its framework proves too narrow. The voices of the wives and professional women in colonial Nigeria – coming through their published and unpublished memoirs, letters, reports, and interviews – suggest a much wider range of experience and awareness to be portrayed and analysed. Restricted as they were, these women were not merely 'victims', but active agents in the

colonial scene. Many of them showed strong resources and
initiatives in going beyond the boundaries of the colonial
hierarchy and stretching their 'degrees of freedom' to the limit. In
their professional and voluntary work and in social life, many
genuinely related to Nigerians. Some considered themselves to be
'rebels' (their designation) to colonial rules and regulations; a few
to colonial rule itself.

To a certain extent, their writings show 'the difference of view,
the difference of standard' that Virginia Woolf attributed to
womanhood (1966, p. 204; Jacobus, 1979, pp. 10–21). As an
example, when Constance Larymore visited Keffi, a town
subjected to a punitive expedition by the British following the
killing of the Resident by its ruler, she records:

> On the summit of a high hill, overlooking the town, was a
> circular wall, enclosing a solitary grave, the resting-place of
> Captain Moloney, and, in the square, outside the Mosque,
> stood a tall white wooden cross, marking the spot where he
> died. All honour to those who placed it there – but that cross has
> always been a sorrow to me; close beside the wall of the
> Mosque, it could not fail to be an offence to a Mohamedan
> community, and, being on the way to the market, each man,
> woman and child who passed must be reminded daily of the
> tragedy that has ruined the prosperity of the town, and wrecked
> so many innocent, humble homes. (1911, p. 39)

As the historian Michael Crowder (1983, p. 14) asks, could this
observation have come from the pen of one of Lugard's political
officers?

One highly successful innovator who broke many colonial
conventions was Lady Violet Bourdillon (wife of the Governor of
Nigeria from 1935 to 1943); she entertained Lagos market women,
among many other groups, and danced with them in the gardens
of Government House. In his excellent profile of this remarkable
woman, Pearce (1983) compiles evidence to support the generally
disparaging view of British women in the Empire; he considers
Lady Bourdillon to be one of the exceptions. She was clearly an
outstanding woman in any setting, yet when designated as an
'exception' to the general picture of colonial women, she 'proves
the rule'; thus Pearce's analysis reinforces the accepted view.

My own research on European women with the Colonial
Service in Nigeria has turned up so many 'exceptions', women of

character and enterprise who took on unusual projects for themselves, both well-known women and relatively unknown ones, that I have to question these underlying assumptions of the 'norm'. The negative stereotype of European women in the colonies itself becomes problematic. This study, then, begins with the ethnography of European women within the imperial culture of Nigeria and goes on to examine why the negative images of colonial women have persisted for so long.

2 Imperial Representations of Gender

*John Stuart Mill cannot help claiming the suffrage for the Negro –
and the woman. Such conclusions are the inevitable results of the
premises whence he started* ... [*and their*] reductio ad
absurdum.

(*Anthropological Review*, IV [1866]: 115; quoted in
Hobsbawm, 1975, p. 251)

RACE, CLASS AND GENDER

Following the industrial revolution, European nations threw
themselves into intense competition for political control over vast
areas of other continents in order to secure markets for their
manufactured goods and receive supplies of cheap raw materials.
In Britain, this economic imperative and the perceived
population surplus gave strong impetus to military conquests in
foreign lands, the imposition of imperial administration and,
where the climate proved congenial, colonial settlement.
Numerous writings on imperialism have traced the dynamic
economic, political and demographic developments of this phase
of aggressive foreign exploitation and analysed the ideology of 'the
civilising mission' which legitimated the forms of power exercised
over the colonised peoples. My concern here is the limited one of
examining the life-world of this small and closed society of British
colonial rulers: their self-definitions, rules of social behaviour, and
in particular their concepts and practice relating to sex and
gender.[1]

Imperial views on gender roles formed part of the more
comprehensive system of ideas held by the dominant ruling group
in Britain in maintaining its own power and interests. At the turn
of the century this belief system derived its discourse from such
diverse sources as social Darwinism, evolutionary anthropology,
medical tracts and treatises on psychology, as well as myths of
chivalry, boys' adventure stories, 'muscular' Christianity, and the

literary tradition of empire. The central unifying assumption behind its diversities in rationale and practice in regard to race, social class and gender was the acceptance, often unstated and unconsciously held, of the 'natural' superiority of the English gentleman. 'Science' attested to this self-evident truth.

On issues of race, the arguments drawn from biology, anthropology, and sociology during the Victorian and Edwardian eras are complex and conflicting; yet, whether these are considered 'racist' in setting out the Negro as a separate inferior species or 'philanthropist' in positing a common humanity with the Negro classified at a lower evolutionary level, they attributed superiority to the contemporary Englishman.[2] Similarly, upper-class men were considered superior by birth to working-class ones, based on theories of inherited genetic qualities accompanying social evolutionary ones (Hobsbawm, 1975, p. 267). In relation to gender, the scientific writings of Spencer, Darwin, and Galton reinforced the popular view of men's superiority on physiological grounds, women's reproductive functions supposedly limiting their intellectual capacities, which in turn provided reasons for constraining their intellectual and social development (Alaya, 1977; Rosenberg, 1975–76, 1982). 'Science', as in other eras and places, thus reinforced the dominant social order by legitimating social inequalities.

If nineteenth-century British and American anthropology contributed to these ideologies, it is to the credit of the *Année sociologique* group that Robert Hertz, as early as 1909, exposed how social hierarchies maintain themselves by their claim to natural superiority:

> Every social hierarchy claims to be founded on the nature of things, *physei, ou nomo*: it thus accords itself eternity, it escapes change and the attacks of innovators. Aristotle justified slavery by the ethnic superiority of the Greeks over barbarians; and today the man who is annoyed by feminist claims alleges that woman is *naturally* inferior. (1973, p. 3)

Hertz went on to show how natural differences, which allow little basis for ascribing superiority or inferiority, are transformed by social definitions into hierarchical relations.

This chapter examines imperial definitions of male and female identity, the division of spheres between the sexes in colonial life, the assignment of social roles, the codes of speech and silence, and the social shaping of emotions. How was the masculine ethos of imperialism shaped and perpetuated? What were the special qualities required of the 'ideal colonial wife'? It also takes up the official rules on sexual relations across racial boundaries and, finally, how ethnocentric concepts of gender roles influenced the governing of colonised women.

THE VICTORIAN DEBATE ON WOMEN

The dominant model of separate spheres for male and female, generally accepted by European women for the most part of the colonial period in Nigeria, had its roots back in the nineteenth century. Kate Millett (1973) identifies two documents, opposed in their purpose and style, which she considers to compress the whole range of Victorian thought on the topic of women. The first is John Ruskin's 'Of Queen's Gardens', delivered in a series of lectures in 1864 and appearing the following year in *Sesame and Lilies*; the second, John Stuart Mill's *The Subjection of Women*, published in 1869. These continued as opposed positions during the movement for women's suffrage and the fight against this by entrenched groups. As will be seen, imperial ideas were strongly aligned with those of Ruskin.

   In his search for the differences between 'womanly nature' and 'manly nature', Ruskin turns to literary sources to elaborate the theme of female redemptive powers. Describing the romantic image from chivalry of a lady buckling on her knight's armour, her love guiding his honour, he asks whether such a relation to lovers is reconcilable with 'true wifely subjection'. His answer is that the woman has a *'guiding*, not a determining, function' (1970, p. 58). After rejecting the idea of the superiority of one sex over the other (presumably 'true wifely subjection' does not mean inferiority), Ruskin states, 'Each has what the other has not: each completes the other, and is completed by the other.' This is the familiar doctrine of the period: male and female qualities are complementary; they are different in kind, not in degree. He sets out characteristics of the male:

   The man's power is active, progressive, defensive. He is eminently the doer, the creator, the discoverer, the defender.

His intellect is for speculation and invention; his energy for adventure, for war, and for conquest, wherever war is just, wherever conquest necessary.'

Qualities of the female are bounded by what she is *not*: 'But the woman's power is for rule, not for battle, – and her intellect is not for invention or creation, but for sweet ordering, arrangement, and decision.'

While the man has rough work in the open world, encountering peril and trial, he guards the woman 'within the house, ruled by her'. Victorian property laws are thus respected, while the woman is awarded a charter for domestic rule. The home, as described by Ruskin, becomes a symbolic centre: 'It is a place of Peace; the shelter, not only from all injury, but from all terror, doubt, and division . . . a sacred place'. He concludes the romantic image of the domestic angel with a telling profile of her qualities: 'She must be enduringly, incorruptibly good; instinctively, infallibly, wise – *wise, not for self-development, but for self-renunciation*' (my emphasis).

Turning to education, Ruskin explains, 'A man ought to know any language or science he learns thoroughly, while a woman ought to know the same language, or science, only so far as may enable her to sympathise in her husband's pleasures, and in those of his best friends' (p. 65). A clear prescription for stunting women's intellectual growth in subservience to the needs of men. Finally, Ruskin considers the public duty of a woman to be an extension of her private role: 'power to heal, to redeem, to guide and to guard' (p. 72). This is what transforms a housewife into a 'queen', but the metaphors of a walled, private, peaceful garden suggest a limited public role. Ruskin's lecture thus sets out the familiar Victorian doctrine of separate spheres for male and female with complementary roles.[3]

In contrast, John Stuart Mill's essay even today makes a stirring and relevant case for the equality of women, confronting Ruskin's position at every step. Ruskin appeals to audience sentiment by appropriating images from literary sources and the revived cult of chivalry, while Mill bases his argument on reason and a thorough examination of social history and law. Ruskin reiterates traditional gender stereotypes; Mill sets out the necessary educational and legal changes for the emergence of equality between women and men.

Mill's analysis is particularly acute on what would now be

called 'socialisation for sex roles'. Although he considers that
well-brought up youths in the cultivated classes are taught to
respect their mothers and not to domineer over their sisters, the
'immense majority of male minds' are formed differently: 'how
early the notion of his inherent superiority to a girl arises in his
mind; how it grows with his growth and strengthens with his
strength' (1970, p. 218). For Mill, this assumption of male
dominance from earliest youth forms the source for all other forms
of self-worship and abuses of power.

The education of girls, in contrast, teaches them the advantages
of making themselves sexually attractive to men, of meekness and
submissiveness. Mill calls into question the accepted view of the
inherent nature of the female by asking how this could be known
from present relations. He points out, 'What is now called the
nature of woman is an eminently artificial thing – the result of
forced repression in some directions; unnatural stimulation in
others' (p. 148). He advocates giving women an education to
make free use of their faculties. By opening to them the same field
of occupations, a free choice in employment, the same prizes and
encouragements offered to other human beings, the effect would
be that of 'doubling the mass of mental faculties available for the
higher service of humanity' (p. 221).

Perhaps on the basis of his own relationship with the spirited
Harriet Taylor, Mill designates the ideal marriage of persons
'between whom there exists that best kind of equality, similarity of
powers and capacities with reciprocal superiority in them – so that
each can enjoy the luxury of looking up to the other, and can have
alternately the pleasure of leading and of being led in the path of
development' (p. 235). Mill's projection of marriage thus poses an
antithesis to Ruskin's idea of 'true wifely subjection'.

This Victorian debate is central to the question of imperial
representations of gender.[4] At Oxford, Ruskin celebrated the
imperial vision in his lectures on art as Slade Professor,
influencing many future leaders of empire (Howard, 1981,
p. 241). Cecil Rhodes, for example, testified to finding his guiding
principles set out for him in Ruskin's Inaugural Address of 1870
(Sandison, 1967, p. 8). The cause of imperialism was closely
linked to the anti-suffrage movement; Brian Harrison cites such
prominent leaders as 'Curzon, Cromer, Joseph and Austen
Chamberlain, Lyall, Kipling, Mackinder, Lord George
Hamilton, Lady Lugard and others upholding both causes' (1978,

pp. 75–6).[5] A graphic example of Joseph Chamberlain's views on women are revealed in the diary of Beatrice Webb, telling of the end of their relationship that might have led to marriage:

> I *think* both of us felt that all was over between us, so that we talked more *pleasantly*, but even then he insisted on bringing me back from trivialities to a discussion as to the intellectual subordination of women. 'I have only one domestic trouble: my sister and daughter are bitten with the women's rights mania. I don't allow any action on the subject.' 'You don't allow division of opinion in your household, Mr Chamberlain?' 'I can't help people *thinking* differently from me.' 'But you don't allow the expression of the difference?' 'No.' And that little word ended our intercourse.   (MacKenzie, 1982, p. 102)

THEMES FROM A COLONIAL NOVEL

The imperial model of gender relations discloses itself throughout colonial writings. A particularly revealing source is the novel *Gone Native*, published in 1928 by A. C. G. Hastings, who served as an administrative officer in Northern Nigeria for eighteen years (from 1906 to 1924). While Joyce Cary in his novels presents the ambivalence and inner contradictions of colonial experience, Hastings gives an unquestioning, idealised promotion of imperialism. In his descriptive passages, Hastings provides authentic, keenly-observed scenes of the tropical landscape and the surfaces of life in a colony similar to Nigeria. He creates characters as ideal types (in Weber's sense of artificially delimited conceptual types), embodying key roles in the colonial social order.

The main character, or hero, is the man of the title, 'gone native'.[6] He is James Steel, referred to by others as 'a gentleman by birth', now a trader and hunter among a remote pagan group, an unapproachable loner who on occasion becomes depressed and drinks himself into a stupor. For the last five years Steel has lived among the Manti. He has learned to speak their language fluently, knows their customs and aspirations, and retains their trust. His views on economic development coincide with those of progressive officers of the time: he has introduced new seeds, ploughs and other farming implements, and ways to improve stock-breeding. His political views are orthodox: he supports the authority of the aged chief, Tula Mantia, to undertake measures for gradual change. 'Indirect rule' is thus shown in a favourable light.

The Manti had fought as brave warriors for their independence twelve years before, but had now become sullen and intractable. The Resident, Jack Cardew, considers something to be wrong with the administration of this group. The previous year a district officer had been murdered and his friend, Captain Fortescue, had led a severe punitive expedition causing the death of innocent people. The story reveals that the murdered DO had resented a development scheme set up by Steel and had press-ganged the farmers to work on a road during the critical planting season. The DO's successor, disliking the Manti people and his bush assignment, has not even carried out routine visits. The Manti are thus aggrieved and vindictive, open to radical influences.

Lejean, a 'half-caste' (the term itself pejorative), leads a section of the Manti in a plan for vengeance. James Steel gains wind of this and, in order to get further information, undertakes a hazardous journey, testing his physical endurance to its limits. He is thus able to alert the small group of Europeans of an imminent attack on the station. At the precise moment the raid begins, Steel exposes himself before the warriors, speaking in Manti to his friends, in an attempt to persuade them to give up their ill-planned venture. The leader, Lejean, answers by spearing Steel in the chest; Steel, in turn, shoots Lejean dead. With their leader gone, the raiders disperse. Through Steel's supreme acts of moral and physical courage, he has saved the colonial settlement from annihilation: he has at once redeemed his reputation and achieved heroism. But, despite careful medical care given by the Resident, Steel's wounds bring on a fever which places his life at stake.

The roots of Steel's strange alienation go back years earlier to his engagement to a beautiful woman named Pearl, who not only betrayed him by finding an older, wealthy man, but justified herself by spreading rumours that he had 'sought to violate her chastity before marriage' (Hastings, 1928, p. 159). Unable to defend himself honourably against such lies, he decided to find a tenant for his property and set out for Africa. His harsh memories of this episode have caused the bleak periods of depression which have turned him to drink. Such an implausible sequence requires a suspension of disbelief from readers of today and, in certain circles at least, those of 1928.

The Resident of this remote area has invited his sister, Monica, to visit him. The two women, Pearl and Monica, resemble each other closely, so much so that when Jim first sees Monica he mistakes her for the beautiful woman of his past. Beneath similar appearances though, they are divided morally into opposite poles: Pearl who is self-seeking and hypocritical, attracted to a man for his money rather than his character, lying to save her own position and harming another's reputation; and Monica, self-sacrificing, dedicated to the service of others, honest and open in her approach, recognising true character in a man temporarily degraded, expressing genuine love. In its views on women, this novel reverts back to the mid-Victorian female stereotypes of 'angel' and 'fiend' (see, for example, Trudgill, 1976).

In the structural oppositions of this novel, Lejean represents characteristics antithetic to the true Manti tribesman. The son of a reprobate French trader and a Manti woman, Lejean was sent by his father for education at a Roman Catholic mission and proved a problem from the beginning. Recently he has been in jail for robbery with violence; since his release he has undermined the leadership of the old chief by scheming for terrorist vengeance against the colonial rulers. Steel speaks harshly of him:

> He is a half-caste – the worst material in all Africa . . . I don't need to tell you of the evils which result from the mating of black and white. The worst points of both races come out in the half-breed and rarely one of the good. The fusion seems invariably to produce little else than the faults and passions of both parents. In Lejean, we have all this and the additional fact that he has some education.   (Hastings, 1928, p. 132)

In India, a common saying among the British was that Eurasians shared the vices of both races (Ballhatchet, 1980, p. 100); this view was not uncommon among British in Africa as well. A separate factor was Lejean's education: colonial officers often showed a marked dislike for the 'half-educated natives' (in their words) turned out by the missionary schools.

THE IDEAL WOMAN IN COLONIAL SETTING

For the representation of the 'ideal woman' in the colonies, the portrayal in Hastings' novel of Monica Cardew provides the main features. The first view of her shows a beautiful young woman standing at the steamer's rail, ready to disembark at the port city of the tropical colony where her brother is Resident in the remote interior. After two days on the train to the railhead and a further river voyage by stern-wheeler (a familiar journey in the early years of colonial Nigeria), Monica reaches Ingola, where she finds herself the only woman among all the men. She reflects, 'Women were not always welcomed by the men in the bush. Women meant afternoon calls, ties and collars, a sense of social duties often out of keeping with the life of work and play which men lead in the wilds' (Hastings, 1928, p. 55). After a warning from a misogynist Scotsman, 'Forbye it's nae sort of a country for women – white women' (p. 41), Monica resolves to show herself the exception. Before taking over the running of her brother's kitchen, she observes the servants at their work and then imposes her authority without nagging. Her dinner parties are praised for weeks. These dinners are models of 'living on the country' in contrast to the 27 tins of provisions opened for a special dinner by one of the bachelor hosts in the station. She begins to learn the Manti language with the aid of a missionary-compiled textbook, and is soon acknowledged a success: 'She was always charming and hospitable, and her directness and simplicity at all times pleased men to whom frills and affectation were anathema. Monica was never bored by "shop", played a good game of tennis and golf and was a glorious dancer' (p. 61).

Soon Monica undergoes a series of tests to her courage and strength of character. The first comes during a few moments of fatal risk from the strike of a spitting cobra; instead of screaming (the reaction presumably of the typical female), she remains calm while James Steel bravely grasps the snake and kills it. Later, when night is falling in the tropical forest during a hunting expedition, she insists on guarding the body of a tribesman who has saved their lives from a rampaging buffalo while Steel goes for help. Recognising her strong sense of honour, he tells her, 'You are a great woman – by God you are' (p. 171).

She gains her greatest moral stature, however, in saving Steel from his alcoholism and his self-imposed isolation. This romantic novel thus becomes a colonial variant of the myth of chivalry, the hero undertaking a mission of great risk and self-sacrifice to save others, the virtuous heroine taking active steps to redeem the psychologically-flawed hero. In symbolic terms, she becomes the 'knight's lady' of Ruskin's lecture. She nurses him through his fever and delirium after his spear-wounds and works out a strategy for bringing his declaration of love. He holds back through shame and self-disgust; she takes the active role in the courtship. Through this series of tests, Monica proves herself to be not only an 'ideal woman' according to the model of romantic chivalry set out by Ruskin, but also an 'ideal colonial woman' able to conduct herself in the ways demanded in the geographical territory and ideological space of 'a man's country'. Paradoxically, the novel ends with the hero planning to bring her back as his wife to his landed estate in England; Hastings apparently did not view colonial living as suitable for ideal married life.

THE CONCEPT OF THE 'GENTLEMAN'

The phrase 'in the wilds' recurs throughout Hasting's novel in opposition to 'civilisation', each with a significant cluster of meanings. 'Civilisation', identified in the colony's capital city as having a 'counterfeit presentment of English life' (1928, p. 37), is reflected in images of comfortable amenities, social conventions, amusement and frivolity, an implicit decadence. In contrast, 'the wilds' presents 'the real – primitive Africa' and 'the unknown, the mystery of Africa' (pp. 33, 37), with its few comforts and considerable risks to health. Of his first tour in 1906, Hastings writes, 'Life seemed a bit precarious, though not more so than was to be expected in the wilds, and deaths among us were fairly frequent' (1925, p. 20). 'The wilds' represents the setting where true manhood was forged, where the hero who had left England in degradation could achieve moral integrity.

In the novel James Steel is referred to as a 'gentleman' at least seven times, qualified in several instances to 'gentleman by birth', thus being identified with the landed gentry and endowed with special attributes of character. Girouard writes, 'The sources of imperialism and the sources of the Victorian code of the gentleman are so intertwined that it is not surprising to find this code affecting the way in which the Empire was run' (1981, p. 224). The concept of the 'gentleman' drew its imagery and imaginative strength from the myths of medieval chivalry which, as Girouard documents, acquired a new intensity during the nineteenth century in adapted forms. Not only was this code of gentlemanly behaviour a dominant theme in Victorian poetry and novels, but it was dramatised in popular boys' fiction,[7] internalised by generations of public schoolboys and embodied in ideals of service to the Empire.

In her biography of Lord Lugard, Margery Perham points to the moral theme which runs strongly through his reports from Northern Nigeria, 'Lugard and his envoys seem to dash about the country like knight errants, punishing wicked people and liberating the oppressed, overthrowing cruel kings and elevating good ones. This was what Lugard willed to do and what he believed himself to be doing' (1960, p. 52). While Girouard (1981, pp. 292–3) sets the exposure of chivalric ideals and its effective collapse during the 1914–18 war, the memoirs of colonial officers suggest that in the Colonial Service this cluster of symbols retained its inspiration as a source of shared meanings through the interwar period.

Mason writes, 'The pattern of behaviour proper for a gentleman was rooted in inequality. It implied differences of rank and fortune in society as well as differences of character and upbringing' (1982, p. 226). Chivalry represents an idealised doctrine for the dominant side of an unequal relationship, a model of altruistic relations between the powerful and the weak, the rulers and the ruled, the autonomous actor and his dependants, and what was considered to be the strong male and the physically fragile female. For the Victorians and the Edwardians the code of Camelot defined the gentlemanly virtues: gentleness, courtesy, generosity, honour, physical valour and heroic action, the protection of women, sexual purity, concern for the oppressed. How far these high ideals contrasted with the actual practice of the era has been well documented in the high instance of prostitution, the protection of ruling class interests, the invisibility of the poor, and the hypocrisy which attempted to camouflage the gap (see, for example, Marcus, 1966).

By the late Victorian period, public schools had incorporated the spirit of chivalry in every aspect of school life, from organised games as the means of building moral strength through physical exertion and team spirit, to the custom of fagging as a way of training leaders and loyal followers within a hierarchical system (Girouard, 1981, pp. 164–76). This process of shaping young gentlemen required the absence of women: at the age of eight, young boys were separated from their mothers, and during puberty older ones were spared the distractions of girls their own age. Wilkinson writes, 'Public school England was indeed a country of men' (1964, p. 117). Both compulsory uniforms and compulsory games encouraged military virtues and the obligations of empire (Kirk-Greene, 1985; Mangan, 1981). This regime of male toughening served to prepare young men for the more extreme physical discomforts and the long separations from family life in the Colonial Service.

To perpetuate the governing classes, this education encouraged students to perceive self-interest in terms of moral prestige identified with altruistic public service. The humanitarian impulse was genuine as can be seen, Wilkinson notes, in the public school missions to slum areas. He adds, 'But *within* the appeal to altruism, the gentleman ideal, lurked hidden appeals to egoism – the egoism of the patron. It posed public service as a moral status-symbol, the credential of membership in a select social club, enjoying moral prestige as well as political power' (1964, p. 16).

In his study of colonial rulers, Heussler writes that in the view of Furse, who guided recruitment for the Colonial Service for 35 years, the public school represented adult life in microcosm: 'The wider implications of this are that the life for which Public School is preparation is to be male-dominated and authoritarian' (1962, p. 90). Bradley comments that it is small wonder that a handful of men who had this schooling could keep the *Pax Brittanica* right round the world over the teeming millions, because the theory of 'indirect rule' in colonial administration was 'only the prefectorial system writ large, with *mutatis mutandis*, the District Officers as masters, the Chiefs as prefects, and the tribesmen as the boys' (1966, p. 15).

Although not all officers were anti-democratic, there was in general a distrust of democracy and of city life. The colonial society they envisaged was that of the English landed estates: hierarchical, paternalistic, rural. Jeffries points out, 'It has been said, with as much truth (or half-truth) as is to be found in most epigrams, that the Colonial Service is the only profession in which

one can live the life of a country gentleman on the salary of a civil
servant' (1949, p. 101).

The theme of chivalry intensified loyalty to the monarch as its
source of authority and continuity. The exuberant Diamond
Jubilee celebrations in June 1897 marked not only sixty years of
the reign of Queen Victoria, but also the military power and the
commercial thrust of imperialism at its zenith (Morris, 1968,
pp. 21–34). During the Victorian period the great expansion of
the orders of knighthood linked the knights of legendary valour
and those of the titled aristocracy with the newly-knighted heroes
of the Empire.

For the colonial society, the concept of the 'gentleman' served
as a category for mapping the social world, marking the
boundaries between 'gentleman' and 'less-than-gentleman'/'non-
gentleman'. The generalist administrator in the colonial society
could look down on the technical expert in agriculture or the
railway engineer (Perham, 1961, p. 128), and the relation of
administration to commercial was, in the early days at least, as
'Brahmin to sweeper' in the words of Sir Hugh Clifford in his
farewell address as Governor of Nigeria (Gwynn, 1932, p. 258).
These were classifications in terms of degree – 'less-than-
gentleman', but for women the designation was set out in a digital
opposition – 'non-gentleman'. The typically Victorian views of Sir
Leslie Stephen are relevant: 'men must be manly and women
womanly' (Annan, 1951, p. 224). Women were defined, in the
way so perceptively analysed in 1949 by Simone de Beauvoir
(1972), as the 'other'. This cluster of imagery signifying 'the
English gentleman' can thus be seen as ethnocentric in claiming
legitimacy for rule over other peoples and cultures, class-bound in
protecting its own interests and privilege, and gender-biased in
presenting a male-centred vision of human society.

'HER HUSBAND'S SILENT PARTNER'

It was not only male officers, however, who expressed this
imperial model of gender relations. In *Dearest Priscilla* (1950),
written as a series of chirpy letters giving advice to the prospective
bride of a colonial civil servant, Emily Bradley sets out the
subservient role of wives:

You must be happy to be alone, yet glad to put everything aside and be at anyone's disposal. You must be interested in the work, and yet a refuge from it, knowing nothing and yet everything about it. You may shed the light of your charming personality on the company, but more often sink into a shadowy corner, still, anonymous and non-existent, concerned that these creatures are fed and refreshed, with everything arranged so that your triumphs are unnoticed and you are utterly taken for granted. (1950, pp. 119–20)

If this advice seems like an echo from an older world, she explains, it is because the colonies are still remote in time and space from the contemporary world in England where husband and wife both have jobs and share the domestic duties. In the colonies, she states, 'Your husband is "the master", the work is his life. You really are going to a man's world in which you will be very much the lesser half of this imperial partnership.' She notes perceptively, 'Perhaps it is only diplomats, or politicians, or dons, or schoolmasters or clergymen, the professions that are a life rather than a skill or a job, that require the kind of wife who is her husband's silent partner' (p. 116). This statement foreshadows recent studies on wives incorporated in their husband's institution,[8] the essential difference being that these studies question the ideological framework.

Emily Bradley went to Central Africa in 1926 as the bride of a colonial officer; her book thus draws insights from her many years of colonial experience. Perhaps it is only an outsider – she was American – who could be so articulate on the tacit knowledge of this group. She gives detailed advice to the bride on the entire range of her future life in the colonies: setting up a household, touring with her husband, 'dressmaking without tears', managing servants, and developing a flourishing garden. Taking up the long-standing problem for colonial wives of how to combat loneliness when husbands are at work, she presents the man's point of view: 'Nothing is so cruelly disheartening to a man, when he is prepared to enjoy his life and his work in what is still largely "a man's country", than a miserable wife. It spoils everything for him, his home, his leisure and inevitably his work' (p. 85). The wife is to find something positive to do for *his* sake, not for her own artistic development or mental stimulation.

The same terms apply to taking part in the 'social whirl' of colonial communities. She offers no possibility other than entering fully into this accelerated social life. Her book does show a strong stance against snobbishness and an openness to friendship with those from other races.[9] On the question of racial barriers to the European club, she points out that this is rightly resented by educated local people and will in time be removed; she does not, as some of her generation did, admire racial exclusiveness (p. 106).

She turns to the vexing problem of how to live on the pay: 'The universal burden of poverty and debt is perhaps the biggest single cause of dissatisfaction and unhappiness in the Service' (p. 125). Promotion to higher ranks does not help, she points out, because salaries increase arithmetically but expenses seem to increase geometrically. Bradley shows ingenuity, though her suggestions are the familiar ones of sewing the family clothing, cutting costs of food and drink for entertaining, making efficient use of left-overs, and generally keeping watch on the household budget. Hospitality proves to be 'the skeleton in the colonial cupboard that makes it almost impossible for any of us to live on our pay' (p. 132). Taken for granted in colonial circles, this custom provided comfort for officers moving around the country and also a process of genial communication from one station to the next. Wives were meant to be generous with hospitality while pruning the costs.

Emily Bradley advises the young colonial wife to take up work outside the home, not to add to the family income or to develop her own interests, but to free 'one of the lordly ones' from some of the routine drudgeries of the office and give him time for the more creative side of his work. Her job does not excuse her, of course, from her duties as an official's wife and hostess: 'If you are too tired at the end of the day to go out or to entertain your husband's friends and colleagues it will be a loss, and the subject of some criticism' (p. 169). When she is 'given a job' (not 'finds' or 'takes'), this is likely to be a very junior post, probably clerical, and she must not show her talents or assert herself: 'You are now an even more silent partner, a small cog in the machine, anonymous. I need not remind you that you are even more unlikely to receive equal pay for equal work than you would be in England, regardless of your qualifications.' Bradley shows herself aware of women's issues, but following the tradition of Ruskin she counsels women to be 'wise, not for self-development, but for self-renunciation'.

She is thorough in her discussion on the need for voluntary unpaid social work. While pointing out that voluntary organisations can provide the means to reach across barriers of race, creed, politics and salary scales, she fails to note that they can also reinforce these hierarchies, as in cases where the 'senior lady' drafts junior ones to work for her favourite charity. To her credit, she endorses working with professional African women: 'These women govern the African society in which the social work is being done, and to which you will attach yourself, by invitation I hope, as a working partner' (p. 183).

Bradley concludes her book, interestingly, with a discussion of children and separations, placing this topic last – in the same position it held in the dominant system of ideas. As a mother, it might have been expected that she would give a chapter on children precedence. This order comes as additional confirmation of the cosmology of the colonial universe, women being seen as 'wives' but not as 'mothers', children being reared in the homeland. This treatise shows the dominant model for the wife: as 'her husband's silent partner' and 'her children's absent mother' – though the second definition was better left unspoken. She writes in a telling sentence, 'Many people will tell you that separation is the most sinister word in the colonial vocabulary' (p. 228). In women's memoirs the pain of separation flows at submerged levels and breaks through with intense awareness. This was the 'double bind' of a mother, that she had to choose to be apart from her husband *or* her children, though in pre-Bowlby days her place was considered to be mainly beside her husband.

In her fervent dedication to the colonial mission, Emily Bradley manages to gloss over the two losses sustained by colonial wives: their children and their own professional development. Her book circulated in the early 1950s to the far reaches of the globe, passing from one colonial wife to the next. Some of the wives of the generation of the fictional Priscilla accepted her prescriptions, but others were sceptical. Cecillie Swaisland, who joined her husband in Eastern Nigeria in 1949, says, 'Just coming straight from LSE, you know, I felt pretty iconoclastic about the advice given in *Dearest Priscilla*' (Ms., p. 2).

Elizabeth Knowles wrote a spirited article in 1954 for *Corona*, the journal of the Overseas Service, asking whether a dangerous state of 'female parasitism' had not arisen among colonial wives. She points to their wartime service, their high qualifications and their self-supporting jobs before marriage into the Colonial Service, after which they were isolated from any hopes of employment or career. She puts forth a proposal for double postings, with wives working as well, and a central register of women trained to particular jobs. The advantages to the governments, she argues, were obvious: they would have a worker already housed, doctored, pensioned, and repatriated for long leave. But she senses the objections this scheme would meet, 'At the risk of being labelled "suffragette", may I suggest that opposition lies in a certain attitude which dies hard in a man's country?' (1954, pp. 338–9). This was male resistance to married women doing professional work.

'A WORKER, NOT A WOMAN'

Single professional women had their own difficulties. When Dr. Greta Lowe-Jellicoe (née Lowe) arrived in Katsina in 1930, the first Lady Medical Officer to be posted to this far-northern walled city, her job was to begin welfare work with the women in purdah, whom no men were allowed to see or treat. Her services had been requested by the Emir and she could begin only after a meeting with him to outline her proposals for training local nurses and starting an infant welfare clinic. She was told, however, that the Emir declined to meet a woman. Her work was held up for a fortnight until a letter arrived from the DO's office stating, 'The Emir has kindly consented to meet Dr. Lowe, since he regards her as a worker, not a woman' (interview, Lymington, Hampshire, 4 November 1983).

If the Muslim Emir of Katsina performed a semantic exercise in order to accept European professional women, not all male colonial officers were so congenial.[10] Patricia MacDermot tells of her arrival in 1956 as a junior administrative officer: 'On my first evening at the Kaduna Club, X said to me in a very direct and forcible manner (I remember the exact words), "I do not like women in offices. I think women are alright in Bed and Nowhere Else." This was my introduction to Her Majesty's Colonial Service' (Ms., p. 59). She explains, 'I think that some of the Colonial Service men assumed from the start that we would not be much good, but this superior attitude towards women was the outlook *at that time* of many who had been educated at the public schools of England.'

Professional women in the Colonial Service found themselves in an ambivalent category. On the one hand, they had to prove themselves to be 'workers, *not* women' (that is, in the same category as men), and, on the other, as unmarried women, they were considered 'not yet fully women' or 'less than women'. The marriage bar represents one of the great legal barriers to women's equality; throughout the history of the Colonial Service, this ruling was in effect. Whereas there was no line drawn between bachelors and married men, both presenting the norm for the middle ranks of the Service, with bachelors predominant in the lower ranks and married men in the higher, professional women had to resign on marriage. From then on, their work could only be temporary and fragmentary. No doubt many women who married colonial officers took this ruling for granted and did not feel the loss of their professional career, but others did. Some who married were only too pleased to continue their work on contract; other professional women declined to marry. Pat Walters, a rural education officer who arrived in Nigeria in 1953, writes, 'As one never lacked an escort in an area where men outnumbered women by far, it was difficult to decide to chuck an absorbing, exciting job in favour of the usually dull life of the colonial officer's wife, so often a dreary round of gossip and coffee parties' (Ms., p. 8). Male colonial officers, of course, were never required to make this either/or choice.

The marriage bar also maintained a division between the two categories of women, each deprived of what the other had: married women gaining a husband, possibly children, perhaps financial security; professional women retaining their autonomy and the adventure of their work (see Sciama, 1984, p. 53). This did not necessarily mean conflict between individual women in these two distinct categories (indeed, strong friendships are recorded), but the potential fissure was there. During the interwar years, for example, Dr. Lowe-Jellicoe found some wives antagonistic towards her. As a medical officer, her salary was higher than that of a DO, and since rank was based on salary, she was often the senior lady present at dinners and other social occasions. This, as well as her relative freedom at work and her possession of a car, apparently rankled some of the wives. The women who arrived as administrative officers in the last decade of colonial rule remember relations with wives, for the most part, as friendly and unstrained. But there was 'a flicker of patronage occasionally', as Margery Daniels (née Bell) observes. She adds that in those days everywhere marriage for women was felt to be the proper role and, after about the age of twenty-two, a job was a sign of failure (Ms., p. 36).

In the imperial representations of gender, professional work provided men's identity, but for women it held ambivalence, signifying in one sense a 'failure'. Outstanding professional women, of course, were admired and considered 'successful', but the price for this was the acknowledgement of 'a worker, *not* a woman'.

SEX AND MARRIAGE ACROSS RACIAL BOUNDARIES

In 1909, the Colonial Secretary, Lord Crewe, issued a confidential circular expressing strong disapproval of officers becoming involved with local women and setting out penalties (PRO/CO 854/168). Known as the 'concubinage circular', this was provoked by the actions of an officer in Kenya whose affairs with African girls were brought to the attention of authorities and resulted in questions raised in Parliament. In his covering letter to each Governor, Lord Crewe states that 'summary punishment for offences of this character may at any time be applied to individual officers'. The two enclosures, 'A' for officers entering the Service in the future and 'B' for those already serving, have similar wording. Crewe considers the moral objections to such conduct to be generally recognised; he goes on to say that at times such ill conduct between government officials and native women has caused serious trouble among native populations. An objection even more serious lies in the fact that 'it is not possible for a member of the administration to countenance such practices without lowering himself in the eyes of the natives, and diminishing his authority to an extent which will seriously impair his capacity for useful work in the Service'. The distribution of these enclosures to Northern Nigeria was listed as 180 'A' and 600 'B'; to Southern Nigeria, 240 'A' and 800 'B'. Ronald Hyam observes that ironically the French authorities at this time were adopting the exactly opposite policy by *encouraging* their officers to take local mistresses (1986, p. 73).

The reception this 'concubinage circular' met in Nigeria is not recorded in any documents coming to my attention. D. J. M. Muffett writes that Lugard, after becoming Governor-General of an amalgamated Northern and Southern Nigeria in 1914, issued a 'Secret Circular B' along these lines. This had to be hastily withdrawn 'because of its impracticality and the sense of outrage which some of its more pungent observations engendered' (1978, p. 17). One of its more objectionable features was alleged to have been an equation of miscegenation with bestiality. Apparently the last copy of this circular was destroyed in about 1945, but its existence has passed into 'common knowledge and even into Service folklore' (p. 23).

Whatever the contents and fate of 'Secret Circular B', officers throughout the colonial period were clearly aware of official disaproval of their consorting with African women. If in practice such conduct was generally condoned, officers exercised considerable discretion. M. C. Atkinson, who arrived in Western Nigeria in 1939, writes, 'There was a tendency to be boastful and exhibitionistic about one's drinking prowess. In the matter of sexual relationships, most expatriates were totally reticent' (Ms., p. 111). He assumes that with so few white women and so few social outlets, it would have been surprising if a fair proportion of white officials and traders 'did not seek solace regularly or occasionally from black women'. He proposes to honour their reticence.

In general, other colonial officers follow this pattern in their memoirs. After telling an amusing story of adultery in Lagos between a bachelor government officer and the European wife of a trader, Sir Rex Niven observes that the general standard of sexual morality was high between white people with such deterrents as houses very 'open' inside and outside, the silent movements of houseboys, and the visibility of parked cars in open compounds. He adds, 'Many white men had black mistresses' (1982, p. 136). Philip Allison, a forestry officer in Southern Nigeria from 1931 until 1960, stated in an interview with Charles Allen that many bachelors used to have a local woman living with them (Ms., p. 39).

Kenneth Blackburne, who served in Owerri Province from 1930 to 1935, tells of an occasion when a local man and his wife came to seek his help on some matter, 'bringing with them a completely naked and shapely young girl as an offering' (1976, p. 12). Such a gift was completely unacceptable, he adds, not only on ethical but also on medical grounds. When Stanhope White arrived in Maiduguri in 1936, the Resident's interpreter said to him, 'If the Master of the House wishes to have a Fulani or Shuwa virgin, it can be arranged' (1966, p. 11). The interpreter went on to expound the local attitude, that this was a man's world, that all men were the same at heart and it was natural to want a woman, particularly a virgin; some white men had nothing to do with women except their own wives, but others took concubines and no one thought the less of them. White comments that few children were born of such unions.

Observing the child of mixed parentage in a village in 1933, W. R. Crocker writes, 'It is rare, even very rare, to see half-castes in Nigeria' (1936, p. 63). Since he cannot recall seeing more than about half a dozen, even around the mining areas of the plateau where liaisons with African women amounted to rather more than that, he assumes that 'African–European liaisons are usually infertile, a matter of considerable biological, and more particularly genetic, interest.' Whatever the reasons for the few children of such arrangements, popular opinion in the homeland might be judged by the editor's comment on correspondence in *West Africa*: 'We regard the creation of the people neither European nor African as the supreme racial disloyalty' (2 January 1926).

Writing of Benin Province after the Second World War, Ian Brook tells of a married ADO (his wife in England) being thrown out of the country for having an affair with an African girl. The problem was not the affair in itself:

> But instead of being a little discreet, the couple flaunt themselves and are seen in public with their arms round each others' waists, and found lying in a ditch in broad daylight. This is hedging and ditching a little too literally for anyone's taste. The Africans are as offended as the Europeans.   (1966, p. 127)

Discretion and reticence, then, were key concepts guiding officers' sexual relations across racial boundaries.

While records of earlier years give hints of European nurses being disciplined for affairs with married European doctors, I have found no references to any 'problems' of European women officers fraternising with African men. After the Second World War, there is some evidence suggesting that senior officers took steps to avoid any 'incidents' along these lines. Barbara Akinyemi, a nursing sister who later married a Nigerian, writes that there was little social mixing of Nigerians and non-Nigerians when she arrived in Lagos in 1947. She relates that when a group of missionaries and social welfare workers attempted to promote integration by organising moonlight picnics at Tarkwa Bay, two other nursing sisters and she joined in. All three were promptly transferred to separate locations: Northern Nigeria, the Cameroons, and home on leave (Ms., p. 5).

Margery Daniels, a junior administrative officer in the mid-1950s, tells of the idea current at that time that some highly educated African men craved English wives as a status symbol. She knew some Nigerian barristers and one asked her to dinner in his house. She writes, 'An English friend, highly trained and experienced in the colonial service, was so horrified that I was going, that he undertook to drive up and down the road at intervals in case I needed rescuing' (Ms., p. 35). She did not need his 'protection' at all, she says, and found it a curious evening hearing the patrol car on its rounds. These examples show the strong official barrier preventing European professional women from crossing racial lines, as well as the prevailing concept of European male 'protection' for the women of their group.

A very few male officers in Nigeria married African women (even before the Second World War) and there is no suggestion that the officers were penalised, as for example in Uganda, where they were expected to resign (Gartrell, 1984, p. 169), or that the couples were not fully acceptable socially. Again, a very few women officers, nurses and teachers, married Nigerian men near the end of colonial rule or after 1960. The great many mixed marriages of the post-Second World War period were usually Nigerian men who had gone abroad for university studies and returned with British or American wives.

ETHNOCENTRIC PERSPECTIVES ON AFRICAN WOMEN

Although in pre-colonial times women in some of the diverse

societies of Nigeria had been important leaders, when colonial administration was extended throughout the country in 1900, 'it was as though women had been rendered invisible to the exclusively male colonial administrators' (Mba, 1982, p. 38). Under 'indirect rule', these officers dealt mainly with African male chiefs and bureaucratic officials; they assumed African women generally to be in a dependent and subordinate position to men even in areas where women were noted for their independent trading activities and their political power through women's organisations. At certain times during the colonial period, when African women showed signs of protest, they were identified as a 'problem', as for example in 1929 in Eastern Nigeria during what became known officially as 'the Aba riots' and the women themselves called 'the women's war' (Leith-Ross, 1965, p. 20). On the whole, colonial officers projected the gender representations of their own society on their perception of African gender relations and, of far greater significance, on their shaping of the new social, economic, and political order which colonialism gradually brought about. This was not, of course, a calculated European male plot to dispossess African women, but an ethnocentric and unexamined exercise (in terms of gender) of power relations between two male groups, each with its own prestige structures. Western bureaucracy, itself a male-centred enterprise, was being extended to Africa.

Ironically, the general impression among colonial officers was that of improving the conditions of the people, including the position of women, by building roads, introducing cash crops, ensuring law and order, and so on. The stereotype of African women presented by missionary literature, as part of the justification for bringing 'civilisation', was that of the oppressed wife in a polygamous household. As early as 1905, Constance Larymore rejects this view of the 'down-trodden women of Africa' in her observations in Kabba of the women long-distance traders between Lagos and the Hausa States: 'There is not much that indicates subjection or fear about these ladies, sitting at graceful ease among their loads, or strolling about in the hot sunshine' (1911, p. 106). Leith-Ross concurs, 'Speaking in general, the women of Nigeria are seldom of the chattel type and correspond little to the widely held idea of the downtrodden slave or unregarded beast of burden' (1965, p. 19).

Colonial rule brought some advantages for women. In the

opening chapters of the splendid life-story, *Baba of Karo* (Smith, 1954), this Hausa woman tells of the time before the Europeans came to their area when there were raids, abduction of women, and slavery. Pacification and the end of slavery meant a great deal for women's freedom, as this vivid story confirms. In general, however, as Ester Boserup (1970) set out, 'development' or 'modernisation' during the colonial period brought a widening division between male and female of the same social group. When policies were devised to create a scientific agriculture with cash crops, extension services were offered to men, but not to women, despite the fact that in many areas women were actively involved in the production of food crops. With the expansion of education, boys were given advantages, the disproportion between the sexes becoming greater at each level of education. Science and new technologies were introduced to men, while home economics and traditional crafts were deemed appropriate for women. Young men migrated to find jobs in the growing bureaucracy; young women were often excluded.

In some cases, colonised women experienced this loss of economic and political power with particular acuteness (see Etienne and Leacock, 1980). In Nigeria, the Igbo and Ibibio 'women's war' in 1929 erupted in mass protest against the way the colonial administration had introduced 'indirect rule', diminishing women's traditional powers in relation to men and causing women to fear the loss of their fertility. "This was obscured from official recognition at the time by the economic interpretation of women's fear of taxation and their difficulties caused by the international drop in palm oil prices. Sylvia Leith-Ross went with Margaret Green in 1934 to undertake separate anthropological studies of Igbo women in the aftermath of this puzzling women's movement. She writes,

> It is a pity that, from the very beginning, some executive local powers had not been given them. At that time, the men would not have resented it as it would have meant little more than official recognition of powers the women already possessed. Now, too many vested interests are involved.   (1983, p. 95)

She notes not only the initial mistake, but the great difficulty of changing administrative structures once they are in operation.

The educated and highly articulate Yoruba woman, Mrs Funmilayo Ransome-Kuti, stated in 1946 that women had lost more under colonialism than men had (Mba, 1982, pp. 135–64). She was a politician to the bone, in correspondence at the time with the Colonial Secretary, Arthur Creech-Jones. Not only had women's traditional economic and political power been taken away, she argued, but they were oppressed by the colonial system and its agencies such as the Sole Native Authority in Abeokuta. They were denied suffrage and any say in government, yet they were forced to pay tax; this, clearly, was 'taxation without representation'. Her activities and those of other militant women in the Abeokuta Women's Union obtained their demands by 1949 with the abdication of the *alake* (the traditional chief), changes in political administration, and the participation of women in the reformed system.

The colonial government held political control and, in Bourdieu's words, 'the specifically symbolic power to impose the principles of the construction of reality' (1977, p. 165). Viewing the gender division in terms of women in the domestic sphere and men in the public forum, colonial officers created their administration on this basis. They also developed the new political order, in a process of continuing negotiations with African men, along these lines. In some cases, this significantly reduced the economic and political powers African women had previously held in pre-colonial societies; in all cases, male dominance was reinforced.

One of the themes emerging from this research is the part European women played, particularly those involved in girls' and women's education, in attempting to redress this imbalance. They tell of battles with men in key positions, both European and African, who considered the education of African girls to be of little account. Before taking up the work of European nursing sisters and education officers, however, this study will examine the patterns and processes of 'imperial culture'.

3 Power and Rank Made Visible

> [*Political ritual*] *helps to define as authoritative certain ways of seeing society: it serves to specify what in society is of special significance, it draws people's attention to certain forms of relationships and activity – and at the same time, therefore, it deflects their attention from other forms, since every way of seeing is always a way of not seeing.*
>
> (Lukes, 1977, p. 68)

THE THEATRE OF EMPIRE

Posing the central problem of how only a 'thin white line' of administrators carried out the extensive colonial enterprise in Africa, Kirk-Greene suggests four answers: 'coercion, collaborators, confidence and competence' (1980, p. 38). To these, Ranger (1980) adds a further dimension, that of 'colonial ideology', and in the context of Northern Rhodesia explores the elaborate rituals expressing the persuasive ideology of 'Imperial Monarchy'. This chapter takes up this theme in a wider frame of analysis, that of 'imperial culture' and its pervading patterns of power and knowledge. The negligible place of European women can hardly be approached without first considering the generative principles of the cultural production in which they played their supporting roles.

Metaphors of theatre abound in colonial memoirs and the studies of historians. When Sir Charles Arden-Clarke arrived in Ghana as Governor, for example, he wrote to his wife, 'It seems that out here they love panoply and plumes. Wherever I go I am expected to hold a Durbar in full uniform, and give huge sundowners and garden parties etc.' (letter, 14 August 1949, quoted in Rooney, 1982, p. 89). He had the impression, he tells her, that they wanted a strong Governor, one they could see and talk to, one who would give them pageantry and ceremonial. He goes on, 'What an enormous amount of play-acting there is in all this, the Governor's state, the doctor's bed-side manner, the all-in-wrestler's ferocity – and the people see through it but love it.' He appeals to her for support in this imperial drama: 'We have a new role to play here, darling, and I'll need your help a lot.'

But it was not only a question of metaphors. When the young Curzon made his exploratory journey to Kabul, he prepared for his visit to the Amir of Afghanistan by calling at a theatrical costumiers in London 'and for a modest sum hired a cluster of gorgeous stars of foreign orders, mostly from the smaller States of Eastern Europe. To these he added an enormous pair of gold epaulettes in a case the size of a hat-box' (Rose, 1969, p. 268). On his journey he gathered a 'glittering pair of patent leather Wellington top boots', 'a gigantic curved sword with ivory hilt and engraved scabbard', plus a cocked hat and a handsome pair of spurs. Now he considered himself appropriately outfitted for his audience with the Amir. Later, as Viceroy of India, Lord Curzon was to prove himself one of the most gifted producers of imperial spectacle.

Imperial culture developed in symbiotic (if always asymmetrical) relations with the specific societies and cultures it dominated. While in general terms its basic objectives were the same everywhere, its manifestations necessarily varied in India, Malaya, the Pacific or Caribbean islands, East or West Africa. The imperial culture of Nigeria differed from that of Northern Rhodesia, the example of Ranger's study, for several important reasons, among them Nigeria's fortunate situation in having no white settlers, no foreign plantations and no deeply entrenched commercial interests.

In its elaborate rules and formal rituals, the Colonial Service articulated its symbolic order into every aspect of daily life for those within its ranks. This was a circumscribed world: authoritarian, stratified, bureaucratic; in a sense more rule-governed for the rulers than for the ruled. Joyce Cary, for example, wrote to his wife, 'Prestige is important to every white man in Nigeria, so important there are a thousand rules made to support it that are not needed in more civilised places' (25 November 1916; Mahood, 1964, p. 31).

Taken as a 'total' symbolic world (not excluding of course the possibilities of contradictions, anomalies, internal criticism, self-parody), imperial culture in Nigeria structured official space and time, prescribed social relations between Europeans and Africans and within the European group itself, set out rules of etiquette and appropriate dress, created a special lexicon of words and mode of discourse (which, among other aspects, classified the African world in terms of European categories), and developed elaborate rituals serving simultaneously to evoke mystical authority and to invite African participation in the continuing imperial tradition. The case might be argued that imperial culture exercised its power not so much through physical coercion, which was relatively minimal though always a threat, but through its cognitive dimension: its comprehensive symbolic order which constituted permissible thinking and action and prevented alternative worlds from emerging.

THE DURBAR IN NIGERIAN TRADITION

British officers played imperial roles with what might be seen as a talent for theatrical improvisation. Appropriate ceremonies were developed and elaborated, drawing from numerous sources: established military and state rituals, the displays of power staged in India at the turn of the century and, in Nigeria, some of the more regal cultural practices they found on arrival. These ceremonies provide an excellent corpus of what Hobsbawm and Ranger (1983) in their impressive collection of essays have called 'invented tradition'. It is apposite here to note Lukes' critique (1977) of neo-Durkheimian functionalist explanations of political rituals for their too simplistic notion of 'social integration' and their failure to take up a whole range of significant questions on the cognitive dimension of power in pluralistic societies. This cognitive role is brought out in Cohn's analysis of how the imperial rulers of Victorian India defined and expropriated Indian civilisation in their representation of authority. He writes, 'Colonial rule is based on forms of knowledge as much as it is based on institutions of direct control' (1983, p. 182).

Margery Perham (1960, pp. 24–5) describes the relatively modest but 'well-staged ceremony' which marked the birth of the Protectorate of Northern Nigeria (and the first official use of the name Nigeria). This ceremony took place in Lokoja near the confluence of the two great rivers, the Niger and the Benue, and it started shortly after daybreak on the first day of January 1900, the dawn of the new century. The symbolism of this moment and this place is not likely to have escaped the notice of the leading figure who designed this ritual.

At 7 am General Lugard (to become Sir Frederick the following year) walked on to the parade ground to read the Queen's Proclamation to the assembled units of the Royal Niger Constabulary and the West African Frontier Force. The flag of the now defunct Royal Niger Company was drawn down, and the Union Jack raised as the visible sign of British authority. Guns fired in noisy salute and then the military band struck up the chords of the national anthem. Next, the Nigerian troops gave three hearty cheers for their new sovereign, Queen Victoria. After Lugard had been sworn in as High Commissioner, the troops executed a march past and were praised for their excellent appearance. Both during this event and the two days of sports which followed, the Nigerian troops and the watching crowds showed intense enthusiasm. This impressive celebration served at once to display mystical authority and to incorporate the Nigerian military units and local populace into the British Empire.

This was the first official 'durbar' held in Northern Nigeria, the model from which the more elaborate later celebrations emerged (Kirk-Greene, 1959, pp. 15–20). The word itself deriving from Persian, this ceremony had its origins in court rituals of the Mughal emperors in India. Spectacular durbars were staged in India during the visit of the Prince of Wales in 1877 for the proclamation of Queen Victoria as 'Empress of India', again in 1903 celebrating the accession of King Edward VII, and in 1911 for the coronation of King George V (Cohn, 1983, pp. 167–72). Transferred to Northern Nigeria, the durbar added the cavalry traditions of horse and camel divisions of the Fulani emirs. The royal salute, the *jafi* and *jinjina*, became its dramatic climax. By the time of self-government in 1959, the durbar had become 'a ceremony symbolising not only the quintessential North but also springing from the very inspiration of the Northern peoples' (Kirk-Greene, 1959, p. 16).

Discussion of what has been called 'the Lugard myth' (Nicolson, 1969) cannot be attempted here, except to note that he asserted British sovereignty over Northern Nigeria by conquest rather than by treaty and his steps to bring the Fulani emirs into his hierarchy of military command had profound political consequences at a later stage. He employed the durbar as a regular feature for imperial celebrations. This is a somewhat jaundiced description of this splendid event in Kano, arranged in Lugard's honour in 1913 to mark his appointment as Governor-General of Nigeria.

> Here was militarism triumphant, with no unwelcome trace of merely utilitarian progress – instead, provisioned at heaven knows what cost to the country through which they had marched for weeks, there were 'some fifteen thousand horsemen, and an uncounted number of footmen, each grouped around their chief'. There were 800 West African Frontier Force, and about 300 mounted infantry, with turbans and lances, and there was the galloping 'Salute of the Desert', with Emirs dismounting to kneel and make obeisance to him. (Nicolson, 1969, p. 199; quoting letter from Lugard to Lady Lugard in Perham, 1960, pp. 449–50)

Durbars for royalty in Nigeria were staged in Kano in 1925 for Edward, then Prince of Wales, and in Kaduna in 1956 for Queen Elizabeth. Before 1956 no reigning British monarch had come to Nigeria. The durbar in Kaduna thus represented the spectacular tribute of the emirs and chiefs of the Northern Region to their Queen, at the time when Independence was already on the horizon. Aside from public accounts of this magnificent display, an intimate touch is added by Lady Sharwood Smith (Ms., p. 216) who writes that the chiefs made a special request to the Queen to wear full evening dress and tiara; she graciously obliged despite the fact that the event was held in the morning when the heat was already shimmering.

OTHER IMPERIAL CEREMONIES

Lugard set out elaborate directives for incorporating Nigerian leaders into colonial rule. Ruling chiefs were graded, those of the highest classes being installed by the Governor or Lieutenant-Governor and carrying a staff of office symbolic of their power derived from the imperial government. In this 'invention of tradition', he shows an astute awareness of the significance of symbols. He writes, 'The personal wishes of the rulers must rapidly become identified with those of the controlling power' (1922, p. 210).

A key ritual was thus the installation of an emir. Northern

rulers not only complied with but strongly supported these great mass rituals enhancing their own prestige and, through the years, these ceremonies became more and more embellished. Sir Rex Niven describes the installation of the Shehu of Bornu in 1937:

> The Governor, Sir Bernard Bourdillon, came up from Lagos to preside in blue uniform with silver lace and flying cock's plumes. Twenty-five thousand men and five thousand horses came from all over the Shehu's territory; some of the great stranger rulers came too. There was a vast circle round the low dais. The Shehu was sworn as the King's man, the ancient oaths to his own kingdom were administered and he was lifted on to a great shield of pure white skin . . . Then the leading men came up in their grades to render allegiance.   (1982, p. 163)

He adds a significant detail, 'All this required some tough rehearsal for a couple of days.'

Governors were central to this scene, combining the functions of King, Prime Minister, and head of the Civil Service. The House of Commons had no control over the appointment or dismissal of any African colonial governor; his authority derived directly from the Crown. 'As the sovereign's representative he earned and expected nothing less than the recognition customarily paid to royalty' (Kirk-Greene, 1978, p. 224). This extended to the imprint of the Crown on his cars, stationery and official possessions. The Governor took precedence at all times, even being served at meals before any eminent lady guests. On ceremonial visits he was received with the British National Anthem and the Royal salute.

In 1919 Sir Frederick Lugard was succeeded as Governor-General of Nigeria, the position now being designated as Governor, by Sir Hugh Clifford. He was remembered for reorganising the machinery of government and also for his social and ceremonial style. Sir Rex Niven gives vivid examples:

> When Clifford gave parties or balls at Government House, all the men had to wear full evening dress, with starched shirts and collars, white waistcoats and tails . . . I remember one ball at which the great staircase was lined on each hand by soldiers wearing scarlet and gold zouaves and fezzes while the Governor received at the top.   (1982, p. 21)

On a memorable day in March 1922, Sir Hugh Clifford gave the Battalion its new Colours. As I have said, Clifford was a great man for ceremonial, and I can never forget the sight of those lines of scarlet zouave jackets and khaki shorts and puttees and glittering bayonets, the faultless manoeuvring and counter-marching of their splendid band . . . Clifford, in blue uniform and feathers, was at his best. (p. 32)

Special ceremonies marked the arrivals and departures of governors to and from Nigeria. The triumphant entry of Sir Bernard Bourdillon to the Nigerian scene in 1935 was described:

On the morning of his arrival we all went down to the Customs wharf, the men in white uniforms and the ladies superb in their best . . . The wharf was alive with bunting in a brisk wind. The Regiment mounted one of its immaculate guards of honour and the band played on a flank. The invited guests sat uncomfortably in their finery on hard chairs, carefully arranged in the order in which they had to be presented. The guns (brought specially from Zaria) fired their slow salute from across the water . . . Then the tall figure of Sir Bernard came down the companion way in his blue uniform and plumes, with his dazzling wife. (p. 148)

In Niven's view, this marked a change, 'Nigeria at last had a real Governor, in the Indian tradition, who knew what was wanted and what he had to do and how to do it, with precision and distinction; and he was backed by a superb wife.'

On the ritual in Northern Nigeria, Heussler writes,

The formal drill surrounding the comings and goings of higher-ups was considerable. Lieutenant governors got gun salutes and a private coach on the railway. Their number twos and sometimes others sent messages of adieu and welcome as they left or re-entered the Protectorate. Their tours in the provinces were royal tours in miniature. (1968, p. 89)

And there were many lesser ceremonies as well. Empire Day, for example, called for official celebrations all over the country. Charles Arden-Clarke wrote to his family about how he and another young officer organised a parade for Empire Day 1921 in Jemaa. They erected a flagpole in the centre of the market place, ranging the police in full dress on one side and the native police, messengers and emir's bodyguard on the other.

> We halted in front of the flag. I gave the order 'fix bayonets', 'slope arms'; then we had the salute. The Police presented arms while the bugler blew the general salute. Bulger and I stood at the salute and all the messengers and people got down on their faces and kowtowed. Then Bulger gave three cheers for the King and everyone yelled at the top of their voices.   (letter of 29 May 1921, quoted in Rooney 1982, p. 14)

Arden-Clarke adds, 'The office clerks all turned out in European dress with their wives, and dazzled the eyes of the Jemaa proletariat with their sartorial resplendency.' It requires only superficial social analysis here to note that the office clerks were very likely to be of a different ethnic group from the local people. If these ceremonies helped to create loyalty to the British Empire, they sometimes served as well to heighten internal divisions of ethnic groups and social classes.

Not all officers were so keen on the show. Stanhope White, who served in Northern Nigeria from 1936 to 1954, writes about Empire Day in 1941 when the Resident called all officers to the provincial headquarters in Makurdi to observe the day in its proper form despite the war. 'So in the morning there was a parade attended by all the Administrative Officers in full dress – white uniform and helmet, sword and all: doubtless a very brave sight' (1966, p. 144). White tells of an earlier stage in Bornu when he hoped to have dispensation from one of the imperial rules:

> At this time we were forbidden to shake hands with any Africans other than Emirs as it was said the latter resented such familiarity with their subjects; on one occasion I said to my then Resident that I wished to ignore the order in my relations with the Galadima, but was told that I must not make an exception in view of the trouble it would cause elsewhere.   (p. 55)

This brief survey has already shown the importance of uniforms. The most magnificent, of course, were those of the Governor:

> But the colonial governor in full dress was a gorgeous sight. He was entitled to wear either a white uniform with white and red plumes in his colonial helmet or, in cooler climates, a dark blue

uniform with a cocked hat and white plumes. Gold and silver gorgets, epaulettes, buttons, and frogging and an elaborately decorated sword completed the uniform.   (Kirk-Greene, 1978, pp. 228–9)

These uniforms could hardly be described as 'utilitarian', since they were an expensive outlay even when bought second-hand, and they were uncomfortable in the tropical heat. The less senior ranks of colonial officers were also resplendent on formal occasions; those who had completed seven years of service were entitled to wear a white uniform with 'Wolseley' helmet, and embellished with a sword.

How a military uniform heightens an image of masculinity is analysed by Laver: 'It gives him a head-dress which exaggerates his height; it puts a stripe on his trousers to exaggerate his apparent length of leg; it gives him epaulettes to exaggerate the width of his shoulders' (1969, p. 73). If the prescribed ceremonial dress of the male colonial officers was characterised by pomp and plumage enhancing masculinity, that of their wives was marked by propriety and femininity. Mary Curzon, for example, took immense pains preparing her magnificent wardrobe as Vicereine of India with the guiding thought, 'She must be ultra-feminine when the men were ultra-masculine' (Nicolson, 1977, p. 138).

To a certain extent, the idea of appropriate female dress was related to the local scene. During the 1920s in Northern Nigeria, for example, Sir Richard Palmer, the Lieutenant-Governor, instructed European women to wear veils at official ceremonies in deference to Muslim custom (Heussler, 1968, p. 134). This was unusual, but for formal occasions wives were always expected to appear in dignified dress (not sleeveless or low cut), a hat, white gloves, and, of course, silk or nylon stockings (sticky in the tropical heat).

IMPERIAL COSMOLOGY IN SPATIAL FORM

In India during the eighteenth and nineteenth centuries, as King (1976) sets out, British rulers developed blueprints for imperial constructions: the layouts of military cantonments and civil stations and the appropriate architecture for administrative purposes and dwellings. His perceptive study of New Delhi shows the transformation of a pre-industrial city into an imperial one with majestic government buildings, splendid ceremonial thoroughfares named after British sovereigns, exclusive residential areas, and extensive recreational facilities, including a race course and polo grounds. Government House in its monumental solidity represented the centre of power and ceremony. King analyses the effect of the symmetrical grid of the new city:

> It expressed total control over the environment, with the power to define boundaries and order the spaces within them; it represented total control over the social structure, the power to order precedence, create communities and control social relations between them. Third, it expressed total control over the process of allocation; once the places were created they would be filled according to plan. (1976, p. 264)

The rulers thus gave spatial form to their conceptual model.

In India, civil stations were laid out in an adjoining area but apart from 'native' cities, thus ensuring both physical separation and social distance between the official elite and the indigenous population. Here an orderly environment was created with spacious bungalows set in large gardens, supplied with drainage, sanitation and a system of roads (King, pp. 123–55). The larger stations had at least one church, a few shops kept by European traders selling European goods, and a club. To the European inhabitants this familiar, rational, self-contained environment contrasted with the unhealthy, mysterious, possibly dangerous, teeming indigenous city. Providing a sense of psychological and physical security, this exclusive location fostered a particular colonial way of living. While this social group attempted to reproduce the middle-class society of the homeland in the new setting, the original culture was subtly transmuted by the exotic surroundings, its required demonstrations of imperial certainty, its undercurrents of isolation and nostalgia, its repression of quivers of unease.

Examining the society of 'the Raj', Charles Allen perceives that the British rulers reinforced their own identity in India and in doing so set themselves further apart from their countrymen back home. 'What could anyone in England hope to make of a world that was bounded by civil stations and hill stations; a world of Governor's Camps, gymkhanas, Gloom Clubs, Black Hearts and

Cold Weather tours . . . ?' (1977, p. 14). In his view, this double isolation helped to fix colonial attitudes, 'preserving, to the point of exaggeration, standards and norms of behaviour long after the same attitudes had been abandoned elsewhere'. This model of pretentious social life, within a structured environment, was perpetuated in colonial societies around the world, though often on a lesser scale.

In the early years of the new century, administrative officers in Nigeria saw themselves as key figures in 'a new country in the making' (Hastings, 1925, p. 12). Lugard set out in his *Political Memoranda* the precise details for laying out a new township consisting of a European Reservation, to be surrounded by a non-residential area 440 yards across. He gives three reasons for this segregation of Europeans, of first importance being 'that they shall not be exposed to the attacks of mosquitoes which have become infected with the germs of malaria or yellow fever, by preying on Natives' (1970, p. 420). Next, this served as a valuable safeguard against the bush fires common in the 'Native quarters', especially during the dry season in the Northern Provinces. And finally, it removed the inconvenience felt by Europeans, 'whose rest is disturbed by drumming and other noises dear to the Native'. These were eminently practical reasons as befitted a pragmatic administrator, but they left unstated certain assumptions at a different level. Physical separation helped to ensure the social distance necessary to maintain imperial authority. It was not racism as such which dictated segregation, though clearly there is ample evidence of assumed racial superiority in the wide acceptance of Lugard's premise that 'it is the genius of our race to colonise, to trade, and to govern' (1922, pp. 618–19).

The growth of European townships in Nigeria can be traced in various memoirs. Hastings, for example, observes Lokoja in 1906:

> Lokoja lay upon some level ground, backed by circling hills, with the flat-topped hill of Patti overhanging the native town. Along a well-made road we passed in the moist heat of afternoon through avenues of limes and mango trees. Compounds well laid out, with paths and flowering shrubs, flamboyant oleanders and acacias, surrounded each their wooden bungalow raised upon piles.   (1925, p. 12).

This same officer tells of the changes in Kano from his first visit in

1909 to his return in 1914. The first time he had ridden in on horseback, passed through the mud city and then a further four miles before reaching the three bungalows and scattered huts of the station. Five years later he arrived by train on the newly completed line from Lagos. 'Civilisation was here at last, dragging itself across the plain between the city and the Government quarters in the form of a laid-out township with brick and stone-built houses of the European trading quarters, stores, canteens and workshops, while broad, straight roads cut through it everywhere' (p. 109).

A quite different interpretation of the nature of this 'civilisation' comes through in the musings of the main character in Elspeth Huxley's novel, *The Walled City*, the title suggesting, though not naming, the city of Kano. As the young district officer rides his pony through the narrow winding streets, he observes that the city is ancient, yet new, because the mud walls of its houses were continually crumbling and continually being rebuilt. He cites an organic simile, 'Like a plant or a man, the city was always growing and being renewed' (Huxley, 1948, p. 7). In contrast, he views the new houses built for colonial administrators: 'rectangular, comfortable and graceless, with corrugated iron roofs and verandas running round three sides'. A dichotomy is thus posed between the living quality of indigenous building forms and the linear logic of colonial architecture and layouts. While this view is expressed by a male character, the novel itself was written by a woman.

At the time of the amalgamation of the Northern and Southern Provinces of Nigeria, Lugard chose a favourable site on the Kaduna River and planned a new capital city on imperial patterns. Here there was strict segregation of European and non-European residential areas, separate cemeteries, a large race track centrally located, a golf course, and a linear grid of roads planted imaginatively with shade trees (King, 1976, p. 279). The city of Kaduna did not become the national capital, as Lugard had hoped, but a regional one of Northern Nigeria, and now of Kaduna State. While its original plan still exists, the city has expanded enormously in response to new social patterns.

In some cases, European settlement dominated an entire area. Hastings relates that by 1923 Jos and the whole plateau had become a busy place. There was now a large township with stores and banks and a flourishing market. On the mining properties good houses had been built, one at least with electricity, and gardens with masses of roses and other European flowers. Light motor roads made by the mines ran all over the high levels and out for a radius of forty or fifty miles. Nearly everyone had a car. 'Life was cheerful, with dances, race meetings and sports of all kinds' (1925, p. 229).

The official residence of the Governor, usually called somewhat unimaginatively 'Government House', required an impressive dignity as a central visual symbol. One of the Governor's perquisites, it was rent-free, suitably furnished, and provided with an array of private staff and household servants. Governor MacGregor writes from Lagos in 1899 about his assigned house, 'It is not old, cost £25 000, has four bedrooms, no library and no bath! I am allowed 52 lbs. of ice daily, a steward, ten servants, gardeners, electric light, a palatial steamer, a horse, carriers, three launches, and so on' (quoted in Joyce, 1971, p. 224). This house was to be refurbished and expanded with successive changes of Governors and with the changes of constitution making Lagos the federal capital. The style of hospitality in Government House was compared with that of an imposing English country house, as were on a lesser scale the Residencies in each provincial headquarters.

Housing for other government officers was closely related to rank. As Dr. Greta Lowe-Jellicoe explains:

> Government houses in the big towns are divided into groups or types known as T1, T2, T3, and T4 and they are allotted according to Salary. T1's are only for the very high and mighty. T2 are supposed to be for the people of about my standing & above. T3's and T4 are for people still lower in the scale.   (letter, 22 August 1928)

The social order was made visible in the conspicuous patterns of material constructions.

'HOMO HIERARCHICUS'[1]

The imperial ceremonies and rituals, the layouts of townships and European reservations, and the architecture giving pre-eminence to Government House present little difficulty in their interpretation. These were the cognitive means for inscribing the

legitimacy of British rule by making its authority visible in
material forms and social processes. The splendid rituals also
gained the active collaboration of Nigerian rulers, whose
traditional powers were often strengthened through the policy of
indirect rule. More puzzling are the distinct social divisions
among European groups and within the Colonial Service itself.

Sylvia Leith-Ross writes of the period between 1925 and 1931:
'In the European society, there were more class distinctions, to
use rather too heavy a term, than there are now. As far as
Government officials were concerned, there were still the
unfortunate Class A and Class B labels; Commerce and
Government seldom mixed except officially; the Missions kept
aloof from both' (1983, p. 85). As a group, colonial administrators
set themselves above missionary and commercial groups, though
leading individuals in missionary and mercantile circles were
placed above junior administrators.

Dr. Lowe-Jellicoe tells of her shock on her first voyage to West
Africa as a missionary doctor in 1925 to find that there was a
missionary side of the boat and a government side and that traders
did not belong to either: each group kept to itself. Her cousin had
introduced her to the Captain of the ship, who then invited her to
sit at the 'Captain's Table'. There was general surprise that as a
young missionary she had been elevated to this much-coveted
position where only senior government officers and the most
senior traders were normally included. From that moment she
decided she was not going to be part of this social division, and
later as a government doctor she mixed with both second-class
government officers and commercial people (interview, 4
November 1983).

The social divisions among European groups can be
interpreted, at one level, as a way of maintaining firm political
control in areas where there might be conflicts of interest. The
issue of assumed social superiority also arises, since British
missionaries and commercial people were more likely to have
come from the lower middle-class with inferior educational
backgrounds. They came from other countries as well:
missionaries from France and Ireland, Canada and the United
States. Business people came from even further afield, including
France, Greece, Lebanon, Syria and India.

As pointed out in the critical comments of these women, the
colonial group itself was divided into two classes. Charles Allen

explains that Class A officials were the administrators, who set themselves not only above but also apart from the rest:

> The division between A and B class officials was the same as that found between officers and men in the services. On the one side were the administrators and, as time went on, more and more officers from various support services. On the other side, with their own B class or second class clubs – and leading very different lives – there were the white 'NCOs', the Public Works Department foremen, railway engineers, civil contractors . . . (1979, p. 53)

This represents to some extent the pattern noted by Margery Perham (among others) that colonial administrators tended to look down on technical officers (1961, p. 128). Here again, differences in social class and educational background in the homeland were magnified rather than lessened in the microcosm of the colonies. Social inequality was institutionalised not only in the separate clubs, but in petty conventions. Dr. Lowe-Jellicoe noted in the 1920s that a first-class official who had become a major in the First World War retained his title, while a second-class official of the same military rank would be plain 'mister' (Ms., p. 1).

Within the Class A group itself, the hierarchical order was rendered visible in the social process of daily life by the elaborate rules of official etiquette. This was guided by what became known in the colonial lexicon as the 'Stud Book', the Staff or Civil Service List setting out the name of every official in the territory in order of seniority. As Erick Berry (wife of a junior administrator during the interwar period) observes, there were no strangers in West Africa; it was only necessary to look up the name: 'It's all there, his salary, his education, his schools and degrees and war service, his leaves of absence, the stations to which he has been posted, his time in the country' (1941, p. 28).

'Seniority was a matter of more than passing interest,' Niven writes (1982, p. 12). The Staff List disclosed the salary of an officer; those whose salaries were equal were differentiated according to precedence of appointment. He explains, 'You might think this would apply to formal dinner parties, but you would have been gravely, even dangerously, wrong as some found out to their cost.' Forms of address, for example, depended on seniority and young cadets brash enough to call an officer by his first name, no matter that he was senior by only a few years, were quickly reprimanded.

Dinner parties, even at relatively small stations, were carried out in accordance with precedence at each stage, not only in the seating arrangements, but the procession into the dining room, and the line of ladies waiting to enter the single lavatory. Niven states succinctly, 'Pressure of necessity did not override that of precedence' (1982, p. 13). Joan Sharwood Smith tells about her introduction to Minna in 1940. The first party they were invited to, she writes, began with innumerable rounds of drinks:

> At last, there was a signal from our hostess and the women trouped upstairs. We ascended the stairs in strict order of our husbands' seniority, according to the Staff List, the Resident's wife sedately leading. The operation completed, we descended the stairs in the same order and were shown our places at the dining table.   (Ms., p. 37)

The end of the party was also symbolically marked: no one could leave until the senior officer rose to make his farewell.

From the beginning to the end of colonial rule, social life for administrators in Nigeria had greater formality than for comparable professional groups in England, though there were variations between small stations and the large administrative centres and between Northern and Southern Nigeria; and after the Second World War a younger generation of officers brought a more relaxed atmosphere.

A recurring theme in the memoirs of colonial officers is the observance of protocol. In 1927 Niven was posted to Kaduna where he found social conventions well established. He states that 'books' had to be signed and cards left; if this had not been done, the young officer would certainly not have been asked out. He discovered that the prescribed etiquette of 'leaving cards', by convention when those being called upon were out, was not without its risks:

> For example, one day I went with my little card in my hand up the drive of the house of the Station Magistrate, whom I knew a little. His wife was bending over a flower-bed and I wished her a good afternoon. She straightened herself but did not turn round, and said, 'In Kaduna when we are calling we do not speak'.   (1982, pp. 77–8)

A decade later, Nigel Cooke had his introduction to this formal structuring of the social order. He relates, 'When we arrived in Lagos we were taken to sign the Governor's book, the Chief Justice's book, the Chief Secretary's book. And furthermore, when one got to one's station not only did you have to sign the Resident's book but you had to leave cards in the appropriate places' (quoted in Allen, 1979, p. 50). This practice of leaving cards was already beginning to decline when it was prohibited by government directive in 1939 at the outbreak of war. It was not revived.

Social phenomena always encode multiple meanings and invite various interpretations, but here it is useful to risk reductionism for the sake of clarity. This rigid marking of seniority within the administrative service itself cannot be attributed to any differences in social background but to its military origins and authoritarian organisation. To meet the unknown threats as well as the known contingencies of colonial rule, a high degree of internal discipline was considered necessary: the code of etiquette operated in isomorphic detail with the structure of imperial authority. Seniority was inscribed in every aspect of social life. At a time of emergency, the logical hierarchy could readily convert to a chain of military command.

On certain occasions, the social pageant was seen to require an element of 'anti-structure'. Violet Cragg tells about a group of friends who gathered for Christmas dinner in Makurdi in 1926; to avoid seating by precedence, they drew lots for their places at the dining table (Ms., p. 41). Christmas was a special time, with its associations of family and personal ties, to be marked with a subversion of official protocol.

DRESSING FOR DINNER IN THE BUSH

The splendid uniforms required for the great public ceremonies were clearly part of the symbolic display of colonial authority; even the dinner jackets and evening dresses of formal dinner parties projected the ambience of superiority of the ruling group. But another custom of colonial life in the tropics seems peculiar to observers from a later age and, indeed, became an image of caricature in journals such as *Punch*: that of dressing for dinner in a bush station and even when dining alone.

In her memoirs Sylvia Leith-Ross tells of an episode in 1913 when she was travelling up the Benue in a steel canoe, accompanied on the first part of her journey by an Assistant Resident in his own canoe. As the days went by, she relates, they talked endlessly about the future of Nigeria, the duties of the British to establish law and order, and their responsibilities for upholding an empire standing for freedom and justice. She continues:

> In the meantime, we had a problem of our own. We had always dressed for dinner. This was a rule that could not be broken, either at home or abroad, at sea or on shore, in the Arctic Circle or on the Equator. But alas, there was very little space indeed in our steel canoes. A compromise was necessary. Every night, we tied up at the edge of a sandbank and dined – we would not have used a less formal word – by the light of a Lord's lamp, high on its tripod. One evening Armar would change his bush shirt and I would change my khaki skirt; the next, I would change my white blouse and Armar would change his khaki breeches. Between the two of us, we had obeyed our code and had upheld our own and our country's dignity.   (1983, p. 69)

She refers to the American anthropologist Elenore Smith Bowen (pseudonym for Laura Bohannan) telling of her surprise on her first evening alone in the remote village where she had come to do her fieldwork when her British-trained servant laid out an evening dress for her to wear. This she considered unreasonable at the time, but later after she had experienced the distressing death of a friend in childbirth, fierce accusations of witchcraft in the small community, and instances of harsh cruelty, she became depressed and began to assert her own identity. She gave the cook detailed orders for her lone Thanksgiving dinner and told the steward to lay out her evening clothes. She had changed her mind: 'The English were quite right. One had to dress for dinner. One needed a symbol, some external sign, to assist daily remembrance of what one was' (Bowen, 1954, p. 207).

Leith-Ross continues this theme: 'When you are alone, among thousands of unknown, unpredictable people, dazed by unaccustomed sights and sounds, bemused by strange ways of life and thought, you need to remember who you are, where you come from, what your standards are. A material discipline represents – and aids – a moral discipline' (1983, p. 69). Here she serves as a knowledgeable 'native informant', providing the exegesis for the ritual of 'dressing for dinner' wherever the individual might be, whether in company or alone. In the signifying system of this society, the discipline of dress was linked to the discipline of a moral code.

In an earlier section about her brief year in Zungeru as the wife of a colonial officer before he died of blackwater fever, she tells about social life in the scattered cantonment, 'If for some reason our dogcart was out of action, bath-towels were flung over saddles and we rode to dinner parties, I in a long low-necked dress, my husband in white mess jacket and the French-grey cummerbund of Northern Nigeria' (p. 48). She describes a photograph taken in 1907 of a group at a race meeting: 'The men wear helmets and are coated and trousered, collared and tied, or in the most correct of riding kit. The four women present sit in a group apart, in summery but long-skirted, high-necked, long-sleeved dresses, elaborate hats tilted at a becoming angle' (pp. 55–6). The entire group is characterised by correctness of attire. She connects obedience to convention with the courage and fortitude required for their task: 'Ridiculous as it may seem to find moral significance in a casual group photograph, one begins to understand how it was that such a handful of men could dominate the land.' She thus condenses various levels of the colonial vision in the single image of correct dress: personal and national dignity, self-discipline linked with an altruistic moral code, upholding British dignity, the fortitude required for imperial rule.

Yet for all the acuteness of her observations, Leith-Ross does not in this case see beyond the 'folk model' of her own social group. She fails to note the hidden assumptions, the meanings behind the social convention. To the insight of the psychologist Erich Fromm that the lone Englishman who dressed for dinner in the jungle could, by this means, feel at one with his home community, Wilkinson adds that the individual's self-assurance was even more bolstered when the etiquette represented that of a traditionally superior class – in this case, the gentry (1970, p. 134). Interpreted in this wider context, 'dressing for dinner' becomes the visible sign of 'innate' superiority in an elite social tradition transmitted through the special institutions of public school education, the military academies, the universities of Oxford and Cambridge, as well as the Colonial Service itself. Even those officers who had not experienced this privileged background quickly assimilated its unwritten rules and conformed to its code.

A rather more subversive view of this custom is provided by Leith-Ross's contemporary, Mrs Horace Tremlett, who writes of her experience in Nigeria in 1914 as the wife of an engineer for a tin mining company. The title of her book, *With the Tin Gods*, appears innocuous, but it turns out to be a knife-edged pun. She tells of the antagonism existing in government circles to mining enterprise. One reason for this, she acknowledges, is that some uneducated men go out in search of mineral wealth and by their ignorance of native customs stir up a great deal of trouble. But also, she adds in a mildly sarcastic tone, it is affirmed that the prestige of the white man is in danger of being lowered by the arrival of the common person who does not own a dress suit. She writes, 'For they are very punctilious in Nigeria on the question of dress clothes. In other hot countries, a man when he is in the bush, will put on a clean shirt and a pair of flannel trousers, and feel he has done all that could be expected of him. But in Nigeria never' (1915, p. 264).

Her analysis is trenchant. She observes that a 'made up' tie is 'the hall-mark of a bounder' and stands for all those things an official does not speak about but instinctively abhors.

> It is for this reason that he clings so desperately in Nigeria to his dress suit, not because he wishes to look nice, but because he knows he is expected to live up to certain traditions, and because he likes to feel that he is a gentleman – especially if he has any doubt on the subject.   (p. 265)

In her view, colonial officials in Nigeria were not exactly exemplars of a high standard of morals. She writes, 'The white man there is king as he is nowhere else in the world; and a most diverting spectacle he is, playing little tin god to his black subjects' (p. 238).

The practice of dressing for dinner continued through the entire colonial period, although becoming less honoured in certain parts of the country. Catherine Dinnick-Parr, who went as a woman education officer in 1947 to a remote area of the Middle Belt, tells how she did not wear the pith helmet she was told to bring, but 'in an evening in the bush I always wore a long dress to keep up my morale' (Ms., p. 26). There was the added reason that she had to wear mosquito boots to ward off the hordes of mosquitoes and sandflies and a long dress covered these. She remembers occasions when the development officer would join her for dinner – 'he in a dinner suit and I in an evening dress' – and afterwards they would walk along the bush path talking. Everyone gathered to see them, wondering 'why we were all dressed up and covered ourselves when it was so frightfully hot'.

LESSER QUEENS

In this symbolic drama of imperial culture, wives were cast in supporting roles to their husbands whose seniority they were assigned. They had to learn the scripts of social practice through precept and rehearsal; how they played these parts depended on individual inclination and flair. In memoirs and historical studies, women are often described as the upholders of colonial social conventions, but they are also seen as ameliorating the intricate formality of official protocol. This section outlines the experience of those in the prescribed role of 'senior lady' (see Callan, 1984, p. 13).

Margery Perham writes, 'I know well from my travels over many years how much, as a lesser queen beside the gubernatorial representative of the British crown, the wife could help to make or mar her husband's work in the highly sensitive setting of a British dependency' (1974, p. xiv). She goes on to pay tribute to Lady Robertson, wife of the Governor-General who presided at Nigerian Independence: 'with her intelligence, wit and humanity, she has been the ideal partner'. Coming from the Sudan, Nancy Robertson found the British senior group 'very much more pompous than anyone we had had in our part of the world'. She continues, 'In Nigeria, everyone was very conscious of rank, and though everybody was very kind to us and I enjoyed it enormously, I always had the feeling that they were going to put on a hat to come and see me!' (quoted in Alexander, 1983, p. 61). From the beginning she made it clear that she wanted a small car of her own so that she did not need to have a Rolls and a driver just to go out for a cup of coffee. During her period at Government House in Lagos, she presided as hostess to the Queen and the Duke of Edinburgh on their visit to Nigeria and to Princess Alexandra who came as the Queen's representative for the Independence celebrations.

The role of the 'lesser queen' was clearly not an easy one. The Governor and his wife were looked on as the heads of the local society and expected to give garden, luncheon, cocktail, dinner, and other parties at frequent intervals. Added to this, they were required to show hospitality at all times, welcoming a continuous flow of visitors to the colony. 'Many Government Houses are occupied by guests, to the limit of their capacity, day in and day out throughout the year' (Jeffries, 1949, p. 111).

The wife who served longest in Nigeria as 'lesser queen' was Lady Bourdillon, whose husband's term as Governor was extended during the war for three years beyond the normal five-year span. An outstanding woman with a flair for making friends with people from all social levels, she entertained kings and prime ministers in Lagos, without losing the common touch of visiting the local market women in their stalls and inviting them to parties in the gardens of Government House (Pearce, 1983, pp. 267–77). Maintaining 'social distance' with indigenous people was not in her temperament. In India as the wife of a junior officer, she learned Hindustani in order to speak with villagers during her husband's tours, and in Iraq she learned Arabic and requested not to move into the European cantonment but to live in the heart of the Arab quarters in Baghdad. When she came to Nigeria with Sir Bernard in 1935, she had already been 'first lady' in Uganda and had the self-assurance to meet the social demands of this position in her own way. On her arrival at Government House, she stated, 'This house is open to anybody who likes to come into it, and the hall is always open. All you've got to do is come into the hall and call for me, and I shall come down' (Ms.[a], p. 33). With the Governor, she was prepared to undertake the 'performance' of official ceremonies ('you *had* to do it'), she said, but they insisted on separating this formal side from a far more spontaneous social life. 'If there was a review, there we were very grand and glorious, all dressed up with feathers and whatnot' (Ms.[b], p. 11), yet at the same time they invited people informally to lunch, to the dismay of the aide-de-camp who might have arranged the meal for four and found six more were coming. She informed him at the beginning that this was the way they were going to live.

Her day at Government House began with guests coming to breakfast on the veranda. This completed, and her guests embarked on their day's schedule, she went out to the compound, where some 150 people lived, the servants with their wives and families, to see the children and enquire about general welfare. From there she went to the kitchen, where the catering was taken care of. 'It frightened me at first. I was no housekeeper. I had an ADC but, of course, the boy didn't know – and we had to cater for so many' (Ms.[a], p. 35). She found the servants marvellous, but careless, and before guests arrived, she had to go into the bedrooms to check that the beds were prepared and to the dining room to see that the table was properly laid. She looked after the guests, taking people out to bathe in the afternoons or on an excursion, and in the evenings there was always a big dinner.

Whether with Nigerian chiefs or with the ebullient Lagos market women, Violet Boudillon struck up a friendly repartee and a joyful exploration of other ways of living. She said her husband was a man of ideas and a great administrator, which she had no part in, but she did love people. 'I've never agreed with that theory that East is East and West is West. Because I don't believe it. I think that personal relationships and affections outweigh the whole thing. I know it does' (Ms.[b], p. 31).

The wives of Deputy-Governors and Chief Secretaries had their social duties prescribed as well, with intervals when their husbands became the acting Governor and their own role also enhanced. After Kenneth Bradley had been Under-Secretary in the Gold Coast for three years, he and his wife were not sorry to leave. He said he never wanted to work in such a hierarchy again and she commented rather more vividly that she had felt like 'a Victorian wax posy under a glass dome' (K. Bradley, 1966, p. 155; quoted in Kirk-Greene, 1978, p. 255).

When the news came that Sir Bryan Sharwood Smith was to succeed Sir Eric Thompstone as Lieutenant-Governor of Northern Nigeria, a spontaneous champagne party was given by a member of his staff in celebration. Joan Sharwood Smith writes, 'It took two glasses of this potent mixture to drown my inward groans at the thought of becoming a Lieutenant-Governor's wife and of all the awful formalities of Kaduna' (Ms., p. 160). After the Residency in Kano, Government House seemed enormous, with its grounds of over fifty acres and some forty people living within the compound. She doubted whether she would be capable of running such a vast establishment, though she recognised that the last occupant had been a bachelor with only the help of a private secretary. She was sure that a different standard would now be expected with a wife in the picture (p. 162).

She soon discovered that a wife was all but invisible in the view of the staff. When her husband went on an official visit outside Kaduna, she was told by friends who wanted to get in touch with her that the telephone exchange of Government House was out of operation. Questioning the staff, she received the explanation that it was always discontinued when there was (in their words) 'no one in the house' (p. 169).

She found the atmosphere in Kaduna 'claustrophobic', but enjoyed accompanying her husband on tour and giving evening receptions wherever they went for the leaders of society, both black and white. As the Lieutenant-Governor's wife, she automatically became the head of various regional charitable organisations and supported the establishment of a multi-racial school in Kaduna. At the time of the Queen's visit, she was not only hostess in Government House, Kaduna, but escorted the Queen in Kano to visit the Emir's wives and (as a fluent Hausa speaker) to act as interpreter.

As the bride of a Resident, Betty Moresby-White arrived in Lagos in 1936; she soon discovered that everyone had a status. 'And I found if you went to dinner at Government House you sat very strictly in seniority, and you had to be very careful who you walked out behind, or in front of, as you left the dining room, all that sort of thing. Very difficult it was' (Ms., p. 2). Not only in Government House, but at informal dinner parties she found herself seated according to the Staff List next to the Chief of Police who had newly arrived from another colony. They took opposed views about 'the wretched abdication thing' and began to scrap at every dinner until they agreed to ban the controversial topic.

Her next tours were spent up-country in Oyo, where her husband was Senior Resident. Here they entertained all the people who came through, a considerable number during the war, including Sir Stafford Cripps. They also used to tour several times a year, travelling 'in quite a caravan' to visit all the large towns of the province. They went in a Ford V8, a police orderly with the driver in front and she and her husband in the back. Ahead of them went a lorry with all their loads and the servants – the headboy and his two helpers, the cook and his mate, the washerman and his mate. They had to take enough china and glass to serve ten people at dinner because the Resident always had to entertain wherever he went. The servants went ahead to their destination, and when they arrived the beds were made and the dinner cooking. They always wore evening clothes for dinner; she used to take about six evening dresses with her on every tour (p. 6).

Near the end of the colonial period, Elizabeth Purdy was a Resident's wife in Northern Nigeria – in Yola, Jos and Sokoto. She remembers Yola as a small and rather remote station, more 'matey', while Jos was much more formal with its socially conscious mining community. She says, 'The Resident's wife was treated very much the top of the social ladder – which, I'm afraid, slightly amused me' (Ms.[b], p. 16). During this time they entertained quite a number of visitors, not only colonial officers from other parts of Nigeria, but Colonial Office officials, Members of Parliament, university professors, and such well-known authors as Elspeth Huxley, Alan Moorehead and John Gunther. This was one of the perks of being a Resident's wife, in her view, meeting the interesting people who came through. She recalls one year when they went from September to Boxing Day without a meal to themselves. Her days were very full – taking care of small children, planning menus and arranging parties, sewing clothes, writing letters. She adds, 'It might seem trivial but the flowers had to be re-done every day before breakfast, and in the Residency that was, you know, quite a job' (p. 24).

The wives of different official ranks had the same duties, Elizabeth Purdy explains, at different levels and on a different scale. The District Officer's wife had a position in the district similar to that of the Resident's wife in the province. These supporting roles played by wives of officers in the Colonial Service would seem to be a prime example of the 'person-defining power of organisations' flowing across the conjugal link (Callan, 1984, p. 5), at the same time allowing improvisation and unique performances.

Part Two

Women in the Professions

4   Women in Health Care

It is extraordinarily interesting work but it shows what a wide scope there is for improving the infant mortality of the country. We very rarely get any normal midwifery cases, all abnormal and extraordinary ones at that. We had two deaths of mothers – both having come in almost breathing their last from neglect and unskilled treatment and drugs outside. Really it was too awful to see what some of these poor creatures suffer and a lot of it so unnecessary if they would only come in time.

(Judith Garvey, Nursing Sister in Abeokuta, letter to Secretary of Overseas Nursing Association, 25 January 1926; ONA 140/1/44–5)

'THE WHITE WOMAN'S BURDEN'

At the end of the nineteenth century, nurses found themselves in the privileged position among British women to take up the call of service to the outreaches of the Empire. They were needed to nurse their own countrymen. In the typically pragmatic way various branches of the Colonial Service developed, the recruitment of nurses was initiated and continued to be carried out by a voluntary body separate from, but in close liaison with, the Colonial Office. This agency was started in 1896 at the instigation of Mrs Francis (later Lady) Piggot, wife of the Procureur Général of Mauritius, who had observed that health risks for British officials and settlers in the tropics were considerably heightened by the absence of any trained nurses. Following the philanthropic patterns of the time, she enlisted the help of prominent people to form the Colonial (changed in 1919 to 'Overseas') Nursing Association with the specific purpose of recruiting trained nurses in Britain to work in British communities overseas. At its annual meeting in 1899, Sir George Taubman-Goldie[1] praised the work of these nurses, in a paraphrase of Kipling, as 'the white woman's burden' (CNA Annual Report, 1899, p. 81; ONA, p. 131).

In Northern Nigeria no wives were present at the turn of the century, but a few nursing sisters were serving in Lokoja and Jebba. At the High Commissioner's dinner in Lokoja on 1 January 1900, celebrating the inauguration of formal colonial rule, Lugard invited 53 guests, among them two women, the nurses Miss Carter and Miss Nutt (Lugard Mss. 36/227). In Southern Nigeria, other nurses were working in Lagos and Old Calabar. During this early period they cared for a few soldiers wounded in battle, but the overwhelming number of their patients were officers stricken with the all-too prevalent tropical diseases of typhoid, dysentery, malaria and blackwater fever.

If in the beginning 'the white woman's burden' in Nigeria meant nursing white men, gradually European nursing sisters took up work in African (or 'Native') hospitals as well, and began the training of African nurses, both male and female. Between the wars, the government saw the need for developing maternity care and child welfare for African women and children. 'Lady Medical Officers' and nursing sisters were recruited for the Massey Street Maternity Hospital in Lagos and for starting maternity services in other areas – Katsina, Kano, Abeokuta, Enugu. Finally, during the last phase of British rule, efforts were turned to the vast expansion of health services and the training of Nigerians at all levels of medical and health care.[2]

This chapter deals mainly with the professional group who in 1948 became known as Queen Elizabeth's Overseas Nursing Service, the only branch of the Colonial Service with a membership composed exclusively of women (Udell, 1949, p. 23).[3] This in itself helps to explain why they were present at the beginning of the colonial enterprise in Nigeria, when other professional women were excluded: their work was classified unequivocally as 'women's work'. Not only were these nursing sisters present during the early years, but theirs was the largest professional group of women at all stages of colonial rule.

NURSES IN THE EARLY YEARS OF NIGERIA

The few nurses recruited on an experimental basis to Nigeria before 1900 served in small hospitals under the direction of government medical officers; they had widely varied conditions of service – hours on duty, regulations on uniforms, pay scales and allowances, lengths of tour and leave. The success of this experiment was also valued differently. The Governor of Lagos, Sir William MacGregor, wrote to the Colonial Secretary, Joseph Chamberlain, 'Several, too many, of the nurses have been giddy and restive beyond all expectation' (17 October 1899; ONA 123). In an earlier despatch he had observed that perhaps 'trained nurses of the servant girl class or the members of a nursing religious sisterhood' would be more appropriate for nursing duties in Lagos. The Colonial Office rebuffed the Governor by replying that in both the Northern and Southern Protectorates the nurses selected had been found thoroughly satisfactory. On the question of social class, the Secretary for the Colonies did not think it advisable that nurses in Lagos should be chosen from the class of domestic servants: 'He fears that they would be less able than nurses of somewhat higher social standing to resist the temptations to which they would be exposed in a Colony' (19 February 1900; ONA 123).

These few fragments of evidence place us in the midst of the late Victorian world of moral rectitude and discreet official statements without throwing much light on the nurses themselves. In his report of May 1901, the Chief Medical Officer of Lagos Colony, Dr. Strachan, recorded that the first European nurses had arrived in 1896. When he had assumed duties in 1898, he found few regulations guiding these nurses and, when rules were set out, argument resulted. He considered that 'there was a decided tendency on the part of the nurses to resent any restriction, however salutary – being placed on their movements, or the imposition of any disciplinary measures' (ONA 122). During the four years from May 1896 to April 1900, nine nurses had been appointed to the hospital. Of these, one had died; four had resigned on marriage and another had accepted a position in India; another had gone on leave and would not return; two recently appointed nurses remained. Dr. Strachan adds that it was a great pity the hospital could not be served by a nursing sisterhood; in contrast, he found that these nurses appeared to regard nursing as 'temporary employment before marriage'.

In the absence of further data, it is difficult to interpret these documents on the human drama of nurses in Lagos. The history of nursing (for example, Abel-Smith, 1975, pp. 17–35; Vicinus, 1985, pp. 85–120) cites the foundation of the Nightingale training school in 1860 as the beginning of the period when nursing became respectable as a career for gentlewomen, at that time

almost the only acceptable way for a young woman of the middle
or upper classes to leave the Victorian household and take up an
independent vocation. The school had two means of entry:
ordinary probationers who got free training and maintenance,
and lady-pupils who paid for their maintenance. It was the lady-
pupils who, by taking up the higher positions as matrons and
heads of nursing departments, were able to carry out Florence
Nightingale's nursing reforms. This movement was designed to
displace the old nurses (the 'Sarah Gamp' stereotype), hired from
the domestic service class and trained on an *ad hoc* basis by
hospital doctors, with educated women trained by senior nurses in
a defined field of knowledge and skills. As nurses gained a new
professional identity and enlarged role, institutions required new
organisational arrangements. This process was not without
conflict: medical opposition lasted for many years in hospitals
throughout the country. Doctors feared that educated women
would undermine their authority: the line was still not clear
between the matron's supervision of general nursing and the
doctor's responsibility for medical treatment. Eventually nursing
became established in its own domain, subsidiary to medicine.

In Lagos two points appear to be relevant: the nurses
apparently did not respond to the disciplinary measures of the
Chief Medical Officer and led a more active social life than
approved of by him or Governor MacGregor. Certainly the
marriage rate was high, with four of the nine nurses resigning to
marry before they had served as long as two years. Clearly in
endorsing nurses from a religious sisterhood or from a lower social
class, the senior colonial officers were advocating the 'prescriptive
model' of nursing at that time as a calling for dedicated single
women (see Maggs, 1980, pp. 18–40).[4]

In Northern Nigeria during this period, nurses were faced with
altogether more rugged demands. Two of those serving with the
West African Frontier Force, Miss Ward and Miss Neville, were
drafted to work at the base hospital of the Ashanti campaign in the
Gold Coast and received favourable mention in a despatch to the
Secretary of State (CNA Annual Report, 1901, p. 8; ONA 131).
From Jebba, Lugard reported to the Colonial Office on the
European nurses employed in the Northern Protectorate, quoting
the late Principal Medical Officer:

The employment of nursing sisters under such rough conditions and so far from civilisation, was an experiment which was fully justified by the results. The manner and extent of their training in a large London Hospital naturally rendered them superior in nursing ability to the Non-Commissioned Officers. I am of opinion that several lives were saved by their care. (14 June 1900; ONA 122)

The Principal Medical Officer in Old Calabar also gave high praise to the European nurses who had come into government service in 1895 on an agreement with the United Presbyterian Mission: 'Since the hospital had opened in December 1895, 241 cases had been admitted, most of them very serious and many of those which recovered of such severity that no power on earth could have saved them if they had been without the constant skilful care which can only be obtained in a hospital with well-trained nurses' (ONA 123). These nurses had very long hours on duty, as M. M. White wrote to the Secretary of the Colonial Nursing Association:

When I was in Calabar we took 8 hours duty at a time, which gave us every other night in bed, but as there are only two nurses in the hospital I consider these hours in such a trying climate much too long, as every other day we were on duty 16 hours out of the 24. (1 February 1900; ONA 123)

Based on these reports, the Colonial Office in 1902 issued a brochure: 'Information regarding Appointments for Nurses in West Africa' (ONA 123). Conditions of service were now made more consistent, although some local variations remained. Preference was to be given to applicants between 25 and 35 years of age with recent training in a large general hospital. The salary began at £100 a year, rising by triennial increments of £15 to £130 a year. Appointed first for one year, a nurse could be sent to any station; after satisfactory completion of probationary service, the appointment could be confirmed on recommendation of the Governor; she then became eligible for a pension or gratuity.

The list of uniform articles has a definite period flavour:

6 or 8 white skirts
6 or 8 white blouses
12 linen aprons
1 waist belt (navy blue silk petersham)
1 hat ribbon (navy blue silk petersham)

1 navy blue silk or alpaca dress
1 pair mackintosh over-shoes
3 white sailor hats
1 blue bonnet (for full dress)
12 collars (turn-down)
12 pairs cuffs
12 caps (Sister Dora or Indian Army)
1 helmet (optional)
1 mackintosh cloak (long)
1 white umbrella

Photographs of the time show that the white uniform skirt reached the floor and the blouse had long sleeves, hardly designed for comfortable work in the humid heat of West Africa. Full dress uniform (to be worn at all official functions) consisted of navy blue silk dress, collar and cuffs, waist belt, and bonnet or cap. In Lagos, special rules applied: 'Every nurse shall wear uniform when on duty and when off duty.' This rule was relaxed in 1904 to allow nurses to wear individual dress for private occasions.

During the early years of the colonial period in Nigeria, the number of European nurses gradually increased. The 1910 Annual Report of the CNA notes that nurses were serving in Lokoja and Zungeru in Northern Nigeria and in the new hospital at Baro, the starting point on the Niger River for the railway to Kano. In Southern Nigeria they were working in Lagos, Calabar, Onitsha and Warri. A series of letters from Ida Evans to the Secretary of the CNA provide vivid details of the nursing scene in Northern Nigeria at the time of the First World War. She writes from Kaduna, sending a photograph of their makeshift hospital with four beds:

> The Governor Sir Frederick Lugard visited the hospital and our quarters last time he was up, and seemed awfully pleased with all he saw. Ours are the only stone buildings in the place. All officers etc. have mud and grass houses. They are quite nice in dry weather, not so in the wet . . .

> The site for the future capital of all Nigeria is about four miles away from here, and there I believe the hospital will be big enough for 12 beds and quite up to date. Government House is going to be built first and then the hospital. Already they have miles of roads made and are starting Botanical Gardens, etc.,

rather strange for West Africa, when you see nothing but thick bush everywhere and every direction the same . . .

We have Mrs. Carter – the Colonel's wife for a week or two and it makes a very nice change. We see a great deal of her, unfortunately she is going back as they only have a mud house which only means one room and a verandah all round. We very rarely see any of our own sex, so we gladly welcomed her. (5 April 1914; ONA 140/1/15–18)

Her next letter is dimmed by news of the global war (18 August 1914; ONA 140/1/5–7). She was to have been presented with her Silver Badge (awarded for five years of meritorious service) by the Commandant with a parade in her honour, but the troops had left for the German Cameroons. Her leave has been postponed; she has volunteered for active service at the front. But in the letter following she states she is not likely to go to the front since Duala has surrendered. 'I'm afraid we have lost some excellent officers on the German frontier and some that we know very well in Kaduna' (2 October 1914; ONA 140/1/4).

The war also brought casualties among nurses. Two were bound for West Africa in 1915 when their ship was torpedoed by a German submarine; one nurse was drowned, the other returned to England and sailed on the next ship to join the Expeditionary Force in the Cameroons (CNA Annual Report 1915, p. 16; ONA 131).

NEW WORK BETWEEN THE WARS

While some nurses continued to work in European hospitals after the First World War, increasing numbers were assigned to African hospitals, where the training and supervision of African nurses, both men and women, became one of their main tasks. In addition to these general hospitals, the government set out a programme for maternity and child welfare services: opening Massey Street Dispensary in Lagos, providing maternity wings in the new general hospitals, organising midwifery training, and initiating welfare work for Muslim women in purdah in a few cities of Northern Nigeria.

The ONA Annual Report of 1920 lists 26 nurses serving in

Nigeria, with a total of 43 in West Africa. The interchange of postings in West Africa was formally recognised in 1928 with the organisation of the West African Nursing Staff – comprising The Gambia, Gold Coast, Nigeria, and Sierra Leone – for the provision of unified service conditions. By 1930 the number of nurses had more than doubled, with 60 nurses now serving in Nigeria (five of these on the permanent staff) and 105 in the WANS. With the depression, however, this number remained the same during the next decade (ONA Annual Reports; ONA 131).

On the application form of the Overseas Nursing Association, the question was now included: 'Do you understand that you may be in a hospital where all the patients, assistants and servants are coloured and that you may be required to work under doctors of a different race from your own?' The notes in 1938 summarising the interview by the ONA committee for a candidate state, 'Understands about climate. Has had coloured patients. No feeling against them. Does not think would mind coloured doctors – is used to coloured students' (ONA 130/26). But even with this screening, the occasional unsuitable selection was made. One nurse posted to Nigeria in June 1937 resigned in December 1942, ostensibly because her parents needed her, but the following remarks were recorded after her phone call to the Secretary of the ONA: 'She is sorry to break her career but doesn't really care for nursing natives – finds the partly educated West African difficult and dishonest. Doesn't stand the heat very well!' (ONA 130/12).

Letters from this period give graphic accounts of professional work and social life from within the medical setting; these also show imperial attitudes typical of the interwar years. Like officers in other branches of the Colonial Service, nurses did not get their assignment until their outbound ship touched in at Accra and even then they could not be certain. Mary Lucas writes that when she got to Accra she had orders for Kaduna, but on arriving at Lagos they were short-handed and kept her there. After a few months, she was posted to Onitsha, 'the most beautiful spot a human being could wish to live in although the living is a trifle primitive in parts' (2 April 1925; ONA 140/1/34–9). Here she was the only nursing sister on the station, where about ten government officers lived on a hill overlooking the River Niger. She describes

a curious and rather happy life. Everyone working all day absorbed in their various jobs, and then soon after 5 p.m., everyone gets equally busy playing tennis or golf, and then a much needed drink and exchange of views to others at the club or in someone's house and after that dinner about 8 p.m., and early to bed.

Her next letter was written during the rainy season from Calabar, her third station in eight months: 'Here it rains and rains and rains and the sun seems to have forgotten how to function and the stars are lost to us' (10 August 1925; ONA 140/1/35–7). She tells about the journey on her own from Onitsha to Calabar: 'The Station Magistrate at Onitsha lent me his car for the first stage as far as Aba – 140 miles – very interesting trip though the road was very bad in places. It took me from 8 a.m. to 4 p.m. and I did not see a white man the whole way.' She stayed the night with friends and the next day was driven on to Oron by Works transport. To get to Calabar she had to take a ferry; she tells of long delays and her arrival in total darkness at a landing several miles from where friends were expecting her.

She is not impressed with Calabar: 'I think it ugly. The Native Hospital is an ugly building and looks the worst at 7 a.m. after a hurriedly bolted breakfast at 6:30 and a horrible jolting ride of nearly a mile downhill in the hammock.' Her work she describes as 'endeavouring to care for my black brethren, or rather trying to teach them how to care for, or nurse each other'. This she finds 'a job more suitable to a direct descendant of Job than an ordinary individual, for it requires patience and again patience and then more patience for at least eight good hours every day.' She analyses the difficulties with some insight: 'Some people say that the average African is a phenomenal liar and incapable of speaking the truth. I don't think that exactly. I think that their knowledge of English is so inaccurate that mostly they quite fail to understand you and just answer yes or no and trust to luck.'

Her final letter tells of transfer to the European Hospital, 'a most blessed place in comparison' (26 December 1925; ONA 140/1/40–1). Mary Lucas looks back on her experience:

Thank Heaven I have finished my bit in the Native Hospital! Six months is more than enough for anyone to do there without a break! The Native Hospital was an amazing place and is a great credit to the Doctors and Sisters who have organised it . . . I have never in all my years of nursing seen such a succession of horrible cases, 'never seen' did I say? – rather, never even imagined anything like them. I used to dream about them. And then the Native staff. A doctor said to us the other day, 'It is not the climate that kills, it is trying to teach the Native to work.'

A letter written from Port Harcourt and published anonymously in *Nursing Notes* of March 1927 (ONA 132/8) gives an account by the sister in charge of the Native hospital there.

The work is very much like that of a general hospital at home, medical and surgical cases, gynaecological and midwifery and the usual out-patient queues. We do from 10 to 12 abdominal cases weekly, and have 60–100 out-patients daily. I do theatre always, instruments and ligatures and sutures, and the rest of the work is really more supervisory, stores and linen occupying at least two days a week.

Her comments on 'native nurses' are conventional for the time:

Some of our native nurses have been here 20 to 25 years, and are excellent. One in a dozen is a genius in a way, the others take months of patient teaching. They need very strict supervision even to their administration of castor oil, their own love of it being apt to lead them into the temptation of swallowing it themselves. They love it, and any other drinking medicine as they call it. In many ways they are children, and their brains are undeveloped as ours were when the Romans came to Britain. Now they are becoming much keener on education knowing that all vacancies are filled by sixth standard people.

Writing from Kano in Northern Nigeria, Mary Macdonald reports on the expected visit of the Prince of Wales. The European hospital has been busy and the number of beds will be increased temporarily for the royal festivities. 'There are to be a great many visitors to Kano for the Durbar which is to take place then, and as it is the worst month of the year just before the rains come, there is sure to be a lot of sickness' (24 March 1925; ONA/140/1/30). A temporary isolation hospital was also being set up for the 'Natives', since the Emirs and their followers from all over Northern Nigeria would be coming to take part in the celebrations and were likely to bring in infectious diseases.

In Ibadan, Dorothy Purvis was in charge of both Native and European hospitals, with five male nurses working under her. She describes the setting: 'Our compound is a large one, comprising two hospitals, dispensary, my house, the Senior Medical Officer's house, the dispenser's house, Native and European kitchens, nurses' quarters, an infectious block for smallpox cases etc., an isolation hut of four rooms for syphilitic cases, ulcers etc. and all the outhouses' (1 June 1926; ONA 136/3/12–13). Her work began every morning at 7 am with the difficult dressings in the Native ward. She writes of a particular case:

> Last night we had a Native soldier brought in at midnight with a terrible shattered leg, the result of a shooting affray after gambling. He nearly bled to death on the way from the Barracks and by the aid of lamps (alas no electric light!), his leg had to be amputated at once at the knee. He is really doing well, in spite of the awful shock.

And another in the European hospital:

> At present I am having a very anxious time with a young Englishman who is very seriously ill with typhoid, dysentery and other complications. This patient has been running a temperature between 104 and 105 for 22 days and we are wondering how much longer his pulse will hold out.

She makes the point: 'One cannot rely on the native nurses for really serious cases, they have no initiative and are not reliable in any way.'

Her next letter describes the training for nurses: 'I had a two days exam paper for my 15 probationers (my original four have now risen to 15, including three girls of whom I am very proud). They look very neat in their blue cotton frocks and VAD caps . . . I have now got all the men in white ¾ coats which is a great improvement' (28 December 1926; ONA 136/3/14–16). Unaware of any cultural imposition, she tells about Christmas celebrations:

> The Native Hospital I decorated with scarlet paper decorations from Derry & Toms, with lanterns and large yellow bells hanging from them. The excitement early on Xmas morning was intense when I distributed toys from England for the children and gave round Illustrated London News and Xmas cards for everybody (including the servants, labourers and even the policemen on duty guarding the prisoner patients of whom we always have a number) . . . At midday they had a special dinner of a sack of rice, treble portion of meat in their soup and

tomatoes and fruit all round, which was repeated again at 4 pm. The children were very thrilled over the first crackers they had ever seen.

Announcing her engagement to the Senior Conservator of Forests in Southern Nigeria, she describes the parties given for them:

> My SMO (Senior Medical Officer) had a dance and bridge party in his house to celebrate our engagement in November. It all went off very well. There were 75 people there and the compound looked like fairyland all lighted up with 500 little oil lamps with floating wicks. Everybody has been extraordinarily kind and nice and we have had a whirl of dinner parties to go to including one at Government House.

Dorothy Purvis takes for granted her resignation on marriage and the end of her nursing career: 'I shall be terribly sorry to give up my work here. I have loved every minute of the time.' Nurses were in great demand as marriage partners, as these letters show. Mary Macdonald, for example, writes, 'Miss Parson's marriage was a great surprise to everyone. She is living in Lagos and I hear looking very well. I heard the other week that Miss Anderson who came out on the boat with me is engaged' (24 March 1925; ONA/140/1/30).

The information bulletin issued by the Colonial Office in 1937 on the West African Nursing Staff gives the conditions of service at this time (ONA 136/3). Pay had risen to £350 a year for a nursing sister on her first tour, increasing to £400 after eighteen months' service with annual increments up to £480; for senior nursing sisters to £500 a year with annual increments; and for matrons to £700 a year. The list of uniform articles had changed little from that of three decades earlier, although now the duty uniform had short sleeves. For ceremonial occasions the uniform dress had changed to fine white drill with long coat sleeves to be worn with white kid gloves. Despite the tropical heat, the requirement for wearing white stockings on duty was not lifted until the Second World War brought shortages and the principle of common sense ruled over that of maintaining the established professional image.

LADY MEDICAL OFFICER

In 1925 the first of four 'Lady Medical Officers' recruited to develop maternity and infant welfare services arrived in Lagos. One of these was Dr. Greta Lowe-Jellicoe (née Lowe), whose story derives from personal interviews as well as from her collection of nearly a hundred letters written from Nigeria to two women medical colleagues in England. Born in 1898, Dr. Lowe-Jellicoe entered medical school in Manchester near the end of the First World War when there was a big demand for doctors and the largest proportion ever of women was accepted, ten out of a class of eighty. She qualified in 1923, winning a much-coveted medical prize. Missionary work appealed to her after reading Dr. Schweitzer's account of the hospital in Lambarene; she held posts in mission hospitals in Freetown, Sierra Leone, and in Ilesha, Nigeria, before joining the Colonial Medical Service.

She was sent first to Abeokuta, where the government had taken over the Roman Catholic Sacred Heart Hospital, to work on the women's side, mainly maternity cases. Some of these, here and later in Lagos, were very difficult, when women were brought in in an advanced state of labour, having been given all sorts of treatments by 'Native doctors'. She and the nursing sister were able to save the lives of many of these women and their babies. It was rewarding work: 'I liked producing a live baby when it wasn't expected' (interview, 4 November 1983). The circumstances were far from easy. One of her letters from that period notes, 'We have had several night calls lately & I do dislike doing a forceps case by the light of a hurricane lamp' (letter, 2 March 1930). Part of her duties, here and in Lagos, was the training and supervision of local nurses in midwifery courses.

Later, Dr. Lowe-Jellicoe was sent as the first woman government officer to start medical work among the Muslim women of Katsina, where all except the poorest were confined in purdah. She wrote to her friends about the hazards of her journey from Abeokuta, some 800 miles by train to Kano and then by car and lorry to Katsina. Here she was 'dumped' in a rest house for a few weeks: 'The swallows and lizards & flies & an occasional scorpion still bear me company' (letter, 31 May 1930). Having moved into her fifth house within a few months, she told how she heartily hated that part of colonial life. Her job, however, was beginning to take shape:

> After much consultation I have taken over the women's side of the existing general hospital. My job is to look after that, to visit purdah patients in the town & to train some illiterate Hausa girls & make nurses of them. I can't get any females between fifteen and forty – they are all busy being wives. I have just obtained six between 10 & 15 years old. They were the dirtiest little urchins you ever saw the first time we met & the whole thing is just a passing game to them. They don't know one word of English . . .   (letter, 25 July 1930)

She designed a uniform for the nurses, white kerchiefs on their heads and a simple dress made of local cotton in a 'biscuity' colour. She says, 'I was very much against Europeanising them, which all government sisters and the mission sisters did, giving them European names, which I always thought was such a pity. I became very fond of them' (interview, 4 November 1983). Soon she was visiting the women in the Emir's palace, finding this a small village in itself – each wife with her own little mud house and her own wealth measured by a pyramid of brass bowls. Here she gave various medicines, did a lot of teeth extractions, and began infant welfare work. Her Hausa improved. One of the Emir's wives, she remembers, was very charming and had a good sense of humour.

Suddenly she was posted back to Lagos to replace another LMO on leave. She preferred working in Katsina, but was never able to stay for a long period. After a later change of posting, she told her friends:

> I have just received news that I am to transfer to Lagos in the first half of January. I very nearly wept when I read the notice. Lagos I loathe, Katsina I like. The job there I detest. The job here is creative, interesting. I have just finished – only just finished unpacking and now I have to repack my 60 odd cases.   (letter, 26 December 1933)

Lagos brought her back to 'civilisation'. Her small, modern house located on the lagoon had luxuries long forgone – electric lights, a telephone and an electric geyser for hot water. Her work was also quite a change:

> Nominally I have the Massey Street Clinic to run. It consists of an Out Patient Dept. for women & children with a daily attendance of between 90 and 120. The antenatal & infant cases

are given precedence. There are two wards one general and one maternity. I believe we have about half a dozen abnormal midder cases a month & twenty normal but am not sure yet. The training of midwives is one of the aims of the hospital so that entails lecturing. Three afternoons a week I have an Infant Welfare Clinic to attend. Three at Massey St. & one at Ebute Metta about five miles away. In addition to all this I have charge of the two female wards at the African General Hospital.   (letter, 17 April 1932)

This was a well equipped hospital: 'Its building would put to shame many of the same size which I have seen in England.' Two very good senior medical men were in charge, with five European nursing sisters. She admits feeling rather lost amid such efficiency:

The Path. lab. is most obliging & efficient & the X Ray dept. just at hand. I had almost completely forgotten what functions these last two possessed. It is difficult not to lay oneself open to the scorn of the fortunate members of the staff who have not been hidden away in the bush for the last six years.

On her last tour in Lagos, a new assignment came her way. She wrote to her medical friends, 'To my great trial at present I have to lecture to 4th year Medical Students (a new College has been opened here) on Midwifery & Gynaecology – I had one day's notice. Oh! Heaven's it is a trial. What do *you* remember now about choriodecidual spaces and diseases of the syncitium now, I ask you?' (9 February 1934). This was the Yaba Medical Training College, which began in 1930 for training medical assistants and continued until 1948; because its training was not recognised by the British Medical Council of Britain, considerable discontent arose among Nigerians (Schram, 1971, pp. 203–6).

The worldwide recession had dire effects in Nigeria. Dr. Lowe-Jellicoe reports that the levy on their salaries was to be continued; staff was being cut down. 'Things are very bad here & there is talk of more & more & more retrenchments. Two out of the four LMOs have resigned & they are not replacing them' (letter, 3 August 1934). Before long she had difficulties with her eyes and was herself invalided home.

During her service in Nigeria, she found some of her male medical colleagues to be misogynists, others friendly and helpful. In Abeokuta and Lagos she had held responsibility for extremely difficult maternity cases and in Katsina had pioneered medical care for Muslim women in purdah. She had lectured in the first Nigerian medical school. All of this varied work she had enjoyed, and she had always wanted to return. When she hears criticism of colonial officers, she asks whether the Nigerians whose lives she saved, or their children or grandchildren, would really say they wished she had never been there (interview, 4 November 1983).

NURSES AND WOMEN DOCTORS: COMPARISONS AND CONTRASTS

Although they were both engaged in health care in Nigeria, the position of nurses contrasts with that of women doctors. In her trenchant analysis, Gamarnikov (1978) shows how nursing provides a vivid case of the sexual division of labour within the patriarchal context. When nursing was established as an occupation, it posed a threat to the male medical profession; in order for nursing to preserve its own space, a gender ideology was developed identifying it with femininity and placing it in a subsidiary position to medicine. Doctor–nurse–patient relationships were represented as essentially homologous to the family structure. The equation of the patient with a child requiring care provided the ideological image for depicting doctors as 'fathers' and nurses as 'mothers'. Doctors were associated with science and authority, nurses with caring. Florence Nightingale placed emphasis not so much on the nurse's skill, competence or education, but on her 'feminine' character, a set of moral qualities (patience, humility, gentleness, sympathy, obedience) differentiating women from men. The division of labour was thus set out within the familiar Victorian gender ideology of hierarchical complementarity. In the Nigerian colonial context, the feminine role of nurses reinforced the established cultural order by emphasising the masculine role of doctors and colonial administrators.

During the period after the First World War, women doctors were the few exceptions in a male profession; they were seen as anomalies and found themselves in a marginal and vulnerable position. They had gone through the same training, passed the same examinations, and were capable of the same range of work as their male colleagues, but they constantly had to prove their abilities. When Parliament pressed for the development of maternity and child welfare for the colonies, women doctors were considered appropriate for this work with indigenous women. In the Colonial Medical Service they had the same conditions of service as the men and the same increments, but they met difficulties relating to perceived gender roles.

The Medical branch held a privileged position in salary and rank within the Colonial Service. As early as 1902, the reorganisation of the Medical Service placed African doctors (those trained in the same medical schools as Europeans) on a lower pay scale and they were never to have seniority over even the most junior Europeans (Schram, 1971, p. 130).[5] The dividing line between the races was thus firmly set out at an early stage; between the sexes the boundary was drawn as well, but in a different way. European women doctors were recruited for a specific area of medical practice (women and children) and in this early period, Dr. Cecily Williams (who served in Ghana) states that there was no promotion for women doctors (interview with Dr. Daphne Roe, 8 November 1980). While nurses were seen, thus, as a properly subordinate group carrying out a complementary role to (male) doctors, women doctors were perceived as problematic. The experience of these first Lady Medical Officers suggests that they appeared as a 'danger' (subverting the 'natural' order) both to their medical colleagues and to other male officers.

This difference was reflected in the social life of the two groups. Nursing sisters were conventionally housed in group quarters near the hospital and had a communal 'mess', while women doctors had individual houses. Many of the nurses married government officers in Nigeria, but none of the women doctors did during this early period. This was not a question of age, since Dr. Lowe-Jellicoe joined the Colonial Service when she was in her late twenties, the same age as many of the nurses, but more to do with seniority. As she pointed out, most men older than she was were already married and those of her own age were likely to be earning much less. One man said to her, 'I can't ask you to marry me because I'm earning less than you are' (interview, 4 November 1983). For her, there was also the question of giving up her work commitment for the role of a dependent colonial wife. Interestingly, women missionary doctors in Nigeria at that time were able to continue their medical practice after marriage.

NURSING DURING THE SECOND WORLD WAR

The year 1940 marked the creation of the Colonial Nursing Service, which brought the nursing staffs of the great majority of the colonies into a unified service on the lines of the Colonial Administrative Service, Colonial Medical Service and other branches. This step made it possible for nurses to go to a colony with the prospect of a long-term career not necessarily in one colony.

Again, the war brought dangers for the passage to Nigeria, with shipping lines crowded and convoys required. Casualties among nurses began in 1941 with the news that G. E. Hayes was not among the survivors when the ship she was travelling on from West Africa was sunk by enemy action; she had worked in Nigeria since 1934 (ONA Annual Report, 1940–1). Five nurses were going out to West Africa on the SS *Accra* when it was torpedoed; they were saved and eventually went on to their posts, but lost all their possessions.

In Nigeria the war brought tremendous changes to the country, as British, American and West African forces were deployed there during the desert warfare in North Africa. Military hospitals were built and army medical personnel brought in. Malaria became a serious problem, although after the change from quinine to mepacrine in 1943, this threat abated. Barbara Schofield (Ms., p. 5) reports that when the war began in September 1939, Europeans in the government service received a letter from the Colonial Office stating that each person was to continue in his post; no resignations were allowed.

Labour restrictions at home caused difficulties during the war years. In April 1943, all nurses and midwives were required to register and, in September, this was followed by the extension of the Employment of Women (Control of Engagement) order to include all nurses and midwives under 41 years of age (ONA Annual Report, 1943). Now each individual nurse's application had to be referred to the Ministry of Labour before she could be offered appointment; only a proportion of the State Certified Midwives could be released to go abroad. Nurses with public health qualifications were also in short supply. The most serious shortage coincided with the growing demand for qualified sister tutors who were needed for training nurses in the UK, as well as for the expanding training programmes overseas. These restrictions were not lifted to allow free movement of nurses until June 1946.

TIME OF EXPANSION AND HANDING-OVER

When the war was over, the time for assessment arrived. In the words of the Ten-Year Development Plan in 1946, the medical and health services in Nigeria were found to be 'far below the average in the Colonial Empire and, in some respects, as bad as anywhere in the world' (Nigeria Government, 1946, p. 15). Colonial Development and Welfare funds were now allocated for the rapid expansion of the medical services including the building of hospitals and health centres. As the political scene moved closer to Independence, emphasis was placed on training Nigerians at all levels to enable them to take over. The training of nurses received high priority. In 1946 the status of Nigerian Registered Nurse gained official recognition; this required an initial six months in a Preliminary Training school in Lagos, Aba or Kano (and, by 1952, Ibadan), followed by training for three years in an approved hospital. Beyond this qualification, Grade 2 midwives needed 12 months of specialised training and Grade 1 a period of 18 months.

For women in the Colonial Nursing Service, to be designated in 1948 as Queen Elizabeth's Colonial Nursing Service, new opportunities arose as health visitors, sister tutors in specialised areas, and matrons of the newly-established hospitals. Some now served under Nigerian doctors and worked closely with Nigerian nursing colleagues. By 1948, eighty nursing sisters were working in Nigeria. Numbers rose during the next decade to 95 in 1952 and 98 in 1958, the great majority of these serving in the Northern Region. By the time of Independence, the number held at ninety, but by 1965 fewer than twenty were left (ONA Annual Reports).

Barbara Akinyemi, a health visitor arriving in Lagos in March 1947, provides sharp observations on the medical and social scene. She tells of the experience of another health sister from the West Indies of African descent, who had arrived at the same time with the same qualifications:

> In a short time I was fixed up with a nice flat, car, proper salary and a bank account opened, while she was being treated as a

locally recruited person with no transport, or accommodation
and a salary far below mine. Eventually, I took her secretly into
my flat in Ikoyi.   (Ms., p. 5)

Official concessions were made 'grudgingly', but later this woman
became the Chief Nursing Officer.

Barbara Akinyemi's work as a health visitor brought her to a
local clinic, where she found the bright headties of the waiting
mothers resembled a flower garden. She was now in 'the clinical
world of enlarged spleens, fevers, "jedi-jedi" (piles) and umbilical
hernias' (p. 7). Here she found the typical colonial time lag:
leaflets were being distributed with clocks illustrating infant
feedings at intervals of three or four hours, while in England
child-care authorities were now advocating the demand feeding
that Nigerian women traditionally practised. Her interviews had
to take place through an interpreter, a tedious exercise involving
many misunderstandings. She wanted to learn Yoruba, and
friends sent along a young man as teacher; six years later they
were married in England.

The first qualified midwife tutor in Nigeria, Marion Hooley,
was posted in 1951 as nurse administrator and tutor to the Massey
Street Maternity Hospital in Lagos, where Grade 1 midwives
were trained. The consultant obstetrician in charge of this
hospital was now a Nigerian, Dr. M. A. Majekodunmi, and after
six months a second obstetrician arrived from training in the UK,
Dr. (Mrs) Awaliyi, one of the first Nigerian woman doctors. For
midwifery training, Marion Hooley tells that her pupils practised
taking case histories in the ante-natal wards, usually conducted in
pidgin English with the patients, including such questions as
'How many moons you no see flower?' (blood) to help indicate the
date of the patient's last menstrual period. Pupils were also given
bedside tuition in the post-natal wards and instruction in the
general care of the babies, both normal and those 'at risk'. She
moved to a new setting in July 1960 when the new Lagos Island
Maternity Hospital was opened, with 236 beds and modern
facilities. Here she was in charge of the teaching unit of 110
student midwives with two other midwife teachers, one European
and one Nigerian. There were now two large classrooms fitted
with screens for film projection, blackboards, and an abundant
new supply of teaching aids. She stayed until the end of 1962,
deciding it was time to leave since trained Nigerians were ready to

step in. She concludes, 'It was a pleasure to work with all the Doctors in Massey Street. Dr. Majekodunmi set the pace and the others followed. I would describe him as a pioneer in his own country' (Ms., p. 10).

After war service with the Royal Naval Nursing Service and experience with the National Health Service, Phillis James went in 1952 to Northern Nigeria to serve for nearly ten years. She was not alone in finding the official list of required items useless:

> The list included mosquito boots, white stockings, that I never wore, and a topee; this really caused me great trouble. At the end of the afternoon I called into the office where I found a very helpful secretary, told her my trouble, she had one look at the list of requirements and said it was obviously made out in Lord Lugard's day and had not been updated.   (Ms., p. 1)

She vividly remembers her introduction to Makurdi African General Hospital:

> The Hospital was in a very run down state – overcrowded – patients and families sleeping together in beds and on the floors. The stores were full of unused equipment. Rolls of mackintosh for draw sheets all stuck together, ant hills growing out of specimen jars, blankets rotting and everything had layers of dust. An X-ray machine still in its original crate was found in the compound, had been there some considerable time; no electricity was available in the station. Bats were in abundance causing much damage to ceilings and generally the place was in a most untidy and unhygienic state.   (p. 4)

Soon a visit from the Medical Director prompted the appointment of another doctor and nursing sister, extra financial help was granted, and the hospital reached the required standard. Later, after promotion to the grade of Matron, she was assigned to Katsina where she found goats continually wandering into the hospital and even into the operating theatre. She comments, 'I could not imagine the Matron of my Training School chasing goats!' (Ms., p. 6). But, she adds, 'We just carried on, in spite of shortages of drugs, antibiotics and other medical supplies that frequently happened.'

Arriving in Maiduguri in 1955, Muriel Holmes describes the wards at that time as 'old, attractive, mud-built and primitive' (Ms., p. 7). Neem trees gave welcome shade to the compound during the trying heat of the dry season. During this period there was a water shortage, the hospital being supplied twice a day by lorry and patients being rationed to one pint morning and evening. At that time there was no maternity clinic and no trained Nigerian midwife. She relates, 'Our senior midwife was a wonderful old Kanuri woman, illiterate but very devoted and much loved. She had made the pilgrimage to Mecca so was addressed as "Hajja". Her midwifery, bad as it was, was from all I was told infinitely better than the native ways' (p. 5).

One nursing sister served over twenty-five years in Nigeria; this was Elizabeth Paterson, who arrived in 1951 after five years in Cyprus. Her first tour took her to various hospitals in Eastern Nigeria – Aba, Ikot Ekpene, Calabar and Port Harcourt. At Aba, where there was a training school for nurses, one of her duties was giving simple lectures in nursing and hygiene. She remembers Dr Femi Pearce, the Nigerian Medical Officer in charge, telling her, 'What is wanted from an expatriate nursing sister is discipline, well-kept stores and good examination results' (Ms., p. 8).

On her next tour she went to Northern Nigeria, where she stayed for the rest of her career. When she was promoted in 1962 to Principal Matron at the Ministry of Health in Kaduna, she had to learn a new type of administration on the job with most evenings and weekends at the office. Besides attending meetings of the Nurses Council and the Midwives Board, she enjoyed touring and inspecting some forty government and mission hospitals throughout the region. When this post was Nigerianised, she returned to Jos. Later she became Chief Nursing Officer of Borno State; after two tours she again handed over to a Nigerian, this time a male nursing officer with three wives and thirteen children – quite a change, she comments, from the conventional single female officer (p. 3). Her services in Nigeria gained her, in 1968, the award of an MBE. Another who received recognition was Barbara Schofield with an MBE in 1950; she went on to become Matron-in-Chief in Tanganyika and later in Hong Kong, gaining an OBE in 1963.

THE CHANGING ROLES OF COLONIAL NURSES

As the only group of professional women serving for the entire period from 1900 to 1960, nurses in their changing roles reflect the

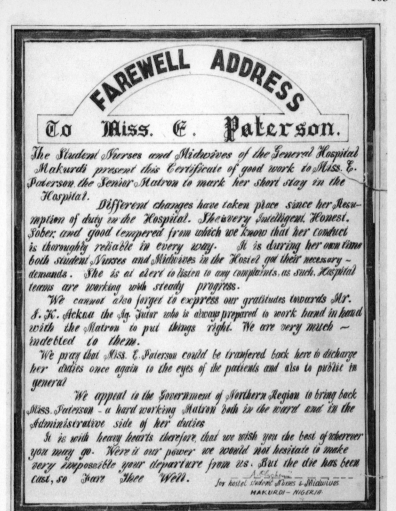

FAREWELL ADDRESS

To Miss. E. Paterson.

The Student Nurses and Midwives of the General Hospital Makurdi present this Certificate of good work to Miss. E. Paterson, the Senior Matron to mark her short stay in the Hospital.

Different changes have taken place since her Resumption of duty in the Hospital. She is very Intelligent, Honest, Sober, and good tempered from which we know that her conduct is thoroughly reliable in every way. It is during her own time both student Nurses and Midwives in the Hostel got their necessary demands. She is at alert to listen to any complaints, as such, Hospital teams are working with steady progress.

We cannot also forget to express our gratitudes towards Mr. J. K. Ackaa the Ag. Tutor who is always prepared to work hand in hand with the Matron to put things right. We are very much indebted to them.

We pray that Miss. E. Paterson could be transfered back here to discharge her duties once again to the eyes of the patients and also to public in general

We appeal to the Government of Northern Region to bring back Miss. Paterson - a hard working Matron both in the ward and in the Administrative side of her duties

It is with heavy hearts therefore, that we wish you the best of wherever you may go. Were it our power we would not hesitate to make very impossible your departure from us. But the die has been cast, so Farr Thee Well.

for hostel student Nurses & Midwives
MAKURDI – NIGERIA.

Plate 1: Student nurses often showed their appreciation to favourite matrons by presenting special certificates, such as this one, as a farewell gift.

successive phases of colonial rule. At first, they were nursing only Europeans in the small hospitals built to reduce the high mortality rate of colonial officers. Part of their work entailed training African nurses, many of whom were male. After the First World War, they began working in African hospitals, one nursing sister often being in charge. Their training of nurses became more systematic; standards were set and examinations centralised. With the development of maternity services in the period between the wars, they began midwifery training, an area reserved for female nurses. Given the limited educational opportunities of Africans at that time, it is not difficult to imagine the communication difficulties between European nurses with little or no knowledge of indigenous languages and Africans with imperfect English.

Following the Second World War, nurses took on a wider variety of duties. As matrons of large Nigerian hospitals, they had greater authority and enlarged responsibilities; sometimes they complained that keeping track of the stores took more effort than dealing with patients and nursing staff. Health visitors now travelled to small clinics throughout a province, a particularly rugged job in some areas of Northern Nigeria where distances were vast and roads few; those with duties to places beyond roads were compensated with horse allowances. With the opening of new hospitals and enlarging of old ones, the training of nurses expanded throughout the country. The need for new professional expertise was met by sister tutors, who developed training programmes and organised examinations.

How far was the colonial model of gender relations in the medical profession imposed on the Nigerian scene? The equation of nurses with female and doctors with male met considerable cultural resistance. Because Nigerian boys had educational advantages over girls, young men came forward in the early years for training as nurses. Added to this were the social customs approving male nurses for men's wards and female nurses for women and children. In the Muslim areas of Northern Nigeria, nurses' training for girls hardly got under way because girls' education was not encouraged and they were expected to marry at an early age, while in Western and Eastern Nigeria the proportion of girls in nurses' training rose significantly only during the last decade before Independence. Here Nigerian women (some of whom were trained in the UK) took over as matrons of the government hospitals, but in the North men moved into the highest administrative positions in the nursing profession.

As for doctors, Nigerian men went into medical training long before women because they were given advantages in education both by Nigerian families and by the colonial government. After the Second World War, a few Nigerian women went abroad for medical training. In the societies of Western and Eastern Nigeria, women traditionally worked outside the domestic scene after marriage and during their childbearing years; they followed this pattern in continuing their professional careers. When Nigerian governments took over, service conditions for professional women improved with the introduction of maternity leave and benefits.

This chapter would not be complete without mention of the University College Hospital at Ibadan, which opened in 1957 as the showpiece of a well-equipped modern teaching hospital in Africa (Schram, 1971, pp. 263–74). In one sense, this might be considered as marking the post-colonial phase. While planning took place during the period of colonial rule, the hospital was built by Nigerian funds to match their aspirations for a medical school equal to the highest international standards. British medical specialists (women as well as men) were recruited, along with qualified Nigerians, to make up the entire range of medical expertise. In the years following Independence, fully qualified Nigerians gradually replaced these expatriates.

At the same time, a School of Nursing was established for training at a higher level than the recognised Nigerian Registered Nurse, with a British principal in charge and a full complement of British nursing sisters devoted to teaching (Schram, 1971, pp. 275–6). This might be seen as a 'second Nightingale reform' taking place a century later and in a different country. The Principal, Louise Bell, and many of the nursing sisters, had trained at the Florence Nightingale School in St. Thomas's Hospital in London, including Mrs E. Pratt, who later became the first Nigerian Matron of University College Hospital and Chief Nursing Officer for the Federation. They were committed to nursing as a field exclusively for women and to new methods of training for reaching higher standards of patient care. The patient was now to be considered not just as a medical case in the ward, but as a whole person within the social and physical environment of his home and community (Tattersall, Ms., p. 9). This new training programme was vigorous, exciting, and more closely related to Nigerian life. Its recruits had completed secondary school and these young women, the first to qualify as a State Registered Nurse (recognition by the General Nursing Council of England and Wales) on their home grounds, became the leaders of the new generation of Nigerian nurses.

The colonial nursing sisters were superseded, but it is necessary to see them and their work within the cultural world of their time and the particular constraints of the Colonial Service. Their posts were changed frequently without advance notice, and as the letters and reports show, they took on diverse and difficult assignments, sometimes in neglected and remote hospitals, often under conditions of no electricity, shortages of water, lack of basic equipment and essential medical supplies. In stations with only one medical officer, they were sometimes left in complete charge of a hospital, and often their range of responsibilities was far greater than expected of nursing sisters in their homeland. For some the return to Britain was difficult. Phillis James writes, 'I felt claustrophobic – I missed the friendliness of people that was so apparent in West Africa. I hated the watertight compartments associated with working in the Hospitals in England.. In Nigeria we did most things that came our way – working set hours was unknown.'

Although there was no obligation for medical staff to learn a Nigerian language, some of these nurses made the attempt in more or less systematic ways. Throughout the colonial period these nursing sisters were expected to conduct nurses' training although few had any training in teaching. Qualified sister tutors arrived in Nigeria only after the Second World War. In the new era of more egalitarian relations with Nigerians, many of the post-war nursing sisters worked under Nigerian doctors and side by side with Nigerian nurses; some were highly critical of those with 'old colonial' attitudes who kept to European clubs and a segregated social life.

Many of these nursing sisters served in Nigeria for a decade or longer; Elizabeth Paterson continued her work for over a quarter of a century, including seventeen years beyond Independence. The numerous testimonials with their reports to the Oxford Development Records Project attest to the warm appreciation of Nigerians. Their work was seen as having long-term benefits in the training they carried on for echelons of Nigerians at various levels of health care. Its immediate value was perceived when patients recovered from illnesses that might have been fatal. In this respect, women education officers, whose story will be taken up next, had a more ambivalent reception.

5 Women Education Officers

As far as girls' education is concerned, obviously we achieved more than we thought we had – we laid a foundation and an attitude on which individual girls have been able to build a life for themselves as soon as Nigeria's rapid development showed them the possibilities.

(Evelyn Clark, Principal, Women's Training Centre, Sokoto, 1949–57, Ms., p. 20)

BEGINNINGS[1]

While nurses often had to adapt to trying conditions and deal with emergencies not met in their homeland, their work was well defined in professional terms, carried out mainly in hospitals or clinics, and wholeheartedly seen as beneficial by the local populace. Women education officers, in contrast, were far more closely engaged in the contradictory and ambiguous processes of social and cultural change. Their work, by its very nature, helped to shape the intellect and consciousness, the skills and habits, of young persons growing up in cultures very different from their own. In a few places they met with opposition from all sides: from the girls coming to school, their parents and grandparents, Nigerian rulers and district heads, a few European administrative officers and even some of their male colleagues in the education department. This led them to searching questions about how to create a congenial atmosphere for learning and a curriculum related to the local environment as well as to aspirations for the future. Mediating between two cultures, they had to improvise and innovate.

Again in comparison to nurses who served in Nigeria from the beginning of formal colonial rule, women education officers arrived relatively late. A few started work during the interwar period, but most were recruited after the Second World War when Colonial Development and Welfare funds became available for

110

the rapid expansion of education. For many of them, 'touring' – quite often in rugged conditions – was an essential part of their job, bringing them in touch with local people in their villages and compounds. Learning a local language became part of the initiation for those in the permanent establishment. Their retrospective reports[2] show their strong motivation for improving education for Nigerians, particularly for girls and women, in the short period left before Independence.

The history of Nigerian education has been presented from varied perspectives, with the wide disparity in educational development between Northern and Southern Nigeria fully analysed. Little attention has been given, however, to the difference between the sexes in the quantity and quality of education provided for them (see Mba, 1982, pp. 61–5). The colonial government, particularly in the early years, considered education mainly in terms of males. Lugard, for example, in two chapters of *The Dual Mandate* discusses education entirely in relation to boys, with the exception of three paragraphs on girls' education. Here he sets out a model domestic science course and concludes:

> The immense value to the educated youth of Africa, of having wives who can share their thoughts and sympathise in and understand their work, is only less important than the influence which the mother should exert in forming the character of her children. Improvement in the standard of private life is fully as important as in that of public life.   (1922, p. 457)

The purpose of female education was thus to make better wives and mothers and to improve the private sphere (the Ruskin model transposed to Africa). This eminent imperialist showed little understanding that women of some ethnic groups in Nigeria were actively engaged in economic production and marketing and held public roles in political and religious spheres. While Lugard's ideas on education in general proved to be progressive in comparison with those of Vischer and some other colonial leaders in Northern Nigeria (Perham, 1960, pp. 489–511), his views on girls' education were essentially those of imperial culture at that time – ethnocentric and deeply conservative.

The Advisory Committee on Native Education in Tropical Africa, formed in response to the increasing demand for review and reform of education, states as one of the principles in its

Memorandum of 1925: 'So far as local conditions allow, women's and girls' education must be attempted wherever possible; care must be taken, however, to see that such an education does not have an unsettling effect upon the people of the country' (Hilliard, 1957, p. 170). This qualification was often cited as a reason for not promoting girls' education more vigorously.

It was almost by chance that, in 1926, the first 'Lady Superintendent of Education' was appointed in Lagos. She was Sylvia Leith-Ross, who had arrived nearly twenty years earlier and had acquired an understanding of diverse Nigerian societies. The Director of Education, Selwyn Grier, invited her to join his department (Leith-Ross, 1983, pp. 88–9). At this time Lagos women's organisations were pressing for a girls' secondary school along the lines of King's College for boys, established in 1909. When the government denied that there was any demand for girls' education, these Lagos women raised £1000 for this purpose. This led to the founding in 1927 of the first government secondary school for girls in Nigeria, Queen's College. While on leave, Leith-Ross was asked to find a principal; she was able to recruit Faith Wordsworth, a great-niece of the poet. The rest of the staff was 'entirely temporary, part-time and voluntary, a marvellously devoted group' (Harwood, Ms., p. 22), including Oyinkan Ajasa (later Lady Abayomi), who had attended Cheltenham Ladies' College. In its first year, there were seven pupils in Form I and thirteen in Form II; the school built a strong reputation which it still holds today.

During her first years, Leith-Ross went on tours of inspection throughout the Southern Provinces, visiting mission schools to see whether their standards were high enough to qualify for government grants. Her next assignment was to Ilorin, in Northern Nigeria, to get in touch with Muslim women for a report suggesting how the government could best proceed with the education of girls. Later, she explained, 'I don't think any of the Northern Residents were in favour of girls' education. Hermon-Hodge at Ilorin had been more or less forced to accept me (as questions had been asked by some busybody in the House of Commons about girls' schools) and Ilorin was the least strict of the Moslem Emirates so less harm would be done if the whole idea was locally repugnant' (letter to Jean Trevor, 26 November 1971; Trevor, Ms. 79A, p. 99). At the end of seven months she was unable to get any local support for girls' education. Next she went to Kano to open a small experimental school. Disappointed at the lack of progress in girls' education, she was invalided out of the service in 1931.

Commander Carrow, Resident in Kano and Sokoto during that period, later wrote about the difficulties of starting education for girls: 'There was no demand for this education, in fact it was against the whole of the African opinion – Emirs, District Heads, Village Heads *and the people*. It was impossible to plan how it should develop' (letter to Jean Trevor, 27 February 1973; Trevor, Ms. 79A, p. 107). Women officers were recruited to open schools for girls where requested by progressive emirs, and the decision was made to admit girls to mission schools in pagan areas. By 1936, the Education Department recorded about 600 girls in schools, 200 in the girls' schools of Kano, Katsina, Birnin Kebbi and Argungu, and the rest in the lower forms of boys' schools (Alexander, Ms., p. 2).

In Sokoto, the religious centre of Northern Nigeria, at the request of the Sultan, a Women's Training Centre was opened in 1939 for training 25 young women from seven provinces as vernacular teachers for the beginning classes of primary schools. The experience of the first headmistress, Miss Booker, points up the conflict between the committed professional teachers trying to do their job efficiently and the administrative officers avoiding any trouble which would upset the rulers, as Jean Trevor records:

She demanded better conditions for her school and her pupils . . . Walls fell down, pupils did not arrive and nobody seemed to help or care. The Recession was on, and the teachers had difficulty in obtaining transport to school, and to go on tour. Miss Booker wished to live at the school with the girls, but the Medical Officer would not allow it. She became frustrated and impatient and she wrote impassioned letters to the Resident and even the Secretary for the Northern Provinces. The Resident wrote that her letters were not in accord with the tone of official correspondence as stated in General Orders, and her behaviour was not suitable to an English lady, and advised her to go on leave . . . Hausa women who remember her call her *mai zaifin rai, mai son mutane* – 'hot-headed, enthusiastic and extrovert', and they loved her and admired her courage in challenging the Authorities for their good.   (Trevor, Ms. 79A, p. 111)

Her test came at the time of the dynastic marriage of one of the pupils, the Waziri's daughter Nana, aged ten. The Resident of Sokoto, Commander Carrow, did not want this to become a special case which would inflame local Muslim views; he had already been assured by the Sultan that the marriage would not be consummated until after the girl had reached puberty. Miss Booker, on the other hand, as Jean Trevor relates, was one of many British teachers who wished to save 'their' pupils from the harshness of their own culture by appealing to international standards. Jean Trevor sides with the administration and its slower approach to change, given that the aims were to accommodate education to the requirements of the traditional elite of Sokoto. She says British women teachers were shocked by child marriage, polygamy, purdah, concubinage and the low legal status of women; they had little understanding that these customs might be 'alternative methods of organising a happy constructive society' (p. 115). Muslim society had long opposed what it perceived to be the degrading effects of Western culture; resistance to the Women's Training Centre strengthened. By the end of the war only five pupils remained.

The situation was different in Southern Nigeria. The new Director of Education appointed in 1929, E. R. J. Hussey, gave strong support to girls' education, promoting the idea of separate schools: 'I felt it was only when African women were holding positions of importance in the country that the population as a whole could be led to value as good an education for their girls as they did for their boys. The best chance of making a success of girls' education was to appoint a competent woman inspectress' (quoted in Mba, 1982, p. 63). In 1931 the enduring Gladys Plummer (known affectionately as 'Plum') was appointed Lady Superintendent of Education. She served for the next twenty-one years, dedicated to improving and extending education for women and girls. For fourteen years, with one assistant, she toured the Southern Provinces, spending more than eight months a year on the road in her kitcar or lorry. She visited schools and women's centres, advising and examining, becoming a familiar figure supporting the work of African and European women teachers. In 1945 she was appointed Deputy Director of Education, a position she held until her retirement (Jeffries, 1949, p. 162). She received an OBE award and is remembered as 'an unfailing source of support and kindness to all her women officers' (Alexander, Ms., p. 2).

COMMITMENT: AFTER THE SECOND WORLD WAR

After the war, the question of girls' and women's education throughout the colonies came to the fore, and in 1947 the Colonial Office appointed Freda Gwilliam as Assistant Adviser to Education, the first woman to hold this position (Gwilliam, Ms., p. 1). She remained in the Colonial Office for twenty years, becoming Deputy Adviser to Education; her mandate covered the whole range of education, but with particular emphasis on women and girls. She helped to recruit women candidates for posts overseas, interviewed them, and continued her personal interest as they progressed in their work.

Education in wartime Nigeria had gone through a difficult period with shortages of European staff, suspensions of building grants, and the deferring of salary raises and pension schemes for mission teachers. But when it ended, Nigerian revenues were increasing and CDWA funds were available for a programme of rapid expansion. Gladys Plummer was now in position to carry on 'an all-out attack on women's education' (Lady Alexander, interview, Redisham, Suffolk, 23 August 1983). This was planned on a number of fronts: promoting girls' enrolment in primary schools, establishing women's training colleges and secondary schools, developing adult education for women, and supporting the work of missions in all these fields. A Chief Woman Education Officer (CWEO) was to be assigned to each region to direct these activities.

In the Western and Eastern Regions where education had spread through mission effort, schools had been opened as communities showed interest and gave their support. In 1930, there were 10 000 girls attending approved mission schools, but 37 000 boys; in 1947, the numbers had risen to 38 000 girls in relation to 114 000 boys (Mba, 1982, p. 61). While the enrolment of girls in proportion to boys had increased, it was still only one girl to three boys. There was no lack of enthusiastic demand from parents and Nigerian leaders; the difficulty was in training teachers and expanding the schools.

In Northern Nigeria the problem was different. Here in the
Muslim areas education at all levels was far behind and if
schooling for boys was not generally seen as beneficial, for girls it
was often considered negative. The person recruited in 1948 as
CWEO, Dr. Constance Geary (now Lady Alexander), had a
background suitable to the task of transforming the situation. For
ten years she had been Principal of Lahore College for Women
(one of the colleges making up the University of the Punjab),
which had a high reputation in science and attracted women
students from all parts of India and from Central Asia, Malaysia,
and East Africa. She brought to Nigeria not only experience in
Muslim women's education, but also a sense of urgency that
Independence would come to Nigeria much faster than some of
her complacent male colleagues considered possible. In her view,
if the foundations for women's education were to be laid during
the colonial period, then the job would have to be done quickly
(interview, 1983).

After some weeks of touring, Dr. Geary became aware that
getting women's education 'off the ground' was going to be even
more difficult than she had anticipated. The girls' schools which
had been started earlier were no longer running; even in the
provinces of the Middle Belt there were only a few girls in the
primary schools. She decided it was necessary to establish the
principle of separate education for girls: this would involve not
only building, equipping, and staffing schools and training
colleges, but creating an atmosphere of learning which would
attract girls to come and complete their courses. Soon five
dedicated Provincial Women Education Officers (PWEOs) were
on the job in the various provinces touring widely to reach Native
Authorities and influential parents in the encouragement of girls'
education.

Within the next decade, notable advances were made. Four
women's training colleges – producing teachers for primary
schools and the lower forms of middle schools – were opened in
Sokoto, Kano, Maiduguri, and Kabba. Eight government girls'
boarding schools – providing a four-year course for adolescents –
were established in Birnin Kebbi, Sokoto, Kano, Katsina,
Bauchi, Maiduguri, Yola and Kontagora. At the same time, two
other types of women's education were being encouraged: helping
girls in missionary schools and organising courses for adult
women. Finally, in 1956 the first government secondary school for

girls in Northern Nigeria (soon to be named Queen Elizabeth School) was opened in Ilorin.

This strong commitment to the cause of girls' education in Northern Nigeria was not met with approval from all British administrative officers. As Henrietta Davies (née Roy) explains, this may have been due to masculine prejudice against the employment of women in anything but a domestic capacity. She adds, 'Another reason was the wish, for the best motives, to maintain the way of life of unspoilt rural communities against a too quick and destructive rate of change, and they considered that the majority of women had little need for education and would only be upset by it' (Ms., p. 21). Some criticism also came from male education officers who did not support the special structure for girls' education within the department or the financial allocations which they considered to be extravagantly excessive (A. R. Allen, Ms., p. 129).

WOMEN IN EDUCATIONAL ADMINISTRATION

The women's branch of the education department developed as a subsidiary to the men's, with a parallel administrative hierarchy. Some of these women education officers served only on the women's side; others moved from one to the other according to their assignments. Here the work of a few women shows the types of administrative jobs they held and the obstacles they met.

Arriving in Lagos in 1946, Joan Russell (née Foster) served over a period of nearly fifteen years in various administrative posts. After a brief introduction as acting Principal of Queen's College, she was posted to Bida in Niger Province as Provincial Education Officer, the first woman to hold this position in Northern Nigeria. She relates how she was summoned by the Resident to be told that he had gained the agreement of the eight emirs in the province to her appointment by persuading them that a woman was capable of doing what had previously been a 'man's job'; he warned her of serious consequences if she, a woman, upset an emir in any way (Ms., p. 3). As PEO, her duties included every level of education in the province: to raise the standards in the primary schools and to encourage the chiefs and parents to allow girls to attend; to get new primary schools built; to supervise the middle school (boys), including the school farm; to arrange for boys (and subsequently girls) to proceed to secondary schools, teacher training colleges, and other institutions of tertiary education; and to encourage adult education classes.

This work involved continuing co-operation with officers from other departments. With the medical officer she pioneered 'school breakfasts' to make sure that children travelling long distances to school were adequately fed. Much of her time was spent touring this large province. Her modes of transport varied from an old Albion lorry to a second-hand Ford V8 station wagon she bought ('somewhat unreliable at times') and included bicycle and dugout canoe; she stayed in bush rest houses. On her next tour she came back to Bida to the newly created post of PWEO in Niger Province, allowing her now to concentrate entirely on the education of girls and women. Later she held a similar post in Katsina. On another tour she was sent to Jos as Inspector of Education for the north-east area, again the first woman in Northern Nigeria to hold that position. During her last three years (1956–9), she served as CWEO for Northern Nigeria. Joan Russell had the distinction, very rare for a woman, of being selected after six years of service for the 'Second Devonshire Course', an academic year at Cambridge or Oxford.

With a degree from Cambridge in the apparently irrelevant subject of music, Henrietta Davies (née Roy) went to Yola in 1953 as PWEO of Adamawa Province. This was a mountainous area far from the centre and considered backward in educational terms; one almost insuperable problem was the multiplicity of languages (Ms., p. 11). Her main task before the Provincial Girls' School at Yola was opened was to prepare the way by 'selling' the idea to teachers, councillors and parents of prospective pupils. She also took part in the general work of the education office and the routine inspection of schools. She travelled mainly in her kitcar, but to get to places inaccessible by car during the rainy season, she went on horseback or bicycle or on the government barge. At no time during this period, she states, did she receive anything but courtesy from the Nigerian officials and teachers with whom she worked. She adds, 'Nor did I ever feel at a disadvantage as a woman working in a partly Muslim area' (p. 14). After four years as PWEO, Adamawa, she spent a few months in Kaduna as Acting Inspector of Education (Women) before her 'resignation on marriage', followed by a further twenty-one years in Northern Nigeria with her husband, a training adviser in tsetse control.

Marian Hepplestone, who had taught in Barbados and Jamaica before going to Nigeria in 1951, spent her entire time in the Eastern Region. First assigned to Calabar, she spent much of her time visiting the girls' primary schools run by the different missions. When she was touring, she remembers it was not unusual to be stuck in the mud on the road or confronted by a chasm where a bridge had disappeared. After similar work based on Owerri and Onitsha, she was posted to Ogoja Province as PEO. Now she became involved in the preparation for free primary education, to be introduced in 1957 when Eastern Nigeria became self-governing. All local government bodies had to be alerted to appoint education committees and it was necessary to attend their meetings; schools (including those in nearly inaccessible places) had to be visited to find how many places were available and how registration of pupils was to be arranged. 'It was a very busy year' (Ms., p. 14). In 1957 she became CWEO for Eastern Nigeria, concerned now with secondary education and teacher training. She was involved with the West African Examinations Council which met annually in Nigeria, Ghana, Sierra Leone or The Gambia, with representatives from governments, universities and schools, and was also a member of the Joint Consultative Committee on Education formed to take up problems common to all regions of Nigeria. Later she became Chief Inspector, Teacher Training, a position she held until 1961 when she returned to the UK.

STARTING SCHOOLS AND TRAINING CENTRES

Evelyn Clark (née Hyde) came to Sokoto in 1949 to take over as Principal of the Women's Training Centre. She soon found problems which nothing she had heard or read had foreshadowed:

> I did know that education for girls was only in its infancy and that there was some parental opposition or distrust, but I was horrified to see girls of twelve or fourteen years being forcibly carried through the gatehouse (into the school) by NA Police and to hear their screams and wails. (Ms., p. 6)

Meeting groups of girls with sullen and angry faces, she immediately resolved that she would find out what lay behind these negative attitudes and 'move heaven and earth to make school life as attractive and satisfying as possible'. She tried varied measures: redesigning the uniform from 'a travesty of the English school uniform of the 1920s' into an attractive blouse and wrap-over skirt more in line with local dress, revising the diet to provide better nutrition and more variety, making the curriculum as relevant as possible to their lives and encouraging teachers to use innovative methods to gain the pupils' co-operation. For the end of the school year she instituted a ceremony at which the Sultan awarded prizes for a wide range of achievements, both traditional and scholastic. These prizes were selected for their high local value – lengths of cloth, jewellery, headties in current fashion, and the bright enamel dishes collected for a bride's dowry.

She describes the WTC in Sokoto as it was in 1949. The classrooms and administration block were built in an open style with colonnaded verandah, while the girls lived in traditional round huts of mud and thatch. Its compound was shaded by trees and enclosed by mud walls ten feet high; the gate was guarded day and night and girls were chaperoned on journeys outside. In 1949 there were three school classes of thirty each and the first intake for teacher training had eleven girls. When she became aware of the narrow range of experience these teacher trainees had beyond their own villages, she planned an educational journey, approved by the Sultan of Sokoto and the CWEO of Northern Nigeria. The girls and their chaperones travelled first by lorry and then by train to Lagos, where they stayed for fourteen days and made visits to the docks, a soap factory, a number of secondary schools, the markets and large department stores, and to the beaches for swimming. During following years, this enjoyable educational journey was repeated with variations. Yet despite all the efforts by her and her staff, opposition from parents and the community remained strong throughout the eight years she was head of the WTC. When her husband was transferred, she continued teaching in Kano and later in Kaduna until 1966.

While education along Western lines in Bornu Province was hardly more advanced than in Sokoto, and the culture as firmly based on Muslim principles, the education of girls met a more favourable response, particularly in the support given by

Shettima Kashim, the Waziri of Bornu who became the first Federal Minister of Education.

After experience teaching in Kano and Sokoto, Annie Cooper (née McGregor) arrived in Maiduguri early in 1952 to start the Women's Training Centre, drawing its students from Bornu, Bauchi and Adamawa Provinces. Before the new buildings were ready, she started teaching the first class of three girls; in the afternoons she took them for a drive in her car or provided some entertainment. Later, when there were more students, they were chaperoned at agriculture shows, race meetings, religious processions and other events in Maiduguri. She relates that their bright orange uniforms, designed in traditional Kanuri style, became part of the local scene (Ms., p. 5).

Soon a new development took place: the WTC accepted girls for training as nurses as well as teachers. A nursing sister with long experience in Northern Nigeria, Alex Cooper, agreed to give the necessary science and nursing lessons and to take charge of a small 'cottage hospital' in the grounds, where the trainees could gain practical experience. When the principal was told that some of the girls, already pregnant, were to be married during the vacations, she decided to allow the students to return with their babies and to provide special guidance in child care.

For teaching practice, the trainees went to local primary schools in Maiduguri. Annie Cooper's first instinct was to get something colourful on the barren walls and the students put up maps, pictures and alphabet-writing patterns. Her next step was to get the passive rows of small children into activities outside; soon they were 'skipping, running, throwing bean bags, and playing with hoops' (p. 13) and the trainees had gained a repertoire of simple games and exercises. Later, arrangements were made for a practice school in the town, with one of their own former students, Gona Gulumba, in charge. Here they were able to concentrate on teaching methods and materials related to the local scene. When she married in 1957, some of the students were her bridesmaids; she continued to teach at her husband's posts until their return to the UK in 1968.

Before the war, Birnin Kebbi had a day school for girls but this was later closed for lack of staff. In 1950, Margaret Burness, as principal, and Pamela Swire (née Godley) were posted there to start a boarding school for girls with the strong support of the Emir of Gwandu. Margaret Burness relates:

Every year, in what would be the Christmas holidays we went 'girl hunting', by car, NA lorry, canoe on the Niger, and horse to visit every primary school in the two Emirates. 'Academic' choice had often to be made from exercise books, since girls either disappeared or froze dumb. Then we would go with Hajiya Kubura, our magnificent matron, to sit on mats in mother's room and talk with mother while the District Head and Emir's representative dealt with father. Kubura promised mother that the girls would be kept in purdah, would do their share of pounding and grinding grain, so that their hands did not get soft, and would be trained in the same good manners as at home.   (Ms., pp. 1–2)

Within a few years the NA Councillor for Education told her that the battle had been won; fathers were offering him bribes to get girls into school instead of to keep them out.

When the girls first came to school, they were given a medical examination. Among the problems found, Pamela Swire recollects, were dysentery, amoebiasis, schistosomiasis, tropical ulcers and leprosy. Most of the treatments were given on the compound in close co-operation with the nearby hospital. Their aim was to create a school within the local culture. Although pupils did not carry water, they helped with food preparation and learned practical lessons in hygiene. Local foods were used entirely, emphasis being given to a balanced diet. With the health care and improved diets, many of the girls felt better physically than they had before; the results showed particularly with the poorer children (Ms., pp. 4–5).

Kabba is located in the southern part of Northern Nigeria. Here in 1952, after two years touring as PWEO, Margaret Chamberlain (née Buckerfield) was asked to establish the WTC. She describes how the first students came, by 'mammy wagon', train, canoe or on foot, with broad smiles and carrying all their possessions in boxes on their heads. They came from varied backgrounds with seven different mother tongues and English as the only common language. Girls competed strongly for entry, about one in nine applicants being selected; most were 16 or 17 years old. Soon they settled into the routine and 'the daughter of an emir could be seen eating quite happily in the dining room next to the daughter of a blacksmith' (Ms., p. 2).

The three-year course trained students for work both in

primary schools and in domestic science centres. Designing a suitable curriculum was difficult, as Margaret Chamberlain explains, because they tried to help the young Nigerian woman teacher be at home in two rapidly changing worlds – the traditional one of village life and the newer modern world. A visit to the cookery room might show one student preparing a full Yoruba meal and another learning to serve English afternoon tea; a history class would concern itself mainly with West African history but also provide an outline of English history. In a similar way on the social side, the students would arrange Yoruba plays and dances one week and English songs and Scottish country dances the next. Emphasis was also placed on helping the young teachers become sensitive to the needs of children within their particular environment and of replacing the prevailing rote-learning with 'learning by doing'.

Problems in practice teaching arose during the rainy season when bridges were washed away and schools could not be reached. The WTC itself was understaffed, making a heavy teaching load for the principal and staff; these were difficulties met in training centres throughout the country. Margaret Chamberlain remained at Kabba for five years, when she became an Inspector (Women) working for two years from Kaduna; from there she went to Uganda as Assistant Director of Education (Women).

SECONDARY SCHOOLS

Girls' secondary schools, as other sectors of education, were advanced primarily by missionary organisations; the government regulated standards, provided grants-in-aid, and established schools where pressure was exerted (as in Lagos for Queen's School) and in Muslim areas where missions were not encouraged to operate. With support being given to boys' education both by colonial authorities and by Nigerian parents who paid fees, the disproportion between girls and boys became even more marked at this level. By 1947 in the Southern Provinces there were 741 girls in secondary education to 8916 boys; in the Northern Provinces, 45 girls to 206 boys (Nduka, 1964, p. 74). The work of women officers in girls' secondary education is illustrated here by the experience of two women who helped to shape outstanding girls' colleges in Nigeria.

Kathleen Player had already served nine years in Nigeria when she was asked, in 1954, to become the founding principal of the first government secondary school for girls in Northern Nigeria in Ilorin. In 1939 Roman Catholic Sisters had initiated the first girls' secondary education in Northern Nigeria, and by 1951 they had established girls' secondary schools in Kaduna and in Kano (Russell, Ms., p. 8). The government school came as culmination of the broader plan to advance girls' education in Northern Nigeria, particularly that of Muslim girls. Its aim was a sound social education, using a wide variety of Nigerian cultural traditions, and academic results leading to the possibility of university entrance or other higher education (Alexander, Ms., p. 6). This was planned as a prestige school, with expensive buildings, good equipment, and a high staff/pupil ratio. Its importance was attested when the foundation stone was laid by the Sardauna of Sokoto, Premier of Northern Nigeria, with notable officials and guests present.

Out of 357 candidates for entry, 56 were finally selected after an interview, two of whom dropped out. The first pupils arrived in May 1956 to be met by the Principal, a teaching staff of four European women and two Nigerian matrons. Some of the girls had not met Europeans before and, as one told Miss Player years later, they had been terrified of 'all those white women' (Player, Ms., p. 9). They were divided into two parallel classes and two boarding houses. The Muslim matron had responsibility for seeing that Muslim girls observed their prayers and other customs. With no electricity for six years, lighting Tilley lamps and bush lamps was a daily chore.

Much of the first term was devoted to improving the standard of English – written and spoken – since it was the language of tuition, a compulsory language for the school certificate, and also the common language among the girls. Special work also went on in mathematics, since several of the Muslim girls had failed in this – though it was rumoured they had deliberately failed because the older women in their families had told them to do so to avoid being accepted (Ms., p. 13). As in secondary schools throughout Nigeria, problems continued with maintaining the teaching staff. Wives of government officers were often available as teachers for short periods; one ran the Girl Guide troop and another the Red

AN ADDRESS PREPARED IN HONOUR OF MISS PLAYER THE LADY SUPERINTENDENT OF EDUCATION FOR ONDO PROVINCE BY THE ST. PAUL'S SCHOOL GIRLS, IKOLE-EKITI.

St. Paul's School,
Ikole - Ekiti,
9th June, 1947.

Our Dearest Madam,

Our immeasurable wishes of joy we so highly elevat to witness Our Sex to the post of a Lady Education Officer.

It is indeed an appropriat adage that 'What a person can d is no more a misery for another', therefore we congratulate you our dear Mam.

Although we may be ignorant of the difficulties which had been inborn with this arduos task, yet we hope with intense desire that Our Race in your time will grow from might to might.

We cannot but assure you that this your honest post will a great deal elucidate the pessimisms our sex inherited from our fathers. We are very much proud of you and we shall continue to be proud of you as Our Sincere Leader, Our Guidian and Mediator. We honestly pray for many more of our desire Sex, both Black and White towards this level, and to greater posts, and we wish you sail back home in the joy of the pillion.

It is with regret that our purse is by far poor than our desires, but with the grace of God we sincerely present you this our poor parcels with buckets of thanks and goodluck.

We are,
Yours very sincerely,
IKOLE C.M.S. SCHOOL GIRLS.

Signed by: E. A. Awopegba.
(Senior School Mistress)

Approved by: _____ (Head Master)

Plate 2: Pupils expressed their delight in the promotion of their teacher by using eloquent language in a farewell testimonial.

Cross in the evenings. After eight years, Kathleen Player returned home to care for elderly parents, but she kept in touch with many of her old pupils, inviting those who came to England to her home or her London club.

Appointed as Principal of Queen's College, Lagos, Margaret Harwood (née Gentle) packed her belongings into her Morris Minor in March 1956 and drove south the 140 miles from Ede to Lagos. Behind her was war service in the WRNS, three years' teaching experience in the famous Achimota School in Ghana and another two in Queen's College, Ede. During its history of nearly thirty years, Queen's College had undergone many changes. The main part of the school having transferred to Ede in 1950, it was now a day school for about a hundred Lagos girls, housed in army huts as temporary quarters while its new buildings at Yaba were under construction.

In 1957 the school moved into its new premises and from a Lagos day school became a federal boarding school of 350 girls from throughout Nigeria, most of them aiming to go on to university. Margaret Harwood admits to harassing the Ministry about staff (and earning the name of 'Pocket Battleship'), but in the next few years fully qualified graduate teachers (Nigerian, British, and American) were taken on, resulting in a reasonable staff/pupil ratio. The new staff, she relates, brought fresh ideas to the college: the music mistress established the tradition of a Christmas service with English and Nigerian carols; there were gymnastics and traditional dancing displays for the official opening of the new school, a careers exhibition, a garden with botanical specimens, a social services society whose members helped in institutions for the elderly and handicapped. She recalls, 'There seemed to be a "blossoming" in those years' (Ms., p. 29). Changes were also taking place in the curriculum: the West African Examinations Council made plans to include Africa in the geography syllabus, local species in biology, and set books in literature by African authors.

In 1963 she planned to retire, with a qualified Nigerian taking over as her successor, but she was asked by the Federal Minister of Education to join the Ministry. During the next five years she rose from Assistant Adviser to Adviser on Secondary Education and acted as Chief Federal Adviser. She took part in the inspection of federal colleges, interviewed prospective teachers, and attended meetings as the Minister's representative. She was a Nigerian delegate to the Commonwealth Education Conference in Ottawa in 1964 and again for the one in Lagos in 1968, when she prepared the Conference Report. In 1968, prior to her marriage, she retired, and in 1969 was awarded a CBE. She stayed on in Nigeria with her husband, returning to teaching in Sokoto and Kaduna. When they left in 1979, she had spent twenty-five years actively involved in Nigerian education, nearly twenty of these after Independence.

WORKING WITH ADULT WOMEN

During the immediate post-war period, a movement for mass education gained strength in West Africa to help prepare the great majority of the people who had never been to schools for taking part in the changing economic and political processes of these nations soon to become independent. In Northern Nigeria the government had sponsored pilot projects and small schemes, but in 1952 a committee was appointed to step up the drive which became known as *Yaki da Jahilci* (War against Ignorance). This became a widespread literacy campaign, with literature published in local languages, training programmes for organisers and teachers, and visual aids for 'public enlightenment' (Coomassie, 1957).

On the women's side, Gladys Plummer, from the time of her appointment in 1931, had encouraged the pioneering work of voluntary agencies in what is now called 'non-formal' education for women, broadly designed to help women improve the conditions of their everyday life. During the depression and the war years, resources were short and government recruitment impossible. But when the war ended, she saw the opportunity to develop this field. Annette Spence, one of the first WEOs to be appointed specifically for work with adult women, had come to Nigeria in 1940 as a missionary to take charge of Ovim Girls' School in Eastern Nigeria. In 1945, she was asked to join government service to promote women's education, first in the British Cameroons and then in Eastern Nigeria. In 1947 three women officers were recruited to work with women in remote areas: Catherine Dinnick-Parr was sent to Benue Province, Frances Taeger to Plateau, and Jane Pine-Coffin (formerly Sandiford) to the Cameroons. Like anthropologists starting fieldwork, these women arrived with their loads and began to learn the local language and the customs of the people. Their colleagues soon dubbed them 'the primitives'.

Catherine Dinnick-Parr had interrupted her medical training during the war to serve in the Women's Royal Naval Service. Arriving in Nigeria in 1947 well prepared for her diverse duties, she was assigned to Mbaakon, a place some hundred miles from Makurdi, headquarters of Benue Province. She tells of following directions, turning off the main road at milestone 40 on to a bush path which came to the local school: 'Then we were told to drive back to a certain tree and to plough through the grass, which was at least six feet high, which we did, and there was this one room with a wooden verandah and a thatched roof' (quoted in Allen, 1979, p. 153). This was to be her living quarters.

She describes her first days learning the language and getting to know the people: 'I was learning all the time, learning by watching what the women were doing, how they cooked, what foodstuffs they put into their various dishes, seeing their babies, talking to the women, listening to the old men telling their stories about former days' (p. 155). Sometimes she had to curb herself. On her first morning when she went for a walk around the compounds, she remembers seeing a man thrashing his wife with a leather strap with blood running down her back. Her automatic reaction was to rush in and tell him to stop, but she realised that before she could do anything to improve the position of the women, she would have to be accepted by the men (Dinnick-Parr, Ms., p. 17).

She never felt any opposition or resentment. The local people would come to her compound night after night to talk; when anybody was ill, she was called out. Babies got bad burns by rolling into the fire in huts at night, and she was able to show parents how to clean a burn and keep it covered so that flies could not get at it. Much disease, she observes, was brought by flies and lack of cleanliness; she tried to get them to build pit latrines with covers so that flies would not get from the latrine into their food. She started a women's class, sometimes with only four there, sometimes with forty or more. Since there was no way of telling the time, they would sound a drum when her car arrived and the women would come. She taught hygiene, child-care and cookery, but 'the bait to get them into the classes was to permit them to sew'

(Ms., p. 18). She opened more classes, going to a different location each day of the week. Slowly she was able to observe results:

> Always there is one women who listens. She may not agree with everything you say, but she does put some of your things into practice. The next time you go to visit her hut, you find it has been swept out . . . She's covered all the food pots so that the hens and goats can't get to the food' (quoted in Allen, 1979, p. 155).

After five years she was posted to Kaduna, first as Domestic Science Organiser for Northern Nigeria, then as CWEO. She left in 1963, having worked in women's education in Nigeria for sixteen years.

Margaret Burness noted that when she was head of the girls' school in Birnin Kebbi, there were never 'discipline' problems, only the disappointing tendency for the very brightest girls to get all their sums wrong after a visit from grandma talking about marriage. She says, 'I there and then decided my life's work would be to see what I could do about grandma' (Ms., p. 2). This work began when she became PWEO of Katsina Province and was given permission by the Emir to work with the older women in the palace. She was now fluent in Hausa. Before long, one of the Emir's wives was teaching literacy to the other women in the palace. Then she was asked to transfer to adult education.

She started work at headquarters in Zaria with 'a wonderful colleague', Hajiya Dada Sare, who for many years remained her closest friend. Their brief was to set up women's classes parallel to the literacy classes for men, in which both literacy and simple household hygiene would be taught by local women, the general aim being to encourage self-development. They met difficulties from unexpected quarters: first from educationists, especially those in domestic science, and then from Ministry of Health officers, who had to approve their hygiene syllabus and insisted, for example, that elementary midwifery was unnecessary since only a first-class midwife could deliver a baby. (She adds that they never discovered what was supposed to happen in the vast populations out of reach of a first-class midwife.) They also met resistance from expatriate administrators, who were apparently afraid they would cause trouble despite the success of their programme in other provinces (Ms., p. 3).

Margaret Burness and Hajiya Dada Sare toured together, trying to visit six of the twelve northern provinces every dry season to explore local needs and attitudes and to hold training courses for instructors. The Native Authorities would provide a large compound, usually with a guard, and women came for training, often with a grandmother or a daughter in the dual role of chaperone on the journey and nursemaid for any unweaned child during course hours. They produced instructors' guides in Hausa, English and ultimately six other languages. She relates:

> Gradually, in the face of expatriates' statements of impossibility, women emerged who would not only teach, but travel to supervise a group of classes. They travelled by lorry, with a child as escort, by canoe, one round Lake Chad by ox. They took to bicycles, clutching a veil in their hands, then tied a residual veil tight over their headties and took to motorbikes. *They* were the pioneers. *They* brought literacy in western script and new ideas of hygiene and nutrition to remote homesteads. (Ms., p. 4)

This involved the work of a team of at most two or three expatriates and four to six northern women, half Muslim and half Christian. Margaret Burness says that when she made her return visit in 1976, several of these women were still on the job.

FEMALES IN AN ALL-MALE PRESERVE

In 1953, Pat Walters was the first woman recruited as a Rural Education Officer, a position considered an 'all-male preserve'. She had taken agriculture and economics for an honours degree at the University of Wales, Aberystwyth, and for four years had travelled throughout the UK lecturing as an education officer with the Agricultural Co-operative Organisation. Her first assignment sent her to Moor Plantation, Ibadan, where the Rural Education Centre was 'a small unit of Africans and British and we had the warmest and friendliest of relations' (Ms., p. 6). The two-year course was designed for male teachers in rural primary schools to teach simple mathematics, hygiene, biology, and agriculture in ways related to the child's environment. These teachers also had to prove themselves in practical terms, showing a satisfactory 'school farm'. Part of their duties, then, was to 'follow up' all the teachers in schools throughout Western Nigeria. She tells of her first experience:

> My very first cook-steward abandoned me without a word in the midst of my first long seven-week tour of inspection in the wilds of Benin. Rashly I attempted to complete the tour on my own – carrying water, gathering and chopping wood, cooking, emptying the latrine, worst of all getting the Tilley lamps to go as darkness fell nightly at 6 p.m. By the time I'd worked my way up to Northern Ondo I was a fever ridden skeleton and collapsed at the feet of that wonderful Welsh missionary Mr. Edward Jones of the Ifaki Methodist Centre as he walked to the car to greet me. (Ms., pp. 3–4)

She was cared for at the mission station until she was able to return home. And she was more fortunate in her next cook-steward, who stayed for her remaining eleven years in Nigeria.

She became Senior Inspector (Rural Education) for Western Nigeria in 1958 and, at Independence in 1960, became Principal of the Rural Education College in Akure. Here were the usual classrooms of a training centre, but also an impressive layout of demonstration farms and experimental plots. She says, 'What the attitude of the African to the single white woman was I don't really know. Mystification I believe. At Akure I was woman principal of an all male college and all-Nigerian staff and students for three years and had absolute loyalty and support from all' (Ms., p. 8).

Jeanne Keene (née Batchelor) had qualifications and experience similar to those of Pat Walters and knew of her work; in 1956 she applied for a vacancy in Northern Nigeria and was sent first to the Rural Education College, Bauchi. Although her teaching of rural science was in English, she soon passed the lower level examination in Hausa. After three years, she was appointed the first Principal of the new Rural Science College at Minna, a position she held until the end of her service in 1964. During these years she visited every province in Northern Nigeria: a two-week tour could involve a journey of some 2000 miles with inspection visits to twelve to fifteen students at their local schools, visits to several teacher training centres for practical examinations, talks to Young Farmers' Clubs, and discussions with Provincial Education Officers. Besides the academic subjects, the students had practical work on an individual half-acre farm with livestock,

vegetable garden beds, and a tree nursery. They also took a Red
Cross first aid course and had practice teaching. With this
training, a teacher in a rural area could teach all subjects –
mathematics, general science, biology, hygiene – through the
medium of the children's natural environment. In her view, the
Rural Education Colleges were an under-rated part of colonial
education (Ms., p. 10).

'NICE GIRLS AND GENTEEL SPINSTERS'

These women officers followed the rules of protocol of the Colonial
Service, as Mary Hargreave describes:

> It was customary during the whole period that I served in the
> North to sign the Resident's book *whenever* in the Provincial
> headquarters, even if only passing through. And upon arrival
> on Station the form was adhered to by greeting the most senior
> officer of Department *and* the District Officer at the earliest
> opportunity after one's arrival. AND one always greeted the
> most Serekin Seriki of wherever one went, even when on tour
> and only spending one day in that place. The greeting of
> Serekin Sokoto was a *very* important act. But even so was the
> same deference and courtesy to a Village Head in the remotest
> bush village.   (Ms., p. 22)

They were posted, as were other officers, according to the needs of
the service. When Iris Congleton did not get the post she had
expected, she complained to the Resident and to the CWEO. She
relates, 'I received a sharp reminder that being in the Colonial
Service was like being in the army, and I had signed a contract to
the effect that I would go where I was required. I decided to write
a letter of apology, as suggested by the CWEO and be prepared to
serve anywhere' (Ms., p. 6).

The officers in the permanent and pensionable establishment
had to pass a lower standard language examination during their
probationary period of three years in order to be confirmed in
their appointment; those on contract did not have to meet this
requirement. Most WEOs in Northern Nigeria learned Hausa
because it was the *lingua franca* of the area and relatively easy.
Henrietta Davies passed the examination in Fulani, the main
language of Adamawa where she was assigned, and felt that

though she never reached fluency the fact that she attempted to speak the indigenous language was appreciated as a courtesy (Ms., p. 6). Jean Trevor (née Cole) spent three weeks' local leave as the only European in a Fulani cattle camp and later had the distinction of passing the higher standard Fulani examination (MacGregor, Ms., p. 46). Ursula Bozman prepared a Kanuri reading course for primary schools; Frances Teager conducted her women's classes in Birom; Catherine Dinnick-Parr became a language examiner in Tiv.

Housing, as for male officers, depended very much on the post. Teachers were often assigned houses on the school or college compound and shared whatever amenities were available. Many schools were without electricity and piped water. Jeanne Keene, for example, was assigned 'an old Lugard house' when she first arrived in Bauchi in 1956. 'It was a square house with a four sided roof which went up to a point in the middle with matting on the outside to deaden the sound of the rain. It leaked badly, but we put the bed in a suitable place and suitable containers at strategic points when needed' (Ms., p. 3). The bathroom had running water from a tank filled from the well by the garden boy each morning, and the toilet was a 'thunder box'.[3] With no electricity, she used Tilley lamps, a kerosene refrigerator and a charcoal iron. Despite these seeming drawbacks, she found this house quite delightful and stayed there for the whole of her first tour, although she could have moved.

Iris Congleton tells of housing at the girls' school in Kontagora, when she arrived in 1953: 'There were two staff houses within five minutes walk from the school, and two wells from which all water had to be hauled by bucket; in the dry season this meant about 40 to 60 feet' (Ms., p. 7). Soon two more members of staff arrived and they were assigned houses at the 'Bariki', a former army station: 'Neither was in very good condition; one had no doors or windows, the other a far from rain-proof roof, and subject to marches of marauding termites.'

The social life of these women also varied according to their assignments. Catherine Dinnick-Parr, for example, found much of her social life with the village people. In the evenings she could hear the drums and, after a time, began to understand what they were saying, whether it was a birth, or a wedding, or a funeral. They would ask her to join them. 'And I would go down and dance, sometimes dance the whole night . . . It was all so friendly'

(Ms., p. 29). A small town had its compensations, as Masry MacGregor relates, 'Kontagora was such a small place, that when someone of importance, like the resident or a government minister came, *all* the officials were invited, while in Kaduna it might have been just the senior members of a department and their wives' (Ms., p. 51). For those in the regional headquarters and other large cities, social life could be rich and varied. Posted in Enugu in 1958, Marjorie Pears wrote to friends, 'We are by no means without culture and entertainment. Apart from a good deal of hospitality, there is the Club where one can swim, play golf and tennis, go to the pictures three times a week, eat and drink, play cards and gossip' (Ms., p. 8).

But social and professional life had a definite gender dimension. With the title of 'Rural Education Officer', Jeanne Keene remarks that she was the only woman in the education department in Northern Nigeria who did not come under the women's branch, adding, 'For which I was duly grateful' (Ms., p. 4). In a similar position in Western Nigeria, Pat Walters soon discovered the advantage:

> Women education officers usually live 'on campus', the principals of these colleges truly were 'a monstrous regiment of women'. They controlled the lives of their unfortunate subordinates as if they were the Grand Turk himself. Sometimes WEOs were, to their joy, summoned to Ibadan as marking panels. I felt angry and impotent when they described their circumscribed lives to me. How they envied my freedom, though few as they confessed, would have felt able to do the extensive touring in remote bush villages which my work frequently entailed.   (Ms., pp. 3–4)

Some teachers in girls' schools and women's training centres tell of the restrictions they met. Susan Pickering (née Stockford) writes, 'We had to ask permission to leave the station even for half an hour' (Ms., p. 10). While she could see the safety angle in this, since roads were dangerous and an accident could happen, it was irritating to ask 'as if we were children – and accept the verdict'. Jane Sharland (née Stockford) adds:

> There were various edicts we were supposed to obey – including one stating that we are not to allow young men with whom we might be dining alone, to let their houseboys go off duty while

we were there. We might also be told that we were seeing too much of one person or another. Strangely enough, though we complained about such strictures, on the whole we complied with them.   (Ms., p. 8)

At any station it was necessary for all officers to apply for permission to leave, but women principals often considered the boundaries to be the grounds of the school rather than the wider area. And for WEOs, the discipline of the Colonial Service appeared to have 'Mrs Grundy' embellishments.

But why should women principals have the reputation of being 'monsters' when men in similar positions did not? The marriage bar gives some answers. By definition, these women had to be single, and their work often set out the horizons of their world. Some of them were determined to create an institution according to an ideal pattern they envisaged, which required enormous demands on their staff as well as themselves. In Nigeria, the factors of heat, isolation, and lack of communication added to the strain, perhaps accounting for some of the seemingly arbitrary and petty restrictions. A few learned from their own experience as underlings. Margaret Harwood, for example, notes that her first principal taught her, inadvertently, the things that headmistresses should no longer expect of their staff in the post-war world (Ms., p. 20). Later as a principal herself, she placed emphasis on 'staff harmony'.

Yet there was an added factor to the social constraints on women education officers. Masry MacGregor (now Mrs Prince) makes the alert observation that the British shared many attitudes with Northern Nigerians; both societies equated adulthood with marriage. Her schoolgirls insisted that the European teachers were not adults because they were not married, and the teachers in her view lived as much in purdah as their pupils:

There were a great many bachelors around, among the British men, but we saw them mostly in groups at dinner parties and drinks, occasionally we visited them in twos, chaperoning each other, and if some man called by, there was always a Nigerian steward on hand. Doubtless there were some early Women Liberation advocates out in Nigeria, but not among the staff at Kontagora during my time, there and in many other similar institutions, the Women Education Officers were two, now almost extinct species, nice girls and genteel spinsters.   (Ms., p. 55)

ASSESSMENTS OF THE PAST

After an interval of over two decades, what do these women education officers see as their shortcomings and their achievements? Looking back, and remembering how much the teachers gave to the schoolgirls, Masry MacGregor expresses her surprise that they did not make more effort to befriend the Nigerian teachers (Ms., p. 52). The differences in remuneration, she notes, made relations between them and the Nigerian teachers uncomfortable; her own salary after one year of teaching, for example, was higher than that of a Nigerian colleague after six years because she had a university degree and the Nigerian had not yet reached her school certificate. This tension was more evident when the Nigerian teacher came from another part of the country and was as much a 'stranger' on the local scene as the Europeans. Sometimes ironic misunderstandings arose. Iris Congleton tells of a Nigerian teacher who had been trained in domestic science in the UK and disliked the idea of adapting her teaching to the local environment. She 'ordered cherries, raisins, self-raising flour etc. and wanted a Calor gas cooker, saying this was how she had been taught at Bath and I was just trying to keep Africans down' (Ms., p. 9). When the teacher came from the area, she often served as a mediator between the girls and the European teachers, the school and the society. Jane Sharland tells of Jibabatu in Kontagora, 'She taught the youngest class general subjects and weaving and mat-weaving to all the girls, and was a great help to us and to the girls in enlightening us of customs and expectations on both sides' (Ms., p. 4).

One of the central aims of British teachers was to relate their teaching to the daily life of their pupils. Barbara Beswick (née Beeston) writes that domestic science was at an exploratory level when she arrived, and it was necessary to observe how people lived, their usual diet, methods of work, materials available, in fact learn to appreciate their culture before trying to help them with improvements in hygiene, enriched diets and so on (Ms., p. 5). Mary Goldsworthy states that their goal was to base all studies on the environment: 'the history and geography syllabi were started as local work, spreading out from this, language was based on the vernacular, and domestic studies on their own practices' (Ms., p. 6). Some teachers were not always able to carry this out, textbooks were not always available; but, in her view, education was sufficiently correlated to girls' lives for it to have considerable impact. She considers their standards of hygiene, diet and child-care were vastly improved. Joan Russell points out that in comparison with schools in neighbouring French colonial territories, they were doing far more to preserve local traditions, religions, languages, crafts and so on (Ms., p. 12).

In Western and Eastern Nigeria the education system had developed over a century, however haphazard its growth. During the 1950s, the newly-formed Nigerian governments introduced a programme for free, universal primary education and promoted educational advancement at all levels. The part played by these WEOs in this advance was relatively minor, augmenting the work of others in administration and teaching. In a few instances, they had a special role, as did Marjorie Pears who started a pilot secretarial training course for young women secondary school leavers in Aba. It was in Northern Nigeria that they played an integral part in setting the 'infrastructure' for the education of Muslim girls and women and in assisting the pioneer work of missionaries in non-Muslim areas. The provincial boarding schools for girls lasted only a decade before being transmuted into other institutions, but they provided virtually the first educated generation of Muslim women in Northern Nigeria.

Did these women follow the traditional ways of their mothers and grandmothers in purdah or had their schooling opened up new possibilities for them? These were the questions asked by Jean Trevor when she returned to Sokoto between 1968 and 1970 to stay with her former pupils, now married and rearing their own children. The main thing she learned from her return visit, she states, is that in their community a woman can become modern in outlook without behaving in a Western fashion. In the old polygamous compounds, she found some of the most modern-minded women who were raising their children in a new and truly educative way, discussing radio programmes, and helping their friends to read and write. Some were teachers able to carry on their careers because other wives took care of their children while they were at work. She tells of a grandmother at 29 who told her that she had decided to take 'the Hausa path' first and now no one would criticise her when she tried 'the British path'; she planned to enter training college to become a teacher (1975, p. 265).

But if there has been cultural continuity in Northern Nigeria, there has also been change in girls' education. Evelyn Clark observes, 'It was the subsequent careers of those pupils and students of the nineteen fifties which had fired the imaginations of two or three generations later and had also paved the way for the later parents to acquiesce' (Ms., p. 20). The teacher training had a multiplier effect with former students now passing on these skills.

Kathleen Player was one of those fortunate to return many years later to the school where she had been the first principal (Ms., pp. 26–31). The Old Students of Queen Elizabeth School generously invited her to attend the Silver Jubilee celebration and also provided the fare for another teacher from the early years to accompany her. She found now a great increase in students, from 166 when she had left in 1962 to 1500 in 1981, and new buildings in the compound. Most significant of all, she met former students who were now confident women in high positions in government, academic life and business throughout Nigeria. In the Northern States these were the first women doctors, principals of secondary schools, librarians and teachers, as well as pioneers in other fields of activity. Many were wives of leading politicians and other prominent men; they were raising families with care and attention given to their education; many were taking part in voluntary community work as well. The rugged determination of women education officers in the post-war period could now be seen to have had results.

6 Women as Colonial Administrators

There was at that time a great pressure for Nigerianisation. All Europeans were soon to feel the wind of change. Perhaps women on short-term contracts, liable to marry and retire gracefully, were just what the colonial office needed.

(Margery Daniels, Ms., p. 13)

THE LONG EXCLUSION OF WOMEN

During the early years of the Second World War, with the severe depletion of 'manpower', women were finally taken on in the administrative grades of the Colonial Office in London, although only on a temporary basis.[1] The distinguished sociologist, Dr. Audrey Richards, became temporary principal in the Social Service department and six other women were placed as assistant principals in various departments. Then, as an 'experiment' in 1944, women were sent out to the colonies as temporary junior administrators with the Colonial Service. They went first to The Gambia, later to other West and East African countries, to Trinidad and Malaya. During wartime and the subsequent period of decolonisation, these women showed themselves capable of carrying out a wide range of administrative duties previously reserved for men.

While the displacements of war gave women the opportunity, their entrance to administration was not gained without struggle. The Sex Disqualification (Removal) Act of 1919 had opened the way for the appointment of women in the administrative grades of the Civil Service, but when recruitment by examination was resumed in 1925 and the question of women's assignment in the Colonial Office arose, it was agreed internally that such appointments should be reserved to men. The reasons given for this decision reveal the gender assumptions of the time:

(i) the unfavourable effect in the Eastern colonies, etc., if an

       impression were given in those Territories that their affairs
       were being handled by women;
  (ii) that it would be highly impolitic for a woman to deal with
       Africans and Orientals of the uneducated classes;
(iii) the liability and its obvious consequences of service
       abroad.   (PRO/CO 866/25/1085/44)

The Royal Commission of 1931, examining the position of women
in the Civil Service, stated that the permanent heads of a few
departments regarded the appointment of women to
administrative posts in those departments as inadvisable. The
report continues: 'As far as possible all posts should be open to
men and women but it was neither necessary nor desirable to
abolish all the existing reservations in the service generally'
(PRO/CO 850/131/14/20508). Thus, in the genial language of
equality, women were excluded from certain posts.

    During the interwar years, numerous women's organisations –
including the Women's Freedom League, The National Council
of Women of Great Britain, and The National Union of Societies
for Equal Citizenship – sent resolutions to the Colonial Office and
requested meetings with officials. They fought for the admission of
women to administrative posts not so much on grounds of equal
opportunity for British women, but primarily for the interests
affecting women in the colonies. In 1932, for example, the
Colonial Secretary, Sir Philip Cunliffe-Lister, received a
deputation of women led by Eleanor Rathbone MP, who pointed
out that although nearly a thousand women were employed in the
colonial medical and educational services, no women were
employed in the administrative services where they could
influence general policy; she argued that women advisers to
colonial governments would consider women and children's
welfare from the woman's point of view. The minutes of her talk
continue, 'In India we had lost a great opportunity of improving
the lot of women and children in this way, and it would be a
tragedy if we did not take that opportunity in Africa while we had
the power of enforcing policy' (PRO/CO 850/14/2).

    The Colonial Office contined to rebuff these deputations. An
official statement in 1936 reserving administrative posts to men
was elaborated in a letter replying to various women's
organisations: 'Administrative duties have often to be performed
single-handed, among remote and backward peoples, where the

appointment of a woman would not be understood or workable; even in special missions, the employment of women in these dependencies would often be impracticable' (PRO/CO 850/131/14/20508). Although this argument was countered by citing that women doctors, teachers and others had little difficulty working among the indigenous people, the Colonial Secretary maintained that the stage had not been reached when women in these tropical countries 'could be armed with executive and judicial functions'.

Women were not the only excluded group; no men of non-European heredity were employed during this period. Sir Cosmo Parkinson, an official in the Colonial Office from 1909 to 1945, writes, 'There has not, so far as I know, ever been any colour bar. But in practice, the question did not arise' (1947, p. 105). Kenneth Robinson points out, however, that precautions were taken in 1925, when recruitment by examination was resumed; discussions involving both the Civil Service Commission and Treasury made it possible to declare a particular candidate unsuitable. By 1936, thus, of the fifty-eight members of the administrative class in the Colonial Office, 'all of them were white, none of them were women' (Ms., p. 6).

With women's organisations continuing to exert pressure, the authorities began to doubt whether they would hold to their position. By 1938, with the India Office now allowing the admission of women, C. J. Jeffries of the Colonial Office wrote in the confidential files: 'If it were decided to abandon the reservation, I think it would have to be on the understanding that we retained the right to restore it during any period when the number of women for the time being employed was considered to have reached the maximum compatible with efficiency' (PRO/CO 850/131/14/20508). The entry after this reveals:

> I agree. I begin to think that it would be better to open a sluice or two now rather than wait until the dam bursts and we are swept away by the torrent. Also I am not at all sure that we can maintain indefinitely the position that it is impossible to send a Woman Administrative Officer in the CO to a Colony. She could not of course be put on to District work, but there are other things she could do.

Then, at a meeting of the permanent heads of the Colonial Office and Dominions Office, Sir Cosmo Parkinson announced that he did not think that the reservation of administrative posts to men could be maintained any longer. (His wording shows little support for women's employment – rather, the reluctant recognition that the barrier could no longer be defended.)

Finally, in December 1938, the Colonial Secretary, Malcolm MacDonald, announced in the House of Commons that he had decided to remove the restriction to the admission of women to the Colonial and Dominions Office on an experimental basis, to be reviewed in a few years. Parkinson comments, 'It has been remarked on as a curious circumstance that, not until there was a bachelor Permanent Under-Secretary of State to advise and a bachelor Secretary of State to take a decision, did this change of policy come about' (1947, p. 104). He adds, 'It has been hinted that it may even have been done through ignorance of what the Colonial Office would be letting itself in for, once women got a foot inside it.' Such sexist remarks appear to have had general currency at that time. In an article in the *Crown Colonist* on the withdrawal of the restriction for women, for example, C. J. Jeffries writes, 'Although the new decision marks a break with tradition, it would be absurd to suppose that it heralds an era of petticoat government for the Colonial Empire' (February 1939; PRO/CO 850/151/21/20570).

With the outbreak of war and the suspension of permanent appointments, 'women became practically the only source of recruitment for junior administrative posts' (ibid.). They could now be admitted on a temporary basis. At the same time, the Colonial Office took on coloured men for administrative work, two in the Welfare Department and two in the Economic and Financial Division (Parkinson, 1947, p. 105). It was this period of emergency, thus, that opened the door for these two subsidiary categories previously excluded from administrative posts in the Colonial Office.

During the war, such organisations as The National Council of Women of Great Britain and the National Women Citizens' Association pressed for the immediate appointment of women to senior posts in the Colonial Office to assist in development and welfare; they were particularly concerned with questions affecting women in the colonies. More women were now taken on at junior level. After the war, two women in particular held senior posts relating to women in the colonies: Florence Udell as Chief Nursing Officer and Freda Gwilliam who became Deputy Adviser to Education. The post-war decolonisation period also extended the wartime opportunity for women to take on administrative posts in the colonies.

WOMEN AS AN INTERIM GROUP

Between 1953 and 1957, with the transfer of power under way in Nigeria, women were recruited as 'temporary Women Assistant Secretaries' (an administrative category distinct from the clerical one usually associated with women) in the Secretariats and, with reorganisation, the ministries of the Federal Government in Lagos and the Government of Northern Nigeria in Kaduna. A very small number were posted to the provinces. In all, about twenty-five women served in this junior administrative capacity, most for two tours of roughly eighteen months each.[2] A few stayed on to work for a year or two after Nigerian Independence; the more usual pattern was marriage to a colonial officer with several further years in Nigeria as a wife.

From 1948 to 1960 the political movements and constitutional advances towards Nigerian Independence accelerated with ever greater intensity. During these years, the process set in motion by the revision of the Richards Constitution transformed what I. F. Nicolson calls the 'administocracy' of colonial rule into the apparatus of a federal, parliamentary government, with Nigerian ministers and a 'Nigerianised' public service (Nicolson, 1969, pp. 251–300). This was a period, as well, of rapid economic and social development under a ten-year official programme with funds provided by the Colonial Development and Welfare Act. While greater numbers of professional and technical officers were required to plan and implement the designated projects, the Colonial Service was now consciously phasing itself out of existence.

The recruitment of European women thus solved a number of related problems. While the immediate post-war period brought the rapid recruitment of officers being demobilised from war service (a group now drawn from a wider social range than previously), by the early 1950s qualified young men in the UK were not coming forth in sufficient numbers to fill the vacant posts in Nigeria (I. F. Nicolson, 1969, p. 261). Although overseas recruitment on pensionable terms did not cease until the end of 1955, potential candidates were aware of the lack of permanence and were not attracted by the starting salaries which could barely cover living costs. Women graduates, however, were willing to risk the uncertainty of short-term contracts and, for most of them, the salaries offered were higher than their earnings in the UK. These women were placed in the Secretariats, thus releasing experienced men for what were considered the more arduous tasks in the districts. Some evidence suggests that Nigerian ministers and civil servants, suddenly raised to positions of much greater authority, found it easier to give orders to these women new to the scene than to the experienced men who might recently have been their mentors.

These women officers thus formed an interim 'buffer' group between two separate structures of male prestige,[3] the departing British Colonial Service and the advancing cadres of Nigerian politicians and civil servants. Their reports suggest that they worked with considerable efficiency and with a non-paternalistic approach to their Nigerian colleagues. In this setting, the 'meaning' of their presence in Nigeria as administrators cannot be interpreted in terms of 'equal opportunities for women' so much as providing the Colonial Office with a temporary and non-threatening group aiding the graceful exit of the Raj.

According to the terms of recruitment, these women were required to be single, to have university degrees and general office (preferably administrative) experience. While many came from middle-class professional families with a tradition of service overseas, some came from poor families and brought a different perspective to the social hierarchy of colonial life. Simply by taking university degrees, these women belonged to the educated elite of less than one per cent of women in their generation (Bryne, 1978, p. 12). Yet professional opportunities for women graduates in the late 1940s and early 1950s, outside teaching, were not so easy to find. Since more jobs were accessible for those with secretarial skills, many of these women had taken secretarial courses and found jobs as graduate secretaries. Others had worked in the Civil Service, personnel management in commercial firms, the news division of the BBC; one had been a research physicist.

Despite the variety of their personal histories, many of these women shared the recognition at a certain stage that their jobs were no longer rewarding and offered little future. They began to search for a change of work, another location, a new direction in their lives. Janet Longden (née Lloyd) sums up:

> Like most, if not all, the women who took up administrative posts in Nigeria I found myself there more or less by chance as an escape from a previous existence. For us the Colonial Service had not previously offered openings which could have led to its having been considered as a career, and most of us had leapt at an opportunity to get away from jobs we disliked, from over-close family ties or from frustrated love affairs. (Ms., p. 1)

In many reports the refrain comes through: 'If the VSO (Voluntary Service Organization) had been in operation then, I should probably have volunteered for service.'

PREPARATION FOR NIGERIA

These women unanimously record that they were given no briefing or special training before departure. They had very little idea of the jobs they would be required to undertake or the responsibilities these entailed. While their male colleagues (recruited for the permanent and pensionable establishment) were given no specific training, they did have the benefit of a year's course in colonial administration at Oxford or Cambridge on the famed 'Devonshire' course, which brought them in touch with serving officers. Patricia MacDermot writes, 'It would have been enormously helpful if the Colonial Office had invited me to a two-day study session, at which I could have read and digested various papers on the set-up of the Administration in Kaduna, and of the various amendments to the Constitution' (Ms., p. 7).

As for health precautions and personal effects, the Colonial Office provided more specific advice. All of these women received – and remember vividly – what is now laughed and talked about as the 'Green Book', a pocket-sized green-covered book smelling of its insecticide-treated binding. Called *Hints on the Preservation of Health in Tropical Africa*, this had line drawings of different types of mosquito with notes on how to recognise the malaria-bearing anopheles, as well as information on how to take a blood film, deal with snake-bites and dig privy pits. Its most memorable health hint was the dire warning not to let alcohol take the place of an evening meal. While this quaint book clearly remains a symbol in the collective memory of this group, most women at the time took its admonitions without misgivings.

The Crown Agents sent leaflets about luggage shipment, insurance, forwarding mail, and passage arrangements, as well as information about the climate, required clothing, facilities for shopping in Nigeria, household items to bring and so on. A kit allowance of £60 was provided, which most officers say covered the recommended list. The typical experience was to spend a whole day in London at a well-known departmental store buying clothes, bed linen, china, kitchen items, to be packed by the store or by a reliable firm and sent to the ship. Those who cautiously included a tour's supply of sanitary towels look back in amusement at using them for packing fillers and supplying their friends for months.

The important omission in the information, mentioned by nearly all these women, was the necessity of having a car in Nigeria and of being able to drive. Marjorie Daniels (née Bell) writes:

> The business of a car was important. I had never owned one, but here it was essential. Interest-free loans were available for car purchase, so I bought a Standard 8 for £420 new. We didn't pay purchase tax, so it was a good buy, but to me alarming, as I had never borrowed so much, and couldn't drive the thing anyway. I started driving lessons. (Ms., pp. 6–7)

She was not the only one who had never driven. The stories of failed driving tests provide humour in retrospect, but at the time undoubtedly made adjustment to the new setting difficult.

Travel by sea was customary for the first tour at least. Janet Longden feels she was fortunate in meeting a group of senior officers who, once they knew she was a new recruit, 'were kindness itself in taking it upon themselves to tell me as much as possible' (Ms., p. 3). Morag Corrie adds a sociological note, 'Shipboard was where I first appreciated the rigidity of the social stratification of the community I was about to join and this remained an absorbing study throughout my stay' (Ms., p. 2).

WORK WITH THE FEDERAL GOVERNMENT, LAGOS

Lagos in the mid-1950s presented a scene of commercial bustle and accelerated political maneouvring towards self-government.[4] The successive constitutional advances of this rapid transition period required the reorganisation of the Secretariat into Federal Ministries, with 'Nigerianisation' a high priority. The first women assistant secretaries in Lagos, Mary King (née Beaton) and Christine Prince, took up their posts in November 1953. They were joined during the next year by a handful of others to work in the various ministries.

Of this group, Mary King, with previous experience in the Colonial Office, held the post noted by others for its interesting scope. During her first tour she worked in the Chief Secretary's Office, her schedule of duties including a wide range from information services to ceremonial functions and labour relations. Her most difficult and most interesting work, she recalls, was as Clerk to the Privy Council. With the Governor presiding, the Council comprised the Attorney-General, Chief Secretary, and three eminent Nigerians. Part of her job was to greet the Council members in the anteroom; the first to arrive was usually the Hon. Abubakar Tafawa Balewa (later Nigeria's first Prime Minister), who would talk while they waited for the others (Ms., p. 4).

The 'information' work she found much less demanding, but rewarding in the interesting people she met. She had the privilege of working with the noted Nigerian historian, Kenneth Dike, on the first draft ordinance to preserve archives. He invited her to give a lecture to the history society of University College, Ibadan (in 1960, Dr. Dike became the first Nigerian Principal), and she remembers spending a happy weekend with his family. Among her other duties were visits to exhibitions of painting and sculpture arranged by the talented Art Adviser, Ben Enwonwu.

Her responsibilities for ceremonial functions were 'episodic and instructive'. She recalls 'struggling with the mysteries of naval protocol' to draft an itinerary for the courtesy visit to Lagos of the Commander in Chief, South Atlantic, in HMS *Leopard*. This work was more than rewarded, she writes, 'by a fairytale evening which began with a party on board the flagship, followed by dinner in Government House at which the Admiral proved to be a witty raconteur and a charmingly unpompous guest of honour' (Ms., p. 5).

Phyllis Treitel (née Cook) was posted to the Financial Secretary's Office, to be followed after nine months by Margery Daniels (née Bell). They were each in turn responsible for a heavy work schedule which included among others the Losses Schedule, the Tenders Board (serving as secretary), and expenditures of certain large public corporations, such as Nigerian Railways and the Ports Authority. On her first day Phyllis Treitel was shown to her office by a senior officer who announced that it was a bit of an 'Augean Stable'. She found not only the walls lined with files to the highest possible level but the desk piled high and the area around the desk. She learned what she could from her predecessor, who was going on leave, but files came in faster than she could get them out. Some days later a sympathetic colleague came in to show her how to get through the work. 'This was my training', she says, 'and I was very grateful for it' (Ms., p. 4). About half-way through her tour, she was posted to Buea in the Cameroons.

Margery Daniels followed her in this post. She was met off the mailboat by Phyllis Treitel, told of her assignment, invited to stay in her flat for a few days and eventually inherited not only her job, but her flat, her steward, and her curtains. She writes, 'Phyllis looked after me, and eased me into Lagos life, both social and professional' (Ms., p. 5). As their immediate superior, both served under a Nigerian, Chief S. O. Adebo, who later went to the United Nations. They were told he was abrasive and found him so in the beginning, but also a 'meticulous worker' and 'a delightful boss, very straightforward and tough and kind' (Ms., p. 8). Margery Daniels tells that she was invited to his home, where everyone sang hymns while Chief Adebo played the harmonium.

After several years in Kaduna, Aileen Clayton (née Morris) was posted back to Lagos, where she worked in the Ministry of Commerce and Industry, taking home 'piles of files' each evening. She comments, 'It never ceases to amaze me that the people in the UK are under the mistaken impression that colonial servants have an easy time overseas. Compared with their UK counterparts, they work incredibly long hours under arduous conditions' (Ms., p. 5). After her marriage, she was asked to continue her work, gaining promotion to Senior Assistant Secretary. Later she was assigned to work on a seminar on constitutional legal reform with some of the most famous legal experts of the Commonwealth; she also helped the Ford Foundation set up a management study course (Ms., p. 7). Another woman administrative officer, who stayed on after Independence, reached the highest position in Class I (Deputy Permanent Secretaries and Deputy Secretaries) in 1966. This was C. B. Etty-Leal, who came to Lagos in 1956 after working in Northern Rhodesia and was awarded an MBE in 1963 (Nigeria Staff List, 1966).

WORK FOR THE GOVERNMENT OF NORTHERN NIGERIA, KADUNA

As a setting for work and social life, Kaduna contrasted markedly with Lagos. Although in the 1950s the city was expanding with new buildings and an inflow of people, it still retained some of its earlier ambience of slow-moving dignity as the governing centre of the Hausa–Fulani emirates of Northern Nigeria. Lugard had planned the city with a vision of colonial spaciousness, if not quite imperial majesty, with major government buildings, a race course serving as polo ground, and its roads planted with flowering trees. During this period of political transition, the Secretariat disappeared; departmental activities were subsumed within the newly-created ministries. In the corridors of power, the objective was not 'Nigerianisation', but 'Northernisation'.

When Sheelagh Wrench (née Lynch) arrived in November 1953, she was assigned to the Lands and Mines Section of the Chief Secretary's Office, known in earlier days as 'the training ground of the promising' (Niven, 1982, p. 79). Before long, she was elevated to the position of Acting Crown Counsel. This came about because she was the only one with legal qualifications who could be spared when the Attorney-General made his search for legal talent. At the end of her first tour, she was encouraged to gain qualifications making her eligible for a substantive appointment in the Attorney-General's Department; but she was thinking of another direction to her life. She writes, 'It was the first wedding of its kind in Kaduna – "Admin. Officer weds Admin. Officer!" (Ms., p. 3). Shortly after, her husband was posted to Plateau Province. She writes, 'I had neither the opportunity nor the inclination to work again as I was blessed with three children all born in Nigeria.'

Elizabeth Purdy (née Sharp) was originally hired as Personal Assistant to the Governor, Sir Bryan Sharwood Smith, but a few months after her arrival in January 1955 she took over the work of Assistant Secretary (Security and Defence) in the Governor's Office and was upgraded to this status. Part of her job required touring to each of the twelve provincial offices in turn and writing, in co-operation with each Resident, a report on the security arrangements of the province. When the Queen's forthcoming visit to Nigeria was announced, she was attached to the Royal Visit office to do all the Governor's personal secretarial work in connection with the visit. Carried on in addition to her regular work, this involved an interesting variety of details. She also did verbatim reporting at times of heavy work pressures when the House of Assembly was sitting (Ms.[a], p. 1–10). She came back from leave for her second tour, delighted to find she was posted to the same job. This she continued for ten months before resigning to be married; as wife of a Resident, she spent six further years in Nigeria.

Jill Whitfield (née Forrest) arrived in mid-1955 to take up the post of AS (Lands) in the Lands and Mines Section of the Civil Secretary's Office, a position held in succession by a number of these women. Under the Land and Native Rights Ordinance of 1954, all land in Northern Nigeria was held in trust by the Governor for the natives. The work of AS Lands had to do with processing the requests of non-Northerners, whether Southerners or expatriates, for rights to land and writing minutes about each case to be sent up the administrative hierarchy. When a request was approved, special documents were prepared, signed by the appropriate authorities and duly registered. While she was on tour in Kano to look into various applications, she viewed some 'fellmongering plots' (where the curing of skins into 'Moroccan leather' caused foul smells), a description she had been puzzled about. She also went on official work to Jos in Plateau Province, driving the 180 miles of untarred corrugated roads with her servant accompanying her. 'No one seemed to think that it was at all dangerous for a woman to drive around; the only worry was mechanical breakdown' (Ms., p. 4).

Half-way through her tour, she broke her contract to go back to the UK to marry a fellow administrative officer. Her husband was posted next to Zaria. She writes, 'After the interesting work I had had and the feeling of being an integral part of the administration of the country, I did not greatly take to the role of a mere wife with a social round and not much else' (Ms., p. 5). Soon however, her husband was posted back to Kaduna, and she was immediately requested to take up administrative work in the newly-established Ministry of Health. She did not now receive expatriate allowances and originally lost the increment she had gained before her marriage, but after campaigning, she succeeded in getting it back again (letter, 23 May 1984). She stayed in this post until she was six months pregnant. During her husband's last tour, she considered herself fortunate to get a job on local radio filling in a slot for a quarter of an hour each week with a topic of her choice, occasionally an interview with a prominent person. This brief profile shows the work career of a WAS in Kaduna, one of a number re-employed in an administrative post after marriage, and then finding a part-time job for 'mental stimulus' after the birth of a child.

During 1956 and 1957 twelve more women came to Kaduna as junior administrative officers before the Executive Council ceased recruitment. They were involved in a wide range of duties in all the newly-established ministries. The official hours on weekdays were from 7.30 to 2.30 (less an hour for breakfast between 9.30 and 10.30) and on Saturdays until 12.30. But, as in Lagos, workloads were heavy and often required overtime. Training for the assigned work depended on the availability and willingness of the officer handing over. Anne Wren writes, 'I can't remember any training except reading some piece of paper telling new officers to write brief minutes and not to try to be funny (hard to resist sometimes)' (Ms., p. 2). Patricia MacDermot was told by her senior officer that the best way to learn was 'to go slap into the files'. She comments, 'In most jobs I also have found this the best way of learning – but I would gladly in *this* case, have been given a couple of days' instruction in order to get the hang of things' (Ms., p. 8).

Departments varied in their efficiency and work conditions. Carol Davies tells of the difficulties:

In spite of our re-organisation, files continued to get lost and letters to disappear and urgent telephone calls could not be made because the line was out of order or, as happened on one occasion, because the operator 'had gone to the latrines,

Madam'. A sense of humour was absolutely necessary to avoid a nervous breakdown. (Ms., p. 7)

Besides their regular schedules of duty within each ministry, these WASs were called upon from time to time to undertake special assignments. Zelma Fottrell, for example, was asked to draft an official history of the country from the standpoint of the Northern Region for the approaching celebration of Northern Self-Government. During the sessions of the House of Assembly, all the assistant secretaries shared the job of editing Hansard on a rota basis. This involved checking proofs produced by the verbatim reporters and working late to get the day's edition in to the Government Printer; this miraculously appeared the next morning on every Member's desk in English and in Hausa.

Another special duty was taking part in Boards of Inquiry, as Anne Wren recalls on two occasions:

> one when Government property was destroyed by fire in a house, which embarrassingly boiled down, I think, to whether its occupant had a lover who smoked, and on another occasion having to take an inventory of the Deputy Governor's house. Equally embarrassing as his lady took it badly and stayed in bed. (Ms., p. 3)

Official visitors from overseas required special attention. Janet Longden states, 'I accompanied the Colonial Social Welfare Adviser, Miss Mercer, round the region when she came out from the Colonial Office and took her to see work with women, a purdah clinic in Kano which operated after dark, a reformatory, etc.' (Ms., p. 8).

When Nigerian ministers first took office, some of these women acted as private secretaries. This entailed such duties as writing speeches, making official arrangements for their wives (in the case of Muslims, up to four), and organising official entertaining. Carolyn Jenkins recalls, 'One of my first tasks as Private Secretary was to arrange a cocktail party. I was told that a good deal of drink might be stolen if I left everything to the African stewards so I and two of my women friends acted as barmaids' (Ms., p. 5).

SOCIAL RELATIONS IN A MALE BUREAUCRACY

In their assessments, nearly all these women officers recount helpful support from their seniors, British and Nigerian. Mary King, one of the first to arrive in Lagos, found a pleasant working atmosphere with good relations between British and Nigerian members of the Service. Not aware of resentment or discrimination against women at any time, she views her appointment as Clerk to the Privy Council as evidence of fair-mindedness. This was delayed to find out whether she would be acceptable to African members, particularly the Muslim member, the Hon. Abubakar Tafawa Balewa, who affirmed that the only criterion was the ability to do the duties involved – being a woman was irrelevant (Ms., p. 8). In Kaduna, however, when Zelma Fottrell became AS Ministry of Internal Affairs, one of her scheduled duties was that of Secretary to the Privy Council. It was decided that she should not, as a woman, attend the meetings although it was in order for her to prepare the briefs. This was the only example of sex discrimination she encountered during her service (Ms., pp. 15–16).

Phyllis Treitel describes the friendly atmosphere in 'F Branch' (as the Financial department was known) in Lagos as the best thing that happened to her in Nigeria. She recalls:

> it was their practice, B.B. and the Assistant Secretaries, to go to the Rest House for drinks every Saturday after work ended at 12.00. They always included me, just as they included me in their car sharing scheme even though for months I either had no car or had no licence to drive one. I mention this because I think it was unique and it was invaluable to me in helping me to understand the jobs they did and thus, my own. (Ms., p. 5)

Janet Longden writes of the helpful attitude senior members of the administration had towards these women officers. She adds:

> I think it must be said that this was partly earned. We women were a hand-picked group, and generally more intellectually able than the average male ADO. We were therefore able to adapt easily to work in a ministry in the regional headquarters, and probably more suited to this type of work than less academic ADOs of similar age group, whose general interests were more suited to work in bush.[5] (Ms., p. 8)

These ideas were reflected, she found, in the comments frequently made by their permanent secretaries that they had never had such efficient assistance before, and for frequent requests for these women to return after leave to the same posts.

While these women officers report work relations with British male officers as reasonably harmonious on the whole, a few sensed an outlook of superiority on the part of some of the men and others record specific experiences revealing sexist attitudes. Margery Daniels relates an incident in Lagos. Her salary was increased by a few increments because of her previous experience in the Treasury. Soon two men in the department, one a senior administrative officer and the other on her own level with a wife and two children, came to question her about this; while not being unfriendly, they showed that they felt it wrong for a woman to earn so much with no wife and children to support. She writes, 'I felt there was a distinct impression on their part that, as a woman, I should have been paid less than my male counterpart. I did, in fact, partly support my mother' (Ms., pp. 12–13). It is hardly likely that these men would have questioned an unmarried male colleague in the same circumstances. Patricia MacDermot tells of 'one blatant case of discrimination against women': a woman officer was apparently deprived of an acting allowance (for doing a more senior job while someone was on leave) simply because she was a woman (Ms., p. 59).

Halfway through her tour, Phyllis Treitel was posted from an enjoyable assignment in Lagos to a trying one as ADO in Buea, in the British Cameroons. She writes of the puzzling way a senior officer treated her (her colleague ADO was Kenneth Shaddock):

> It sounds incredible but X would not address me. He would come into our office and say to Shaddock, in my presence, 'Oh, Ken, I want Miss Cook to do so-and-so'. Once I had a quick query for him (and we were so terribly behind with everything) and tried to enter his office but Ken told me not to: it must all go on the file. I couldn't understand it. I worked all day, every day, Saturdays and Sundays to begin with, but never really got on top of the work and finally gave up trying.   (Ms., p. 7)

Explaining that some officers came to the Cameroons because they liked bush life where women had no part, she concludes, 'Buea was a perfectly appropriate posting for a woman but the men there never really accepted it' (Ms., p. 8).

The only overt antagonism from Nigerian men was recounted by Phyllis Treitel. This came from Members of the House of

Representatives in Lagos after a session she attended in the officials' box to supply information on behalf of her superior. She relates, 'As I left, these two Africans cornered me and in angry tones asked me what had become of the great British Empire if all they could send out was women. If there were no men left, then Nigeria could supply them' (Ms., p. 8). A British male colleague dashed to her rescue, making exaggerated claims about her qualifications and 'we all left the building together in a happy party'.

Aside from this incident, these women emphasise that their work relations with Nigerians, both senior officers and junior staff, were courteous and without any evidence of prejudice. Carol Davies, describes the situation she found in Kaduna:

> When I first worked in the Ministry of Lands, our Minister was the Sardauna of Sokoto, who was also the Premier, but later on the portfolio was taken over by Mallam Gashash, a Northern trader, whom I always found to be very pleasant. The Permanent Secretary, Mr. Cartland, was English and the Senior Assistant Secretary, Mr. Olajide, was a charming Yoruba who retired while I was working in the ministry. The clerks were all Nigerian and with a few exceptions were male. On the whole I found them agreeable to work with and Mr. Olajide was extremely helpful and patient with the many stupid mistakes I made.   (Ms., p. 6)

Carolyn Jenkins states that the Nigerians she worked with accepted her readily enough. 'The more able had spent some years in England and that may have made them more used to working with women than the senior Europeans were when we arrived' (Ms., p. 8).

In their work with newly-appointed Nigerian Ministers, Janet Longden analyses the reasons why she and others found it an advantage to be a woman. Because the Ministers were generally known by the British senior administrators in earlier years when they were in junior posts or served as district heads, the Ministers understandably tended to guard their new positions of authority. Sometimes this resulted in obstinacy and refusal to agree with proposals from permanent secretaries, despite the attempt by the latter to approach tactfully the reversal of roles. The WASs were in quite a different position since they had never known the Ministers in any other roles. She relates, 'If the permanent secretary was doubtful whether the Minister would agree to approve a document, it was often given to me to take in to him' (Ms., p. 9). A male officer has commented that because these women had not served in the districts and did not know Hausa, they understood little of the political intrigue going on. But recognition of merit, as well, would seem to have contributed to the favourable standing these women officers had with their Ministers. Janet Longden adds, 'It was also clear that the Minister trusted my decisions completely, as he told this to the Nigerian who was my last permanent secretary.'

OFF DUTY: SOCIAL LIFE AND LEISURE ACTIVITIES

Beyond their heavy work schedules, these women in Lagos and Kaduna took an active part in the lively social round of these colonial capitals. Elizabeth Purdy writes, 'Socially, the life of an unattached female was all one could have wished' (Ms.[a], p. 14). She continues:

> The Club was the centre of social life in Kaduna. It was close to the CRH (Catering Rest House) and from five o'clock in the afternoon the tennis courts (which had a laterite surface) were busy. Incidentally, tennis balls came in vacuum sealed tins. Every Saturday evening there was a dance, often preceded by a private dinner party, and one wore a long evening dress and the men dinner jackets. We had Scottish dancing one evening a week . . . I joined the Kaduna Players and was soon involved in the forthcoming production of 'Affairs of State'.

In a sense, like the tennis balls, this energetic British social life was packed into what was generally perceived as a cultural vacuum. 'There was no TV of course, and no obtainable radio, and no readable local newspapers and none from UK except weeks late,' Anne Wren recollects. 'We were as cut off as men on the moon, by today's standards. Post from home was very important . . . . There were no restaurants or public transport' (Ms., p. 5). In Lagos, communications were closer to the homeland, the waters surrounding the island provided exciting swimming and sailing, but even in this more cosmopolitan scene, the patterns of social life were similar.

Aileen Clayton was one of the few women who took up polo; she learned in Kaduna and continued to take part in matches in Lagos. In the late afternoons, sports simultaneously provided various forms of necessary exercise and entry to different social groups. And in the evenings, as Patricia MacDermot remembers, 'The Europeans entertained each other endlessly' (Ms., p. 63). They soon became aware of the social hierarchy. Elizabeth Purdy notes, 'The Administration was at the top of the social league, followed by Education and Medical officers. Members of the PWD (Public Works Department) and commercial companies were, with a few exceptions, seldom included in dinner parties' (Ms.[a], p. 15). Christine Prince sums up her experience in Lagos, 'Funnily enough I think that social relations with Africans were better than those with PWD, commercial organisations etc. We had become briefly (I hope) frightful snobs and tended to mix only with our peers' (Ms., p. 2).

Morag Corrie writes, 'This social stratification seemed bizarre to those of us without colonial or military background and acclimatisation was necessary' (Ms., p. 7). But even those with previous experience in military and colonial circles found Kaduna extreme. Aileen Clayton says she was regarded 'as a Southern heretic by the dyed-in-the-wool Northern administrative officers' (Ms., p. 77). They criticised her for 'actually daring to refer to certain of my senior officers in Lagos by their Christian names'. She soon learned that while such familiarity might be acceptable in Lagos, it was not done in Kaduna. Having been awarded an MBE for her intelligence work during the war and not considering this of any social value, she had another surprise:

> One evening, before dinner, my hostess – the wife of a Permanent Secretary – showed me her seating plan and knowing her punctilious regard for the Staff List, I queried where she was proposing to seat me. Was I not the lowest form of animal life – a very junior administrative officer? 'But my dear, no,' she reprimanded me, 'Remember you have the MBE.' I nearly giggled.   (MS., p. 2)

Senior wives dominated the social scene. Carolyn Jenkins notes, 'They were conscious of their duty to see that single women were not left too much alone when they first arrived, and they were ready to advise about health and household matters and so on. They occasionally disapproved of some of the things we did, for instance when we acted as barmaids at Ministerial cocktail parties' (Ms., p. 11).

The women officers who worked in Lagos remember social relations between Nigerians and British as happy and relaxed during this period. Mary King relates how Government House gave a strong social lead in this multi-racial society:

> I met one of my closest Nigerian friends at a dinner party in Government House – the barrister, Sonnie Adewale, who had served in the RAF. Sonnie introduced me to two young Yoruba women barristers, Aduke Moore and Gloria Rhodes who belonged to old Lagos families who had their own proud traditions and 'cosmopolitan' outlook. Through these new friends and the Nigerians I met in my job, I gained a fairly wide circle of Nigerian friends and acquaintances. (Ms., p. 13)

In Lagos, quite a number of Nigerian men were coming back from abroad with university degrees, or graduating from the newly-established University College, Ibadan. While their wives were generally less well educated, they did attend official and informal parties with their husbands. In Kaduna, however, the Islamic culture created a different climate of social relations. Educational levels were considerably lower; few of the men who moved into high positions had more than secondary education, if that. The wives of Muslim leaders were generally kept in seclusion. Only rarely were Europeans invited to Muslim homes. Some of these WASs, however, were invited to tea by senior Nigerians and remember being treated with friendly courtesy.

After a few WASs had acted as barmaids for a party given by one of the ministers, he showed his appreciation by inviting them as a group with several of his Nigerian friends to dinner at the Rest House. Carolyn Jenkins writes, 'These dinners became an occasional feature of my life in Nigeria' (Ms., p. 5). In both Lagos and Kaduna these women officers were invited to 'High Life' dances. Margery Daniels remembers, 'We were a kind of secretariat goodwill delegation. The dancing was rather like rock and roll, and the Africans were marvellous at it' (Ms., p. 35). Sheelagh Wrench recalls, 'As a bachelor girl I was often asked to be the guest of honour at dances in the Sabon Gari, and I was once asked to judge a High Life competition. These forays into the Sabon Gari were always great fun and everyone behaved with respect and friendship towards me' (Ms., p. 4).[6]

Some of these WASs undertook voluntary activities which brought them in closer touch with the local community. Margery Daniels was asked by the British Council to teach an evening class on English literature to African students. She remembers, 'The students were amazingly enthusiastic' (Ms., p. 32). After her marriage, Mary King taught history in a similar arrangement. In Kaduna, Carolyn Jenkins was persuaded by senior wives to help with the Girl Guides (Ms., p. 11).

'Local leave' was a privilege, not a right, as these women reiterate in their accounts. Most of them were granted two or three weeks each tour which allowed expeditions to more distant parts of Nigeria. From Lagos, some of these women travelled by train to Jos on the weekly 'limited' passenger service, a journey that was 'comfortable but slow, rather like the Trans-Siberian Railway except for the temperature' (Daniels, Ms., p. 23). Those stationed in Kaduna were able to explore more widely, sometimes travelling in pairs in two cars as a safety precaution, since mechanical breakdowns were not uncommon on the rough roads. They went as far afield as Kano, Katsina, Sokoto and Argungu (for the famous fishing festival). Many echo Janet Longden's words: 'To me travelling around the country seemed important, partly for my own interest and pleasure and partly because only then would much of my work make sense and be seen in perspective' (Ms., p. 14).

THE PROGRAMME REVALUED

After the passage of a quarter of a century, the WAS programme can be seen as one small step forward in the continuing fight for women's equality of opportunity in professional work, but there are other dimensions as well, perhaps more interesting, in its revaluation. The programme must have been fairly successful from the start, as some of these women note, because the original group was followed during the next few years by more recruits. They attribute its success to various factors: the co-operative attitude of their colleagues, the Nigerian ministers' willing acceptance of women officers, and perhaps most of all the professional competence and flexibility these women brought to their work. Senior Nigerians showed their appreciation by requesting those remaining at the time of self-government to continue for further tours. They also wrote letters thanking them for valuable service. Against the earlier justifications of the Colonial Office for reserving positions for men, these WAS proved themselves able to work with Africans, both senior and junior, in the professional hierarchy. They also showed themselves fully capable of overseas service, if not under the rough conditions associated with duties of district officers.

Did this experiment of British women as administrative officers benefit African women as the numerous deputations to the Colonial Office from women's organisations during the interwar years had emphasised so strongly? As it turned out, their work did not deal specifically with policies relating to the health, education and welfare of Nigerian women. Felicia Wand-Tetley doubts whether the women in administration had any effect on the role of women in Northern Nigeria; in her view, credit should go to 'the Women Education Officers, the Nursing Sisters and even the wives serving with their husbands in the Provinces who would have shown what was possible with education to the women in the North' (Ms., p. 6).

Apart from their work, did these officers, as women, contribute to the Colonial Service? Some noted that the women who went out to Nigeria in the mid-1950s brought with them an atmosphere of post-war England, a more modern attitude than that generated by people who had lived a long time in the colonies. 'We broke up the old rigid structure,' Margery Daniels writes. In her view, 'women took with them a gentler, more flexible, attitude to the treatment of African subordinates, whether in the house or the office' (Ms., p. 39).

In terms of personal professional growth, Janet Longden considers that the Colonial Administrative Service provided a remarkably efficient training in general administrative skills and ability to adapt to different postings and procedures. She writes, 'I would attribute this to the degree of responsibility and self-reliance and need to innovate which the colonial service required even of comparatively young and junior officers. In many ways I have never again in the subsequent 29 years had the same measure of responsibility' (Ms., p. 19). While some of those who afterwards sought jobs in the UK found their experience valued, others met disappointment. Carolyn Jenkins relates,

When I applied for jobs in England, the people who interviewed me were not impressed by my experience in Africa. One English civil servant told me that he did not believe my account of my work at the Ministry of Health; in England such a wide range of activities would be divided between several departments. (Ms., p. 11)

For Christine Prince: 'Nigerian experience was a millstone round my neck for a year or two, as I was considered out of date and certainly colonial' (Ms., p. 2). A few went on to further posts overseas; Patricia MacDermot, for example, later worked in Sarawak, Southern Rhodesia, and Swaziland (Ms., p. 84).

These women recruited on a temporary basis answered the need for qualified 'manpower' during the period of accelerated transition from British to Nigerian rule. They entered this hitherto male bureaucracy only as an interim work force. Since the Colonial Service in Nigeria was rapidly disbanding, these women on short-term contracts at the lowest level offered little threat to the British men or the Nigerians succeeding them. The objective was to appoint women to the ministries to free men for more rugged work in the districts. In a sense, this division of labour reflected the early colonial stereotype: men in 'the wilds' at work demanding improvisation, decisive judgements and physical exertion; women in the civilised centres doing 'domesticated' desk work at the bottom of the bureaucratic hierarchy. Mary King writes,

I did not feel that I was competing with male colleagues, but rather that our roles were complementary. In the first place, terms of service were different; women were on contract while men were on the permanent establishment. This was reflected in the staff list which grouped the WAS appointments in a separate section from Class III and IV.   (Ms., p. 8)

Some male officers with previous misgivings about women administrators eventually praised their abilities, as is deftly expressed in this letter from a retiring officer thanking the WAS who made the farewell speech at his retirement party:

It was very nice too, and a permanent reminder – if I needed it and, of course, I do not – of the superiority of the female section of our race over the male; that at the end of my service, during much of which I had opposed the entry into the family of womenfolk my first girl 'boy' who had demolished all my previous arguments handed me the stirrup cup . . . . From the day you came into the office you pulled much more than your weight and what was even more you were one of the 'boys' as far as I was concerned, right from the first.   (letter, 13 October 1954, to Phyllis Cook from Rowland Baker-Beall)

Yet this Shakespearean play on girl/boy roles, on gender reversals, suggests continuing ambiguities in male perception of women administrative officers.

The women who married colonial officers felt that their years as a WAS contributed to the quality of their later life in Nigeria as wives. Marjorie Davies, who resigned after three years to marry a DO, spent a further twenty years in Nigeria. 'My previous knowledge of the ways of the country and the workings of Government undoubtedly gave me a deeper insight into my husband's job. I had a greater appreciation of all that was happening in those post-Independence years and my husband assures me that my former position as a WAS in Kaduna was of tremendous benefit! (Ms., p. 15).

The position of these WASs who married administrative officers might be usefully compared with women in the police force who subsequently marry male officers, as shown in Malcolm Young's trenchant analysis. As women police officers, they are subject to the condemnation often encountered by those in marginal and ambiguous positions, but are still sought after as marriage partners by the same men who deride their professional abilities. He concludes, 'By reconstituting them as wives, policemen are gaining adjuncts to their own careers, re-inserting these female intruders into the male conceptual space "correctly", and so restoring order' (1984, p. 86). While these WASs did not experience overt condemnation, clearly their transition from the category of 'women colonial administrators' to that of 'wives' represented in the dominant ideology of the Colonial Service an eminently suitable resolution to the ambiguities of women as professional colleagues.

The reports of these WASs show that they did not see themselves, nor were they seen by their male colleagues, as full members of the Colonial Administrative Service. They proved their abilities as capable junior administrators, but did not challenge the conceptual space of 'a man's country'. The masculine ethos of the Colonial Service was preserved.

Part Three

Wives in Supporting Roles

7   Part-Time Wives: before 1940

I had ridden over 3000 miles, learnt a new language, made thousands of new friends in the animal and flower world, as well as valued human ones. I felt as if I had 'enlarged my borders' mentally, and had certainly begun to know and love Africa with a deep affection that, I think, is never lost by those who once acquire it.

(Constance Larymore, at the end of her first tour in 1903, 1911, p. 54)

THE EARLY YEARS

The first two of these three chapters on colonial wives in Nigeria set out their living conditions and social spaces as described in their writings, while the third takes up the varied ways these wives acted within the constraints of imperial culture to create their own identities and meaning. As dependent wives, they drew their social identity from their husband's work and rank. Their days and seasons were structured according to his changing duties and his continuous re-postings; they supported his career not only with 'feminine graces' and 'women's work' but in other, less conventional ways. As individuals, they retained a measure of autonomy, often enlarging their circumscribed role by taking on self-appointed projects, in some cases criticising the colonial order (usually in an oblique way, but on occasion with direct candour).

Many of these wives had a family tradition of service in the colonies. Sylvia Leith-Ross writes, 'My father had been at the taking of Lagos in 1851 and, on the sloop *Pandora*, had captured the last Portuguese slaver; my uncles had been in India, a brother in China, another on the Pacific Station' (1983, p. 41). She also had a brother serving in Nigeria who introduced her to his fellow officer; they were subsequently married. Anne Macdonald visited her grandfather's grave at Bonny and her children played on the beach at the probable location of his 'factory' (Ms.[a], pp. 8, 12).

The first wife to accompany an administrative officer to Northern Nigeria was Constance Larymore in 1902. Having spent four years with her husband in Indian military stations and a brief period in Sierra Leone, she was hardly a newcomer to tropical conditions when she embarked at Freetown on the *Sekondi* bound for Forcados. She writes, 'It certainly was a step in the darkest dark; no Englishwoman yet had gone where I meant to go, or done what I hoped to do' (1911, p. 2).[1] Her claim that no Englishwoman had preceded her is exaggerated in that Mary Slessor had begun her missionary work in Calabar in 1876 and during her thirty-eight years in south-eastern Nigeria had even served in an official position as Vice-Consul and District Magistrate of Okoyong (Oliver, 1982, pp. 95–144), and Mary Kingsley had conducted her extensive travels in West Africa a decade earlier (Flint, 1963; Oliver, 1982, pp. 76–94). But she did, as she says, travel over 3000 miles on horseback through the interior of Northern Nigeria on their first tour alone, recording her observations and encounters. Her memoirs, *A Resident's Wife in Nigeria*, including a complete guide to household management in the tropics, went through two editions.

Lady Lugard also arrived in 1902, a few months later than Mrs Larymore, having travelled to Madeira to marry Sir Frederick and accompany him back to his dedicated work in Zungeru. She was now nearly fifty and, as Flora Shaw, had an impressive achievement behind her as a journalist. Earlier when she had contributed an article, she had been told, 'If you were a man you would be Colonial Editor of *The Times* tomorrow' (Bell, 1947, p. 92). It had taken her three years to overcome the disadvantage of being female. During the entire decade of the 1890s, she worked as a staff member of this world-renowned newspaper, the last seven years as colonial editor. On self-designated assignments, she undertook arduous journeys to the far reaches of the globe. She argued in numerous writings the economic and political case for imperialist expansion, the paper providing an authoritative forum for reaching the influential people of the day. If today we find her ideas ethnocentric and misguided, she deserves a place in imperial history in her own right; she helped to create the ideological field from which events were generated and reputations secured in the period from 1890 through the First World War.

Her biographer writes, 'When she ceased to be Flora Shaw she also ceased to be a woman with a career' (Bell, 1947, p. 250). She marked this change symbolically by discarding the black clothes she had worn for her professional career to wear white dresses in her new identity as the wife of a leading colonial administrator in Africa. Her letters from Nigeria show her great admiration for her husband's work, but she herself did not flourish, soon becoming confined to the veranda with an undiagnosed illness. Lady Lugard was thus to play her strong supporting role in England, rather than by her husband's side. Here she gave prominent lectures and wrote articles as well as a long historical volume on Northern Nigeria (1905). These efforts were designed, in the view of one analyst, for the promotion of 'the Lugard myth' (Nicolson, 1969, pp. 152–78).

Another colonial wife, far more sympathetic to the peoples and cultures of Nigeria, came to Zungeru in 1907. This was Sylvia Leith-Ross, who spent only a year there before her husband died of blackwater fever. Over the next sixty years, however, she returned many times: to compile a dictionary of the Fulani language, then to become the first 'Lady Superintendent of Education', to live among Igbo women as an anthropologist, to work as an intelligence officer in Lagos during the Second World War, and finally to collect and catalogue pottery for the Nigerian Museum in Jos.[2] Isabelle Vischer came to Northern Nigeria in 1912 with her Swiss husband, who had earlier been a missionary but was now serving under Lugard as organiser of education. Her memoirs (1917), in French, tell of their daily life and the people they came in touch with in Kano as well as their travels to Jebba and Bida, Sokoto and Katsina.

During this early period, another colonial wife was Olive MacLeod. She married Charles Lindsay Temple in 1913 and accompanied him to Northern Nigeria, where he was Lieutenant-Governor from 1914 until his early retirement in 1917. Her first travels in Nigeria, however, took place before her marriage – from August 1910 to May 1911. This journey, initiated by a dramatic event, is a story of romantic adventure (Alexander, 1977, pp. 277–90, 1983, pp. 59–60). The younger daughter of Sir Reginald MacLeod, head of the MacLeod clan in Scotland, she had hesitated to become engaged to the explorer Boyd Alexander until he was about to leave on an expedition to West Africa which proved fatal. She decided to honour his memory by taking a cross to Maiduguri to place on his grave. With her on this rather quixotic pilgrimage (vividly publicised in the press of the day) were P. Amaury Talbot (a District Commissioner in Southern Nigeria) and his wife. Olive MacLeod's journal, published in 1912 (1971), tells of their travel for six months through 3700 miles of Africa, all the time engaged in scientific study of birds, beasts, and insects and the collection of plants. She met Charles Temple in Zungeru, where as Resident he had entertained the travellers. She must have found him and his life's work congenial, despite his reputation as a misogynist, since she returned later as his wife. He was a proficient linguist, geologist and artist; she became fluent in Hausa and joined him in serious ethnographic study (Temple, 1922).

PREPARATION FOR THE UNKNOWN

Throughout the period until the Second World War (and even after, in some cases), preparations for the journey had much in common. A personal wardrobe suitable for wear in tropical conditions and sufficient for the entire tour had to be acquired. Lady Lugard embarked with 46 trunks and cases, including her trousseau of white dresses and the household items required for enhancing the new Government House at Zungeru. She was also accompanied by an English lady's maid (Perham, 1960, p. 75), which may have been unique since no other instances were cited in these writings.

For 'what to wear' in tropical Africa, Constance Larymore provides practical advice and a basic list:

Six cambric night-dresses
Two flannel night-dresses
Twelve cambric combinations
Six pairs cambric knickers
Twelve spun silk vests
Six pairs tan thread stockings
Six pairs black thread stockings
Three white petticoats
Two silk moirette petticoats (wears much better than silk)
Two dozen handkerchiefs
Six pairs corsets
Twelve camisoles

One white (washing) dressing-gown
One woollen dressing-gown
Four linen skirts
Two holland or drill skirts
Two muslin dresses
One cloth gown
One tea gown
Two evening gowns
Blouses *ad lib*.
One habit skirt
Four riding coats
Two pairs riding breeches
Two Panama hats
One solar topi
One light coat
One *en-tout-cas*
One sunshade
One mackintosh
One pair thick tan boots
One pair tan walking boots
One pair tan glacé walking shoes
One pair black glacé walking shoes
Six pairs house slippers
One pair tan riding boots.   (Larymore, 1911, pp. 290–1)

A photograph taken in Nigeria shows her in an Edwardian floor-length gown with long sleeves and high neck. It is daunting to think of wearing this in tropical heat with the necessary petticoats and underclothes. She makes no compromise on the requirements of taking at least six pairs of corsets: '*Always* wear corsets, even for a *tête-à-tête* home dinner on the warmest evenings; there is something about their absence almost as demoralizing as hair in curling-pins.'

Mosquito boots were essential. She suggests for ordinary use a pair of black canvas gaiters, buttoned and reaching to the knee; under a long evening dress, these gave protection against the ravaging bites of mosquitoes. These boots continued to be a matter for special comment in women's memoirs. Mary Oake took with her in 1928 a pair of white thigh boots; she viewed these with deep suspicion. Invited to a party in Lagos, she found that only another newcomer and herself had the clumsy lines of these boots bulging under their evening skirts; the other women were clothed in the sheerest of silk (1933, p. 84). But if mosquito boots were disdained by the chic Lagos ladies, they were definitely worn up-country. Erick Berry informs us, 'Guests arriving for an afternoon's tennis and remaining for drinks and after sundown small chop arrive also with mosquito boots . . . It is quite correct to change shoes in public. Between malaria and etiquette there is no choice' (1941, p. 136).

Hats for protection from the sun were considered essential throughout this period; but what began as general advice appears to have turned into rigid institutional rule. Whereas neither Larymore nor Leith-Ross make any special fuss about sun helmets in the early years, several wives coming out later mention the danger of even a few rays of sunlight touching a bare head. While trekking in 1924, Violet Cragg writes, 'Our present hut is large, but not sunproof, so that we have to wear hats all the time, even in the bath!' (Ms., p. 9). Similarly, when they were on tour, Erick Berry's husband ordered her to put her hat on indoors because the thatched roof of the resthouse was not safe. She adds, apparently seriously, 'For a shaft of sunlight no wider than a hatpin can, like a hatpin, strike through to the brain' (1941, p. 36).

The explanation appears to be, as stated by Thorburn, 'In the 1920s no one went anywhere without a sun helmet and, when travelling, a khaki bush shirt with a spine pad lined with red to keep off the actinic rays of the sun' (1958, p. 87). The tropical sun was considered to have the special powers of 'actinic rays' – light rays of short wavelength occurring in the violet and ultraviolet parts of the spectrum and producing chemical changes as in photography. While women were required at all times to protect their heads, they were not, however, expected to wear the spine pads essential to men's outfits (see Kirk-Greene, 1955, pp. 108–11). This prohibition against the slightest exposure to the sun vanished with the Second World War when many soldiers, ignorant of these imperial taboos, survived in the midday sun without protection.

Berry describes two types of hats, the double *terai* and the sun helmet. The first was 'wide brimmed, of heavy felt, and literally one hat over another' (1941, p. 135). In the early morning when the sun was low, she pulled them apart and wore the inside hat, but in the midday sun even the double *terai* was not adequate. This required the pith sun helmet, with the ventilation holes in the crown carefully covered. She found a way to make it attractive:

> I frankly lifted an idea from the chic wife of a tin-mine manager; several lengths of chiffon in bright colours; I pinned on over the crown the one best suited to the costume of the day; tan, white, stop-red, or kelly green, leaving a yard or two to float, Lady of Shalott fashion, out behind.   (1941, p. 136)

Women from this early period discreetly neglect to mention female necessities, though Niven in his memoirs published in 1982 writes of preparations when his bride accompanied him to Nigeria in 1925: 'Specially for the lady was a gallon container of medicinal paraffin in case of difficulty and a gross of packets of sanitary towels (the old kind), as well as a full medicine chest and bandages and the like. Toilet articles had to be bought in quantity, bottles and jars and packets' (1982, p. 60).

But personal effects were only the beginning. Household supplies, camping equipment, medical and food provisions for the entire tour had to be obtained. Mrs H. M. Kirby tells of their consignment of 105 cases, which included a sofa and a piano specially made for the tropics (Ms., p. 1). Leith-Ross describes the loads jammed into the crowded space of the stern-wheeler:

> Stacked in a corner was your personal luggage, for we were in the era of airtight tin cases, travelling baths with their wicker linings, red-lined helmets and green-lined umbrellas, spine-pads and tummy-bands, elaborate filters, water and Sparklet bottles, heavy leather-encased despatch boxes, every kind of wickerwork luncheon basket and – heaviest, ugliest and most invaluable of all – the black jappanned Lord's lamp, complete with its kerosene tank and its Eiffel-Tower-like iron legs. On the decks were the tents and groundsheets, saddle boxes and cook boxes and, swamping everything else, the chop boxes.   (1983, p. 43)

She describes these 'chop boxes' – when packed, each one weighing 56 pounds, the regulation head-load for a carrier. These were named, numbered and padlocked, with contents listed on typewritten sheets, dealt with by several London and Liverpool firms (such as Army and Navy Stores or Griffiths, McAlister). The objective was to be self-contained for the entire tour.

TRAVEL BY SEA AND LAND

During the whole of the colonial period, the journey out by Elder
Dempster steamship continued as common experience, though
the last decade brought the option of air travel. The journey took
two or three weeks, depending on how many West African ports
were visited. Sylvia Leith-Ross remembers Las Palmas as the
dividing line between Europe and Africa, followed by Freetown,
Monrovia, Axim, Sekondi, Cape Coast, Accra, Lagos, Burutu.
The cabins were 'tiny, fan-less and oven hot' and they washed in
'rust-yellow water poured daily into a rusty tank' (p. 39).

Those going to Lagos and the western areas of Southern Nigeria
disembarked at Lagos. In 1912, with the harbour in the early
stages of being built, the breakwater provided some shelter from
the terrific swell. Passengers, however, still had to go through the
traditional ordeal, related by Mrs Kirby, of being hoisted high in
the air in a 'mammy chair' by the ship's derrick to be dumped on a
waiting tug carrying them to shore (Ms., p. 2). All the cargo was
unloaded in this way as well, to be carried off the wharf by porters
(with six being assigned to her piano).

Those destined for posts along the lower Niger and in Northern
Nigeria stayed on board until the ship came to the bar outside
Forcados in the Niger Delta. Here, as told by Larymore, they and
their belongings were transhipped to a 'branch boat', a small
steamer which took 'four or five hours crossing the bar and finding
our way up to Burutu' (1911, p. 4). They were transferred yet
again, this time to one of the government stern-wheelers carrying
mail and passengers up and down the Niger. These little boats,
she describes, had a lower deck loaded with cargo, fuel, and native
passengers and an upper deck reserved for European travellers.
Their first journey was relatively uneventful. But in October 1905
they met a tornado outside the bar at Forcados. With four other
passengers, they donned oilskins, climbed down the ladder from
the steamship, and scrambled into the small boat tossing in the
swirling tides. After breathless moments of being pitched about in
the waves, the boat reached the other ship and they boarded its
dripping decks.

The Larymores came closest to losing their lives in January
1908, on their last tour in Nigeria. This time the transfer from the
ocean ship at Forcados had gone smoothly and they were
steaming up the Niger in a stern-wheeler. After peaceful hours on

deck chairs, they went to their cabins to dress for dinner. The cry went out that the ship was sinking. Mrs Larymore moved quickly in an unsuccessful attempt to save her dogs, then dropped to the barge below. She soon discovered her husband was missing. Boxes and luggage had crashed down on the cabin door, trapping him inside. She rushed back to the deck, finding 'a strength beyond herself' as she tore at the heavy packages to release him. A new danger confronted them. The stern-wheeler was dragging the barge at a dangerous angle and the tie had to be cut instantly. They were saved by the black skipper who dived into the swirling water of the lower galley, retrieved a knife and cut the barge free only seconds before the boat sank. She writes, 'We were alone on the river, staring at the quiet dark blue water, where, five minutes before, had been a busy, lighted steamer, the whole of my possessions, valuable and otherwise, and, deepest sorrow of all, our faithful little Scotch terrier' (pp. 180–1).

Throughout this period, journeys on the Niger and the Benue feature in women's memoirs. They tell of housekeeping being carried on aboard the boat, meals put together by cooks, provisions procured from villages along the way or from the 'chop boxes' they brought with them. Elnor Russell found the halts at villages along the Benue a welcome change, though she did not take a romantic view. She writes, 'The smaller places were all much alike, a collection of mud huts surrounded by half rotten grass mats, an air of poverty, innumerable flies, dirty streets, a restricted area of farmlands and then swamps' (1978, pp. 7–8). Exploring the abandoned station at Ibi, she stumbled over a small heap of cement and mud where once a house had stood and observed that the bush came back so quickly their efforts to create a civilisation seemed almost pointless. She continues, 'We found a broken-up cement tennis court and a cemetery full of European graves.'

Although river travel continued throughout the colonial period, the government stern-wheeler disappeared during the Second World War. And as the railway extended to points north, reaching Kano by 1911, this became the preferred official travel from Lagos to the interior. Noël Rowling describes her first journey on the boat train from Lagos to Kano in 1933 (1982, pp. 8–9). In the evening after dinner they boarded the train for the regular journey of two days and two nights. She was pleasantly surprised to find that their compartment had two beds made up with a wash basin in an alcove. The next morning they had a good breakfast. Suddenly the train stopped; a violent storm during the night had washed away a bridge. This was near Jebba, one of the hottest places in the country and here they were stuck for two days. The fans stopped; there was no escape from the pervasive heat. Not being able to use the lavatories, they had to leave the train to seek privacy among the dust-covered shrubs. On the second day when the food in the restaurant car ran out, the stewards bought what they could from local markets; this was to have disastrous effects for her digestive system. At last they heard cheers and were told that the train from Kano to Lagos had reached the other side of the chasm and they were to tranship. Down the side of the ravine they clambered and up the opposite side to the waiting train, finally to take off on the journey north.

Before cars and lorries were introduced during the interwar period, and aside from the regular train routes, all travel overland had to be on horseback or by horse-drawn carriage (in the tsetse-free areas) or bicycle, on foot, or in a hammock carried by bearers. Loads were transported by carriers. Even when motor transport became available, this depended on the construction of roads, often only 'dry season' tracks subject during the rains to flash floods and bridges being washed away. The story of bring stranded at nightfall on the wrong side of a suddenly enlarged river became part of nearly everyone's repertoire.

Across the savannah and scrub bush areas of Northern Nigeria, horse-drawn carriages were sometimes used for long-distance journeys. Isabelle Vischer, for example, travelled this way with her husband from Kano to Katsina in 1913. She tells how a crowd gathered in Katsina to view two absolutely new sights: a white woman and a carriage (1917, p. 53). These journeys clearly required resilience: on their trip in March (one of the hottest months) over a distance of a thousand kilometres from Kano to Sokoto, Katsina and back, the temperature reached 116 degrees on certain stretches.

THE MOVABLE 'HOME'

Constance Larymore concludes her chapter of advice on the household with the significant remark: 'No English housewife in West Africa – if she is "worth her salt" – will spare herself in the endeavour to, at least, turn "quarters" into "home", even if only for a few months' (1911, p. 203). This makes explicit the common fate of colonial wives: they had to make a 'home' in whatever location they found themselves, however temporary.

The imperative of colonial life in Nigeria was a movable household. Every officer in the field – whether administrative, medical, agriculture or education – had to go on frequent tours of his area, lasting several weeks or more at a time. These could be scheduled and planned for. What continued to be unpredictable throughout the entire period were the frequent repostings during any one tour; quite often, as soon as belongings were unpacked and a 'home' created, the telegram would come with orders to move on to another station to replace an officer taken ill or going on home leave. Then everything would be packed up again and the household loads would be on their way, carried by porters in the early days, later by lorry. Noël Rowling explains, 'So every time we were moved or went on leave, we had to pack up china, glass, cutlery, bedding, cooking utensils and, of course, our own pictures, curtains and cushions and all our camping gear and books' (1982, p. 13). Anne Macdonald tells of the time she had to pack in record time: the Superintendent of Police arrived in Agbor as a guest for lunch with the greeting, 'All ready to move?' They were to go on to Warri with all their possessions that night (Ms.[a], p. 12). At the end of each tour (from twelve to eighteen months), all household goods had to be placed in storage, leaving the quarters free for other occupants.

Whatever the myths about the lavish living of colonial rulers in the tropics, as Mary Oake states succinctly, 'No one could call the home of a junior officer in West Africa comfortable' (1933, p. 47). Lassie Fitz-Henry tells of their arrival in Oturkpo, 'The first sight of our house reduced me to secret tears, as I could not believe that that was where we were to live. It appeared to be a shed not even worthy of a cow' (1959, p. 14). Noël Rowling's husband was posted in 1935 to Shendam to fill in after the DO was taken to hospital with blackwater fever. Her spirits fell on entering their house: 'It had been condemned twenty years before but there had been no money to build another, and so it was still used' (1982, pp. 24–5). Two small rooms were surrounded with an enormous veranda; furniture consisted of two wooden chairs, a chest of drawers and a table. Improvements were made: 'Chas and the staff had a wonderful morning destroying the numerous bats that had made the roof their home . . .' The mud floor was cemented and local prisoners made a splendid floor mat of twisted grass.

These memoirs show variations in housing up and down the scale, from the original mud bungalows to two-storey brick houses with roofs of corrugated iron. Some officers preferred local architecture, as did Hanns Vischer, whose house in Kano, known as *Gidan dan Hausa*,[3] was of typical Hausa style. A visitor in 1913, Sylvia Leith-Ross writes: 'Isabelle Vischer had gathered together the finest Kano cloth and mats and leather-work so that there was not a jarring note in the shadowy rooms, cool and still like pools of water after the violence of the daylight. We slept on the flat roofs, . . . and breakfasted in the garden under the high trees, in a dapple of sunlight and shade (1983, p. 77). She praises this as the first *home* she had seen, 'an intelligent creation based on the country's own riches, belonging to it, issuing out of it, and at the same time harmonising with our own ideas of simple comfort, order and cleanliness'.

In her household advice, Larymore recommends making use of the products of local crafts: brightly coloured native cloths, coloured grass mats and decorative brasswork from Bida, 'charming, quaintly-shaped little burnt earthenware jugs from Ilorin', carved wooden stools from Ibi, and 'the brilliantly tinted Hausa leatherwork' fashioned into cushion covers and other articles (1911, p. 197). If some colonial wives searched for handwoven cloths and other craftwork to bring African designs into their homes, others made the attempt to replicate the English interiors they had left behind.

Many houses required survival skills rather than a talent for interior decorating. Elnor Russell describes their quarters in Jalingo in 1937:

> We had two round mud huts joined together by a covered veranda, a hut for our bedroom, a hut for Sali's pantry and the boxes and the middle part which we used as sitting and dining room. There was the same business we had had in Yola of propping up our packing cases on stones and sheets of iron to keep them from being eaten by white ants, of sorting out essentials without opening too many boxes, of unrolling grass mats at the first signs of a rainstorm to stop everything in our sitting-room from being blown away.   (1978, p. 46)

Better houses were available, of course, for officers of higher rank —

Residents and above. But throughout the period until 1940, and in many areas even as late as 1960, there were few 'modern conveniences'. Berry describes the DO's house at Ibi, once a Residence: 'No electricity, no radio, no electric lights. No running water – we were lucky to have as much as the bath. Our toilet was of the bucket and sand-scoop variety' (1941, p. 54). In a country where darkness falls throughout the year by 7 pm, lighting clearly requires attention: 'whether the candle-lamp which burns an ordinary candle but supports it from wilting in the heat by a sort of metal jacket and spring, or the carbide lamp, or the clockwork lamp, both of which were gadgety and, with native servants, likely to get out of order'.

Another problem was heightened in the tropics. Berry continued, 'Refrigeration we had none. Not even later in the big stations of Katsina and Zaria did we possess such luxuries as ice for drinks and on which to store and ripen meat. Our meat must be plunged into the stewpot as soon after death as possible.' The first refrigerator appeared in 1932 – the 'icyball' – described by Anne Macdonald: 'an extraordinary apparatus, one of whose great balls had to be heated each day over a little kerosene stove and then plunged into a huge bucket of water whereat the other ball, connected by a tube, became frosty and kept the food good for a day or two and the drinking water cool' (Ms.[a], p. 8). By 1936, Joy Bourdillon tells of having a kerosene refrigerator in Zaria, 'It was quite an exciting thing to have a refrigerator, but it went by kerosene, by oil, which was a bit of a nuisance, because it was always smoking and it smelled' (Ms., p. 2). Later, in cities with electricity, electric ones were supplied.

Daily routines appear as common experience: 'All water was put through a ritual of boiling and filtering, even in the big stations where pure water came every day from the Government condenser' (Berry, 1941, p. 54). Bread was home-baked in ovens stoked with wood or coal. The household laundry was washed by hand, often in water carried from a nearby stream or river.

In her chapter on managing the household, Larymore considers seven servants to be necessary – the cook, the cook's mate, head steward, under steward, laundress, *doki*-boy,[4] and gardener. For the Edwardian lady, who might well have grown up in a large household with numerous servants, domestic arrangements in Nigeria came well within her practical experience. It was generally assumed that when an officer brought his wife for the first time, his servants would be unhappy at the new authority in the household and resignations or sackings would follow. A. F. B. Bridges explains that after their initial reaction, the servants were usually pleased because the 'Missus taught all the intricacies of laying the table, waiting, arranging flowers, etc., as well as new recipes, all of which increased a boy's market value and not only enabled him to demand higher wages, but to make a profit from the sale of his knowledge to less fortunate individuals' (1980, p. 28).

Throughout these records, these women tell of faithful servants continuing for many years, with details of their personal problems, their wives and families. They give instances of servants being sacked for misdemeanours, mainly for thefts, but these appear to be exceptions to long-term relations of trust. The evidence confronts one of the received ideas about colonial wives, that they bickered continually with servants. These memoirs, of course, reconstruct past reality and may well show positive selection. But there is support for the view that servant relations were relatively harmonious during this early period. Most of these women grew up in households with servants and were used to the paternalistic (rather than merely contractual) relations that were closer to indigenous custom. On their part, servants felt they were moving up in the world, learning new skills and earning steady wages.

However remote the station, hospitality was a central feature of colonial social life. Guests on tour were welcomed for their company and their relay of news. When visitors were stranded, whether they were personally known or not, they were given meals and sleeping quarters in recognition of the fictive kinship of these European travellers in an alien environment. Direct reciprocity was never expected: generosity and honour were linked in a long chain of giving and receiving.

Throughout their memoirs these women place emphasis on laying out attractive gardens. During her first stay in Lokoja, Mrs Larymore was thrilled with the variety of fruit trees ('lime-trees, mangoes, orange-trees and guavas'). She resolved, 'I then and there took to heart the lesson which I have tried to practice ever since – the absolute *duty* of planting trees everywhere for the benefit of one's successor' (1911, p. 7). This theme recurs throughout these memoirs, the appreciation of well-planned gardens and, for many, the duty of gardening. Besides its aesthetic pleasure and its practical purpose of supplying household needs, the garden served as a rich metaphorical link: English order and productivity amid the tropical chaos of overgrown jungle or scrubby savannah.

WIVES ON TOUR

Erick Berry explains the two meanings in West Africa of the word 'tour': 'One's tour in the country is the length of time between trips home. But to go on tour in the bush is to take carriers and travel through the country itself' (1941, p. 62). These women relate many pleasurable adventures, as well as some harrowing moments on these nomadic forays; something of the 'spirit' of Africa was discovered. On their first assignment, Larymore writes, 'We were very happy at being out in camp, with a good six weeks before us, to be crammed with novel experiences, new flowers, new birds, new butterflies to discover, heaps to learn about everything' (1911, p. 11). She counted this 'a rare holiday'.

Others concurred. 'Travelling was our greatest joy' states Mrs Kirby (Ms., p. 8). As an agricultural officer, her husband frequently toured his area around Ibadan to talk to local farmers, telling them how crops could be improved and suggesting they should come to Moor Plantation to see demonstration plots. While he carried out his duties, she helped with minor medical treatments. 'Children's sore eyes were dreadful, and I'd give out boracic lotion and lint, and show the women how to keep their children's eyes clean. I had salve for wounds, and Epsom salts, but so often I saw terrible cases of gangrene and could only beg them to go to hospital.'

Constance Larymore went on horseback, as did other women in Northern Nigeria, but in the tsetse belt alternative ways of travelling were required. Mrs Kirkby walked during the early part of the day when it was still relatively cool, but later she would take to a 'hammock' (a canvas chair slung on ropes from poles) carried by four porters. If the bush path was too narrow for a hammock, she had to walk the fourteen miles or so they usually did on a day's march. Violet Cragg had a rickshaw, which proved tiring over a long day's journey. When the track was not suitable, she had to walk; she always climbed steep hills out of consideration for the pullers. Some wives were allotted men's

bicycles, the problem being that they were too high off the ground
to dismount easily; this was usually accomplished by falling off.
Erick Berry's usual way of travel on tour was behind her husband
on his motorcycle: 'On the new flapper bracket, designed for the
soft security of English lanes, I bucketed like a rodeo cowboy'
(1941, p. 193). But not all tours were overland. She greatly
enjoyed her husband's tour of inspection up the Benue, when for
two months their home was a government barge.

The usual day on tour began with an early rising, a brief cup of
tea, and a brisk start to the day's march. Not all officers, however,
got off quite as early as Hastings, who tells of getting started from
their camps between 3 am and 4 am on a tour with his wife in
Borgu. To light their way during the hours before dawn, the relief
hammock-bearers tore up sheaves of long, dry grass to be used as
torches (1925, p. 213). The general pattern was a stop for
breakfast after several hours' march, the objective being to reach
their destination before the overpowering heat of early afternoon.

Bush paths had their perils. Mrs Kirby writes of the primitive
bridges they encountered on tour from Calabar:

> Often we would have to climb into a tree by a ladder made of
> vines, usually partly broken, and cross on a kind of hammock
> bridge, a narrow platform of bound twigs to walk on, the sides
> had a lattice work of brittle creepers, the whole thing swayed as
> you moved, and there was a raging torrent below you, really
> quite terrifying.   (Ms., p. 13)

Days of discomfort were reported. At the height of the dry season
the heat built up to an unbearable suspense; the rains brought
cooler temperatures, but also general saturation. Elnor Russell
tells of the 'wettest trek of the lot': 'The path was running with
water just like a small river. We began to walk in shoes but soon
took them off because they squelched in the mud and kept on
slipping off. We slipped and slopped along in our bare feet and the
trees on each side dripped with rain' (1978, p. 32). Sudden and
fierce tropical thunderstorms could bring frightening moments
during these marches, particularly when heavy rainfall flooded
streams and rivers and brought sudden fierce currents.

With servants and porters, sometimes messengers and police,
these retinues often became extended. Violet Cragg notes in 1924,
'We are allowed only eighteen carriers for ten days, two of these
being my rickshaw boys, and we have to take three boys' bedding,

our beds, chairs, tables, bath, food, kitchen box, etc. Our clothes,
linen, medicine box and my needlework are in a tiny steel trunk,
and we have all we need' (Ms., pp. 6–7). She mentions as many as
forty in their touring group at times. Police escort could be
required, as she writes from Umani in Kabba Province, 'We
trekked here on Saturday, uphill all the way, with an escort of
twelve Dansanda (Government Police) to put fear into the hearts
of the inhabitants' (p. 24). Until a few years before, this area had
been closed to Europeans. She adds, 'To tell the truth, the chance
of being shot at with poisoned arrows does not alarm me nearly as
much as thunderstorms, bush-cow and leopards.'

Generally these colonial wives note the friendliness of people
they encountered on their journeys as well as considerable
curiosity at the appearance of a white women. When Constance
Larymore arrived in Bida in 1902, she relates, 'no white woman
had been there before and the Emir and his people were
determined to do honour to the event' (1911, p. 24). Ceremonial
greetings during the morning included a colourful procession of
the Emir and his entourage on horseback and followers on foot.
Visiting the ladies of the harem, she was touched by their warmth
and 'perfect courtesy'. The Emir's aged mother was in charge and
poured forth greeting and salutations, later sending invitations for
her to make a return visit. Often word of their arrival went ahead
and there would be welcoming ceremonies in the villages, as Berry
describes, 'And, expecting us, the chiefs would put on their best
robes, the drummers would turn out in full regalia of tattered but
still recognisably Hausa robes . . . and always I felt like the
Governor being met at the station with a full brass band' (1941,
p. 148).

Rarely were instances of hostility from local people recalled,
though Mrs Kirby tells of an incident in 1916 with her husband on
tour from Calabar. They were pursued by 'a posse of natives . . .
brandishing sticks and cutlasses', fortunately to be saved from
confrontation when they caught up with their carriers who waved
their sticks and shouted 'Government'. It seems they had been
mistaken for missionaries, then very unpopular in that area for
trying to stamp out some of the local customs.

Over the years rest houses of greater or less permanence were
built to provide shelter for touring officers. These varied widely, as
Berry explains, 'from a six feet wide native hut, through two-room
shelters, thatch-roofed and mud-walled, connected by a verandah

like the handle that connects the two balls of a dumbell, to vast barnlike structures of eight or nine rooms, long neglected and falling into disrepair, but once the brilliant scheme of some young DO' (1941, p. 118). While touring the Jada district of Adamawa in 1935, Elnor Russell tells how they were promised at one village a rest house on a most attractive site, overlooking the river and with a lovely view across the valley. This looked so appealing, they decided to stay two days – until they went inside. 'The smell of bats nearly knocked us down. There were bats everywhere, clinging on to the thatch and hanging down from the rafters on the roof' (1978, p. 35). Bats were the permanent guests in more than one rest house, as these memoirs attest. Insects were ubiquitous. Violet Cragg tells of a village rest-house near Bauchi, 'I was stung by inch-long wasps whose nests were all over the walls; the *bayan gida*[5] was full of driver ants; and there were bats everywhere' (Ms., p. 63).

Illness on tour could be even worse than in the station. Elnor Russell had what appeared to be the early stages of dysentery:

> Nothing seems to stop the beastly —— and I can't eat or drink anything. It's hopeless being ill in bush. If one sends for a doctor he couldn't arrive under five days by which time we would probably be quite better and he would be furious. If one leaves it, and one really did get very ill then he'd probably be too late. Answer, we left it and hoped for the best.   (Maddocks, Ms., p. 4)

After she spent the next day in misery, they sent a servant to the nearest mission to ask for medicine; he brought back a tin of arrowroot which helped her to get better.

'It is on trek that the native servant really comes into his own', states Berry (1941, p. 151), a generality acknowledged by others. They describe servants going on ahead to the bush rest-house, cleaning it out, setting out deck-chairs and tables, getting the fire lit for warming the bathwater and cooking the evening meal, and greeting the arriving officer and his wife with a cool drink. They were also resourceful in producing special meals for guests. When the medical officer was invited to dinner, Violet Cragg offered a menu of 'grapefruit in sherry, salmon kedgeree, roast guinea fowl with apple sauce and cheese aigrettes' (Ms., p. 37). She adds, 'Not bad for a bush dinner. We do ourselves well on trek and bring small tables, lampstands, etc. It is a little extra trouble not to live anyhow and I pride myself that I do not mind who visits us.'

During these tours in the early days, wild animals – lions, leopards, elephants, bush-cows, baboons – were often sighted and guarded against, but not greatly feared. When Mrs Larymore woke and heard the awesome roar of a lion for the first time, she shuddered at the inadequacy of their thatched shelter; but, remembering the fire burning outside and the saying that no lion would tackle a mosquito curtain, she took their Irish terrier into bed and slept placidly until dawn (1911, p. 14). Much more fear and distaste were shown for unexpected snakes and the hyaenas who scrounged around campsites at night.

Despite discomfort and risks, these women tell of the special quality of those days on tour in the bush, a heightened appreciation of the natural world and a greater involvement in African life. Violet Cragg writes, 'By a wonderful piece of luck we happened to arrive at Doma yesterday when the annual Boka Festival was taking place. It is a sacred festival to the pagan Aragos, during which the Boka, or juju man, performs a dance that foretells the fortunes of the tribe for the ensuing year' (Ms., p. 46). At other times, as well, they were glad to be invited to observe sacred ceremonies and festive dances. Similarly, Erick Berry tells of the interest she and her husband had in the art forms and dances of various ethnic groups. Wherever they went, they asked for local dancers to perform and, on occasion, they walked forth for miles on a dark night to attend a village dance celebration (1941, p. 151).

SEPARATIONS

Colonial wives in Nigeria endured separations, from their family and friends in the homeland, but of greater immediacy and loss, from their children or their husbands. During the period until the Second World War, a poignant factor in their lives was that their children could not be with them in Nigeria. Then, when they went home for childbirth, they were often separated from their husbands for many months. Even without children, the pattern was for wives to go on leave earlier than their husbands and return later. The tropical climate was considered to cause greater harm to women's health than to men's, though professional women apparently required no special concessions. Children were not brought out for health reasons, real enough with the prevalence of malaria (not effectively prevented until the introduction of mepacrine in 1943) and other tropical diseases.

Lassie Fitz-Henry tells of her misery in parting from her 7-year-old daughter Mick before leaving for Nigeria, 'At these partings, Mick and I persuaded each other that the separation was not going to be for long. It was always far too long. It wrung my heart to know that someone else was going to watch her grow up, and see her develop' (1959, p. 11). Babies, too, were left behind. Niven reports the birth of their first child in 1930; his wife returned to Nigeria within a few months, leaving the infant with her mother under the care of a nanny (1982, p. 100). Noël Rowling's experience shows the difficulties in arranging for children's care and the divided loyalties involved. When her first son was born in 1936, she waited until he was weaned before placing him in a nursery and re-joining her husband. She writes, 'Miss Douglas, who ran the nursery, was a motherly person, and much as I hated leaving my baby, I knew I had to do it and I knew, too, that he would be well looked after' (1982, p. 30). Every wife, after the birth of a child, had to choose between one separation or the other; for the husband, of course, there was no choice. Aside from his leave, when he could be reunited with his family, the demands of the Colonial Service were total: his work came first. He was often both husband and father at a distance.

Separation through death does not find much space in these memoirs, nor the subsequent life of widows and widowers. A. F. B. Bridges tells of trouble in the Nsukka area in 1923 culminating in an ambush in which the Commissioner of Police was shot dead. He adds, 'His wife was in Enugu at the time and went home in the next boat' (1980, p. 15). An entry in Daphne Moore's diary in Lagos on 16 June 1924 records: 'A Marine man died of acute nephritis and was hurriedly buried. Deaths are such everyday affairs in this country that no one takes much notice and they try to get the funeral over before 5.30 so as not to miss the evening tennis or golf' (Ms., p. 43).

SOCIAL SPACES

A wife following her husband on his successive postings could find herself on one tour the only European woman at a remote outpost and, on the next, in a city station with as many as fifteen or twenty other women in a busy colonial social scene generating its own reciprocal cycles of formal dinners and drinks parties. While there were intermediate situations, of course, these two poles were represented then, and are analytically useful now, as the contrasting models of social life. The first required strong personal resources to deal with 'loneliness', a haunting theme of alienation in these writings. Yet this isolation from other Europeans usually offered what some wives considered to be of central importance, a closer companionship with her husband and more involvement in his work. The second model suited the woman who wished to reproduce selected patterns of English social life within the bounded European reservation. She was more likely to find her personal identity in the gradations of the colonial hierarchy as 'wife of' and to count her achievements in terms of maintaining the social process with an eye on her husband's promotion, as portrayed so splendidly in the character of the amoral Amorel Begg, later Lady Begg, in Elspeth Huxley's novel derived from Nigerian colonial life, *The Walled City* (1948).

During this period before the Second World War, as these memoirs show, wives spent most of their time at small stations far from centres of European life. Visiting Sokoto from Lagos in 1925, Daphne Moore tells about the wife of a forestry officer:

> She has done two tours of fifteen months each in Sokoto, where most of the time she was the only woman, and treks everywhere with her husband, being in the fastness of the Bush sometimes for three months at a time, beyond the ken of man and left to her own devices all day, alone in the tent, while her husband scours the forest.   (Ms., p. 67)

Mary Oake went to the Cameroons in 1928, the only white woman in Buea for five months. When two sisters attending the teacher training college came to ask her to teach them sewing she 'was secretly delighted to have the opportunity of seeing something of African women' (1933, p. 29). At that time, she says, it was not considered appropriate to invite Africans to your home. With these two, she started a class for little girls in the government school.

In the early 1930s Noël Rowling was the only white woman in Shendam, Plateau Province, where her husband served as DO for three years. While they were there, four Europeans died: of yellow fever, blackwater fever and typhoid. For her it was a lonely life; when visitors came, such as the Resident and his wife on tour, she found she could not stop talking. She writes, 'But I saw far more of Chas than I had done when he was Station Magistrate (in Kano) and he often discussed problems in the division with me and I loved touring the area' (1982, p. 27).

In contrast, social life in the larger stations was hectic. Erick Berry describes Zaria in the early 1930s:

> Here were tin-roofed, concrete bungalows, and calling cards, and morning bridge for the ladies. There were at least a dozen women here; and afternoon teas, and good roads and everyone had a car, and there were dances once a week, and dinners that lasted till midnight every other day or so. And everyone was bored, and had malaria, and most of them drank too much, and all of them gossiped. And I loathed it.   (1941, p. 178)

She wanted time and concentration to get on with her painting, but the late nights left her ragged from lack of sleep.

She tells of the women: 'They had little to occupy their time save squabbles and feuds, discussion of who was now senior lady in the station, and whose husband had taken who to the weekly dance' (p. 182). Others tell of snobbishness carried to the point of caricature. Anne Macdonald describes Warri: 'Usually the club was the centre of the social life in these small stations but not always enjoyable to juniors. There was the story of a senior wife saying to a nervous newcomer: "Mrs. So and So, we do not split our infinitives in the Warri Club" ' (Ms.[a], p. 13). Elnor Russell considers the difficulties of these wives: 'People talk about idle women with nothing to do but make mischief. Most of the women would love to have a job' (Maddocks, Ms., p. 156). Berry attributes their shallow lives not to personal failings, nor to national characteristics or the colonial situation, but to the constraints on wives in an enclave.

Sometimes women were excluded from entertainment open to men. Kenneth Bryant remembers the excitement caused in Kano in the 1930s when three Royal Air Force planes paid a visit and took some of the men for a 'flip over Kano'. He continues, 'I remember that ladies were not allowed on these flights, but one, more adventurous than her sisters, dressed up as a man and took her place in the queue. She was spotted, however, and sternly turned away' (1959, p. 28). This was a time when women aviators, such as Amelia Earhart, were in the news headlines for their daring flights.

Sylvia Leith-Ross places the two models of social life in chronological order by contrasting the rugged pioneer conditions of her early days in Northern Nigeria with the aggrandising momentum of the colonial social competition she saw in Lagos during the 1920s. For this transformation she sets out an illuminating metaphor: the appearance of the first silver coffee pot. She writes, 'Mrs X's first silver coffee-pot causes Mrs Y to send for a silver salver which had to be outdone by Mrs Z with a silver tray' (1983, p. 84). The competition meant that parties had to become more elaborate; more time and money had to be spent at the club; numerous small items swelled the household accounts. This historical perspective is a key one, since the catalyst of the 'silver coffee pot' required a sufficient density of European wives to transmute the social space. Even during the interwar years, only a few main cities had European reservations with a dozen or more women. Leith-Ross recognised the destructive element, distanced herself from this scene, and directed her own energies at that time to problems of Nigerian education.

Other women, as well, took a critical view and transcended the narrow horizons of social life within the European enclave. Erick Berry, for example, balanced her negative observations of the confined social space of Zaria station with generous appraisal of individual wives:

Among the English wives and over several tours I met a number who sincerely loved the life, some because of its social life, a few, who had been out for years, because of that which interested me, Africa itself. Several spoke Hausa better than their husbands, had acquired an enviable background of native lore, and found it a real grief when life swung them back to England again.   (1941, p. 184)

8 The Domestication of Colonial Life: after 1940

The war was a kind of watershed between two experiences of Nigeria, two different kinds of life, partly because after it expatriates brought their children out as a matter of course so that there was family life which we had never had before, and partly for me because when we came to rest in Lagos, I became Headmistress of St. Saviour's School in Ikoyi.

(Anne Macdonald, Ms.[a], p. 16)

WIVES IN THE WAR EFFORT

To those unfamiliar with the history of the Second World War, Nigeria would seem to have been remote from the centres of communication and scenes of battle; in fact, Nigeria became a strategic location for the movement of troops and was itself vulnerable on all sides to enemy attack. As early as 1938, Gladys Leak (wife of an electrical engineer with the PWD), wrote to her mother about the situation in Lagos, 'Submarines were stated to be lying near and German bombers at Fernando Po, just down the coast. Gas masks were in readiness in an air chilled room at the hospital and Oswald had to supervise fixing up sirens as air raid warnings' (10 November 1938, Ms., p. 150). A few years later, she tells of their house being designated as an air-raid warden's post and its roof being reinforced to allow a gun emplacement; men were on duty all night with the Defence Force and then at their job during the day (7 September 1942; Ms., p. 160).

Not only were Nigeria's coastal cities at risk from enemy action, but as the war progressed its territorial boundaries became exposed to the military intentions of Vichy France. Ships serving as a lifeline to Britain had to travel in convoy to lessen the risk from German torpedoes; some ships carrying troops and civilian passengers were sunk. When Germany took control of the sea between Italy and North Africa, Nigeria became an important staging point for troops on their way to the Middle East and

Burma. The war brought hardship and tragedy to Nigeria, to the British in the military and administration and to the Nigerians who were to serve in military units abroad. Yet at the same time the unforeseen difficulties and displacements provided the space for new life-saving measures in medicine, new ways of thinking – and new initiatives by wives of colonial officers.

In Lagos, Lady Bourdillon became a much-admired 'senior lady' by providing hospitality for many more visitors, supporting multi-racial activities among women, and showing practical concern for common problems. During the war, she recalls, Government House was never empty. Flying diplomats, who could not go through the Mediterranean, came from Khartoum or Cairo to Lagos, and stayed until planes were available for Lisbon and on home. The list of guests who stayed with the Bourdillons during this period includes royal visitors from Yugoslavia and Greece, the Prime Ministers of Australia and of New Zealand, as well as numerous admirals, air vice-marshals and leading political figures (Pearce, 1983, p. 272). But carrying out the prescribed obligations of colonial hospitality did not keep her from giving attention to those on the local scene, British and Nigerian. As patroness of the Ladies' Progressive Club, which met once a fortnight in Government House, she promoted contact between women of all races in Lagos; among other activities the club raised money for the War Relief Fund (p. 274).

When the war started, administrative officers in Nigeria with special qualifications were released for military service; at the same time, recruitment for the Colonial Service stopped. The loss of staff required that all administrative officers had to take on extra duties, and wives came forth to take both paid and unpaid jobs. When Joan Sharwood Smith arrived in Kontagora in the early months of the war, she began to help unofficially in the office: 'Apart from confidential typing and occasional coding and decoding, there was the monthly check on the accounts of the two native treasuries of the division. There were also maps and plans to prepare and statistics to compile' (B. Sharwood Smith, 1969, p. 125).

Before long she had an official assignment. Her husband was placed in charge of an army intelligence unit based in Kano to carry out surveillance across the nothern borders where the Vichy French were now in control. As secretary for this group, she trained herself on the job:

> I was given lessons in filing and card indexing and in such spare
> time as I had I absorbed a book on Office Management . . .
> Codes and cyphers then had to be mastered and finally I had to
> improve my French for one of our duties was to interview all
> French officers escaping from Vichy territory into Nigeria to
> join the forces of General de Gaulle.   (J. Sharwood Smith,
> Ms., p 52)

During this period she travelled with her husband to the border
areas, usually in a three-ton truck, carrying her typewriter in
order to type his reports. Her secretarial duties overlapped with
those of 'wife' when they entertained guests coming through
Kano – including General de Gaulle.

   Later, when her husband returned to civil duties in Sokoto, she
took on the duties normally carried out by an ADO of reorganising the Native Authority Central Office. Mrs Carrow,
formerly an education officer and now wife of the Resident in
Sokoto, took on administrative work not done before by a woman
as acting DO in charge of the province's finances (J. Sharwood
Smith, p. 106). In Kaduna, Noël Rowling was asked to become
Government Censor. She considered this a 'hateful job', because
the letters were written mainly by people she knew. At that time
the West African Frontier Force, with British officers and
Nigerian troops, was sent by sea to Ethiopia, leaving officers'
wives in Kaduna. She writes,

> I was horrified to read how many of the wives grumbled that
> they had been left behind and in letters to England said openly
> where their husbands had gone. For some time, Nigeria was
> without a single soldier and after France fell she could have
> been occupied easily by French forces from Niger
> Colony.   (1982, p. 36)

Diana Brown became head of the Birnin Kebbi Girls' School;
she 'achieved fame as the only woman who managed to get her
husband to join her in Nigeria at government expense'
(Weatherhead, Ms., p. 143). Although General Orders stated
that wives may accompany their husbands with passages paid, no
provisions were made for husbands to join working wives. Her
husband had been teaching at Achimota College in Ghana; when
the war came he served with the RWAFF in Burma and India. On
his return, he was able to reunite with his wife in Birnin Kebbi as
her dependant.

In Lagos all European wives had to register to be 'directed' to work. Diana Bridges worked in the censor's office and also helped in her husband's office during his assignment as Acting Commissioner of the Colony. One of her jobs was issuing the permits for the salt ration to the market women. The hazards of shipping had brought a country-wide shortage of salt with consequent hoarding and high prices; this was regulated by a system of permits and rationing. At first there was a disorderly rush, her husband relates, 'but presently the ladies of Lagos became as orderly and matter-of-fact in their queues as their sisters in England' (A. F. B. Bridges, 1980, p. 52).

Gladys Leak carried out a number of jobs at the General Service Office, including one in the filing office. She writes, 'We do the filing for the whole place and do not get a moment's peace. . . . It reminds me of one of those crazy American business films where clerks and secretaries are dashing about' (letter, 8 August 1943; Ms., p. 186). Later she was asked to return to her profession of nursing for relief work at the hospital. After an extremely busy week, she found that she soon dropped back into the routine and loved it. Asked to join the permanent staff, she did not feel she could do this and run their home as well. She comments, 'Oswald does not think I ought to do it at all so I get no sympathy from him. However I shall continue to do relief work when needed' (letter, 15 May 1944; Ms., p. 212).

In her letters during this period, Gladys Leak tells of the abundance of local fruits and vegetables and improved local meat; she kept chickens and ducks for fresh eggs. But imported goods became scarce. She writes, 'Once more I am down to the last few tea leaves. Unless we get some very soon we shall be reduced to hot water or local cawfee as the Yanks call it. It is quite good, by the way' (letter, 29 July 1943; Ms., p. 181). Even Government House was short, she discovered, when they attended a large garden party and were disappointed in not being offered the expected cup of tea. This general shortage of imported goods prompted two wives in Jos, Elizabeth Pembleton and Joan Boyes, to compile a book of recipes making use of local produce and appropriately named *Live on the Country*. Published in two volumes in 1940, this widely praised cookbook was used to the end of the colonial period by wives, and by bachelors, in bush stations (Pembleton and Boyes, 1948).

Wives did their share of 'good works' during the war period.

Elnor Russell took on the unusual task in Jos of writing letters for Nigerian wives of soldiers serving abroad (1978, p. 129). Gladys Leak notes that on Christmas morning she got up early to make seventy-eight mince pies: 'We gave dinner to 500 at our canteen alone on Xmas night with a sing song after it was a great success' (letter, 31 December 1943; Ms., p. 196). She tells of helping with War Relief Week, the proceeds to be used for African servicemen (letter 25 May 1944; Ms., p. 214). In Port Harcourt, a committee of Europeans and Africans raised money during War Relief Week by setting up canoe races, traditional dances, school sports, a display by the Boy Scouts, a netball match, a tennis competition and a school concert. The week finished with a fun fair and bazaar in the Residency garden, for which Diana Bridges, the Resident's wife, with help from other women, provided tea (Bridges, 1980, p. 58). Throughout the country fund-raising efforts went on, with European wives doing their part.

BABIES AND WARTIME PASSAGES

On 17 April 1941 a notice went out from the Secretariat in Lagos that the demands on shipping made it increasingly difficult to obtain passages from the UK; wives would not be given any priority except in a few cases where they were employed in Nigeria on war work or required for that purpose. Since wives accompanying their husbands on leave to the UK would be unlikely to return, it was suggested that those concerned might wish to arrange their leave elsewhere (newspaper cutting; Leak, Ms., p. 207). As alternatives, some officers and their wives went to South Africa, others to the government 'hill station' in Jos.

A few wives who became pregnant decided to have their babies in Nigeria rather than risk the dangers of the sea journey and separation for the duration of the war. In 1942, reassured by the new prophylactics against malaria and yellow fever, as well as improved housing and sanitation, the wives of two administrative officers – Joy Bourdillon and, a few months later, Noël Rowling – had their babies in Kano. They had no special difficulties and the babies thrived. This choice, by these and a few other wives at this time, resulted in the first semblance of family life among colonial officers in Nigeria.

The war for most, however, was characterised by long periods of separation: husband from wife, parents from children. Shortly after Anne Macdonald went home to have her first child, the war broke out; her husband's tour was extended, and the baby was ten months old before he came on leave. When he went back to Nigeria, she took the baby to Canada to stay with her sister. Many months later when she was allowed to rejoin her husband, she decided she could not part from her small daughter despite numerous warnings that she was not only risking the child's life in the Nigerian climate but also from German torpedoes. She gained passage on an American ship and writes of being so ill that 'I could not leave my bunk but fed my child by dropping her biscuits as she sat on the floor' (Ms.[a], p. 18). Eventually they arrived in Aba: 'My daughter caused a sensation as the first white child to be seen there. I had to stop taking her out in her push-chair as the whole population would follow, crowding round, touching her and laughing and clapping' (p. 15).

Their 'hard-won snatch of family life', she writes, was soon ended, however, when it was discovered that their daughter required medical treatment for cataract. She decided to take her to South Africa, hoping that the journey would be less dangerous than to England. She remembers: 'This time boat drill was properly carried out, even to the extent of the life boats being let down in harbour where we were rowed round. Blackout, too, was efficient so that the cabins were stifling and I dragged my daughter on deck each night with life belts and "panic bags" till we reached Cape Town' (p. 16). She stayed there for ten months while her daughter had five operations on her eyes. Her husband's next posting was to Victoria in the Cameroons where she tells of three and a half happy years, including the birth of another child.

At the end of her first tour, extended by wartime conditions, Joan Sharwood Smith went on leave with her husband to South Africa and stayed on for the birth of her first baby. It was still considered 'the height of folly to take a white child to West Africa', she says, and when the baby was four months old, she left him with a nurse and joined her husband in Sokoto. On their next leave, they went back to South Africa and again she stayed on with the child. When he was past his second birthday, her husband had become Resident in Minna and permission was now granted for them to join him. Aside from bouts of prickly heat, the little boy settled into the routine and accompanied them on tours of Niger Province. He became a great favourite with the domestic staff, who talked to him in Hausa (Ms., pp. 103–17). In March 1945, after a year in Minna, she left for England, a journey of four and a half weeks in a convoy under threat from German submarines. She tells that her parents in Leamington Spa were delighted with their first view of their grandson. She adds, 'But the sight of me appalled them for I was six years older, I had lost a stone in weight and the mepacrine, which I had been taking to ward off malaria, had turned me yellow. To cap it all, another baby was on the way' (p. 127).

Sir Rex Niven tells of two ways of going home on leave during wartime: one by sea taking two or three months; the other (the 'quick' way) by flying boat from Lagos Lagoon to The Gambia, then nineteen hours in the air to Trinidad, and on from there to Baltimore. This was the way chosen by him and his wife in early 1943. After a train journey to New York, where they waited for three weeks in the bitter February cold, they gained passage on a convoy via Greenland and the north of Iceland, taking a month to reach Swansea. He provides the grim statistics that out of 96 ships in their convoy, 36 – mostly tankers – were sunk (1982, p. 190).

Even when the war was over, passages for wives to Nigeria remained hard to obtain. Noël Rowling was assigned to a ship that had carried troops during the war with its holds converted to dormitories. Accommodation was allotted alphabetically; her berth was in the hold. She writes, 'There were eight double-tiered bunks on each side of the room, the porthole was kept shut because we were at sea level and the stench from the dirty lavatories was almost unbearable' (1982, p. 54). Fortunately, she found friends with names beginning with 'A' and 'C' who allowed her changing and bath facilities.

POST-WAR LIVING CONDITIONS

The presence of children after the war brought a distinctive change, but in other ways living conditions remained much the same. The seeming lottery of postings brought its concomitant variations in housing. When Margaret White was finally able to join her husband after the war, they lived first in Kano in *Gidan dan Hausa*, the splendid mud house built by Hanns Vischer before the First World War; next in Birnin Kebbi in a 'miserable cement house condemned pre-1914'; and then in Makurdi in 'a new two-storied Lagos-type house, with its own guest wing' (White, 1966, pp. 192, 202, 241).

Housing was allocated on the basis of seniority, and although new houses were built and old ones improved during the years following the war, the rapid expansion of the Civil Service meant that demand often exceeded supply and, particularly in bush stations, many wives lived in pre-war conditions right to the end of the colonial period. Mary Davies writes of her husband's first posting with the Nigeria Police in 1948 to Onitsha in the Eastern Region, 'where there was no electricity, no modern sanitation, but plenty of mosquitoes & other "creepy crawlies". The kitchen table and the meat safe legs had to stand in small tins of kerosene/water to keep the ants away. Our house was in the European Reservation, and thousands of bats lived in the roof' (Ms., p. 1).

Rosemary Hollis mentions difficult conditions in Azare, but adds that her lot seemed relative luxury in comparison with that of another wife assigned to a 'bush rest house' about forty miles away. She was raising two small children in a house with no doors or windows, but only holes in the walls allowing the wind to roar through, bringing dust or rain according to the season. Hollis concludes, 'There were hardly any necessities, let alone luxuries; but I took my hat off to her – she never grumbled' (1981, p. 51). This was the first imperative for colonial wives: whatever the conditions, never to complain.

The frequent change of posts remained characteristic throughout the colonial period. Wives with young children clearly found these sudden moves even more daunting than their predecessors who did not have to take into consideration their children's needs. Cecillie Swaisland remembers, 'In one tour we had eight stations and ten houses, and I got to the point where I didn't put curtains up, because every time I did we were moved' (Ms., p. 12). This was a specific phase in her husband's career, she explains, but she always kept household goods as transportable as possible and, 'like all wives of that period, we all spent a great deal of time making our own households work'.

These post-war wives matched the earlier ones in resourcefulness, if not in some ways superseding them. No longer at the beginning of each tour did they order the extensive loads of tinned food to bring out by ship. The gradual change to travel by air made this prohibitive while, at the same time, a greater range of imported goods was now available in the main cities of Nigeria in such commercial outlets as 'Kingsway' and 'Leventis'. But many wives found themselves in places remote from the new supermarkets and cold storage units, in conditions hardly changed from those of wives in earlier years. The key difference now was the prevailing attitude, passed on from wives' experience during the war, to 'live on the country'.

'We all cooked a great deal from scratch. One learned how to create the ingredients before you did the cooking,' Cecillie Swaisland recalls (Ms., p. 13). They had to use tinned milk powder and buy flour and sugar by the sack 'and sieve it all to get all the weevils out'. Drinking water still had to be boiled and filtered; the daily bread was baked with palm oil instead of yeast as the raising agent. To cope with the problem of tough meat, she says, 'The pressure cooker was the thing that really revolutionised our lives' (p. 29). Wives helped each other: 'We were always handing round recipes.'

Besides taking care of children and supervising the household, Elizabeth Purdy did her own dressmaking and sewed her children's clothes (Ms.[b], p. 24). Cecillie Swaisland started 'right from the nappies upwards' and tells about sewing heavy coats for the children to come back to England on leave; these were made from one of her own which had gone out of fashion. She sums up, 'All the administrative wives that I knew tended to do these sort of things. We all became very domesticated for that period' (Ms., p. 30).

The same problems with servants were encountered in the post-war period, the same amusing stories of misunderstandings told, the same consideration given to their needs and that of their families. Some of the women arriving just at the end of the colonial period apparently had difficulty dealing with servants. As one experienced wife explains, some were not accustomed to having servants at home and were either too lenient or too strict, 'either asking them in for a cup of coffee or else treating them like slaves'.

As a sociologist, Cecillie Swaisland gradually arrived at her view of a 'complete servant culture'. Servants had their own ideas, for example, about what was appropriate for specific occasions. She relates, 'Dinner parties were quite surprising at times when the crockery that it was served on in your own house patently wasn't your own, and you just hoped that it didn't belong to the people you were entertaining' (Ms., p. 42). Her own china, on a reciprocal basis, would be loaned to other servants who wanted it to enhance a special event in their domain. In her perceptive analysis, servants acquired their seniority from that of the officer they served and stood on their own dignity; for example, they had to be provided with the uniforms required to match this status. They had developed their own notion of a career structure within the servant world.

Health risks in Nigeria continued despite the rapid medical advances of the war years. Although impacted wisdom teeth and boils occur anywhere in the world, Rosemary Hollis tells of her unusual experience when afflicted in a bush station. The drive to Jos over eighty miles of untarred road proved unbelievably painful and the treatment compounded her condition: 'The dentist, who had none of the right equipment, and little experience of this type of thing, succeeded in cracking my jaw, and so a fortnight in hospital was necessary' (1981, p. 33). Later, in Kafanchan, she was attacked by a rabid bush dog and ferociously bitten on her arms, hands and legs. Again she had to be driven to Jos, this time for the painful course of daily injections in the stomach for 21 days, the treatment at that time to avert the otherwise inevitable death from rabies.

A number of wives report sudden confrontations with snakes, the threat remaining constant. Anne Macdonald tells of being bitten twice by a snake. The doctor rushed in from a polo match to inform her that if it had been poisonous, she would have been dead already, but suggested that she have a glass of sherry and stay the night in hospital (Ms.[a], p. 13). She writes that she was lucky enough to escape most tropical illnesses 'except the odd jigger, some worms in the Cameroons and the bite of a fly that lived on the banks of the river in Victoria.' For most people this resulted in filariasis, but hers took a different form, 'making lumps here and there, some of which at the bottom of my backbone made sitting painful so that they had to be cut out when we got to Ibadan' (p. 13). Joan Sharwood Smith tells of getting amoebic dysentery at the same time as another officer's wife; they were discharged from the hospital in Jos looking like shadows of their former selves (Ms., p. 84). While in Sokoto, Elizabeth Purdy had cerebrospinal meningitis, which she found very frightening, but her recovery began as soon as she had treatment (Ms.[b], pp. 12–13). Despite preventive drugs, many wives had attacks of malaria which left them feeling weak and depressed.

'Miscarriages appear to be so common among the colonial wives that one begins to take them for granted,' Joan Alexander concludes after over a hundred interviews (1983, p. 74). Cecillie Swaisland says that wives attributed this frequency of miscarriages to taking anti-malarial drugs and adds, 'Whether this is one of the old wives' tales that grew up, it's difficult to know' (Ms., p. 18). The data on the old-fashioned method of gin and quinine to get rid of an unwanted pregnancy (Trollope, 1983, p. 127), and the presence of quinine as the main ingredient in malaria prophylactics, suggest a connection. Aside from this, colonial life – with travel over rough roads, the tension of unexpected moves, difficulties in getting food for a balanced diet, often a long distance from medical care – hardly provided the ideal conditions for pregnancy.

While the risks of travel were not the same as in early years, they were probably no less in statistical terms. If wives no longer accompanied their husbands in canoes running the rapids of the Niger, now they travelled by road where the legendary Nigerian drivers plied their lorries at top speed and sometimes without adequate brakes. If no post-war wife went through the experience of the sudden sinking of a stern-wheeler, several had frightening moments of air travel. Joan Sharwood Smith was on a flight from Kano to London with her two younger children when a thunderstorm struck with violent flashes of lightning. After three hours of being buffeted about, they reached calm; but an engine failure was reported and the plane had to return through the stormy area to Kano (Ms., p. 157). Rosemary Hollis writes of her journey, when she was five months pregnant, on the Maiduguri–Yola–Jos–Kano schedule only to meet a severe electric storm which tossed the light aircraft 'amidst the most terrifying bangs, bumps, and flashes' (1981, p. 180).

THE CHANGE TO FAMILY LIFE

The salient feature differentiating post-war from the preceding colonial life in Nigeria was the presence of children and the change to family life. This did not happen immediately, nor without resistance from some senior officers who considered men's dedication to their work would be undermined. Not only bachelors of the senior generation, but married officers and even their wives, made clear their view that European children should *not* come to Nigeria. If they cited the lack of medical care in bush stations and the debilitating climate as their main reasons, the hidden message was one of classification: the Colonial Service which had earlier defended itself against the intrusion of wives was now being threatened by an invading domesticity.

The issue of children, more than any other, divided the 'generations' of women. Several years after the war when one young wife (who wishes to remain anonymous) boarded the Elder Dempster ship with her two-year-old son to join her husband in Nigeria, she found herself the target of jibes from older women. They asked pointedly how she could bring a young child out to Nigeria, admonishing her that it would be bad for the child, reminding her that she was young and inexperienced and did not know what conditions were like. She was filled with foreboding; as it turned out, she had no special difficulties. Another wife told of the strong feeling of resentment by older wives who had not been able to bring their own children to Nigeria and had thus had little family life.

Practical considerations were, of course, dominant in the minds of parents. The new malaria prophylactics were more effective than quinine and without the effects that mepacrine had on the appearance. Vaccination now prevented yellow fever, while antibiotics were available for dealing with a range of tropical illnesses which had previously made it unwise for European children to come to Nigeria. Besides considerations of physical health, however, new ideas from child psychologists were gaining ground about the harmful effects of separating young children from their mothers. And, in terms of family budgets, the expense of running two homes or of keeping children in Britain with nannies became more prohibitive.

Cecillie Swaisland had her first baby at home while they were on leave, but the second was born in Port Harcourt; in her view, 'having babies out there was a real revolution' (Ms., p. 40). Although wives in Eastern Nigeria were advised to go home, she remembers, few of them did. In their district in the mid-1950s when their second daughter was born, she recalls that five wives, of ADOs or young DOs, had babies in Nigeria. Like many of their contemporaries, the Swaislands had no nurses or nannies, and the children went with them everywhere. She relates, 'We just packed everything into a lorry and it went off and our steward set up house before we arrived. We followed leisurely. We all went on tour, always' (p. 7).

Fathers could now take a more active part in child-care. Of post-war life, M. C. Atkinson writes that except for tennis and golf, the clubs now ceased to be the focal points of station life: 'One drink and home became the rule and for some of us it was father who stayed at home once or twice a week and looked after the bairns while mother played tennis and had the single drink' (Ms., p. 113). Their daughter was perhaps unique in being given a Yoruba naming ceremony by the Egbado Divisional Council (in Western Nigeria) and christened by an Archbishop in the same month. In accordance with Yoruba tradition, she was given a name by the Oba (chief) of Ado and also by his District Office staff: 'Hence her full name is Katharine Margaret Bandele Omolere Adetoro Modupe Atkinson' (p. 87).

On the question of children's medical problems, Cecillie Swaisland says they were very careful about avoiding malaria by having the children sleep under double nets. She recalls, 'We took all the little things like tombo flies and worm infestations in our stride. We just carried the appropriate stuff around, and regarded it as more important that the children should fraternise and play with other children than that they should be kept sterile' (Ms., p. 20). The family's only real medical problem was filariasis, which they all required treatment for at the 'TDH' (Tropical Diseases Hospital) in London.

As a Resident's wife, Elizabeth Purdy had a heavy load of entertaining, but she took care of two babies without the help of a nurse. The children did pick up worrying tropical illnesses. The elder one had cerebral malaria in Jos when he was ten months old, suddenly running a temperature of 105 degrees; but as soon as he went into hospital he began to recover. And in Sokoto she had an alarming experience: 'They were violently ill, running at both ends, fearful temperature, and Andrew virtually expired. The doctor didn't know what it was. Whether they had eaten something, that was something we never knew. But they very quickly got over it' (Ms.[b], p. 12). In her view, the constant medical worries were the greatest difficulty about living in Nigeria.

Memoirs and letters tell of sudden, tragic deaths of children. Brook writes of the visit to Ado Division of the Resident, who brought his wife and two lively children with him on tour. During the night, one of the children died; they were told she had been attacked by a virulent form of polio (1966, p. 312). A letter from Peggy Watt in Yola to her father tells of the funeral for an 11-month-old baby: 'It was all very similar to our little Anne's death – a mixture of teething troubles, heat exhaustion, and probably some kind of malarial fever, and the complete suddenness of the whole thing too' (8 March 1957, Ms., p. 279).

For many parents, schooling came as the dividing line: at about the age of six, children had to be sent home. Only in the 1950s in a few large cities were suitable schools set up. Joan Sharwood Smith (Ms., pp. 174–5) tells about the multi-racial 'Capital School' in Kaduna, the dream of the first Minister of Education, Makaman Bida. This started in temporary quarters with half a dozen British children, including their daughter, and about twice that many Nigerians. Within a few years a new building had been constructed, a boarding house added, and the numbers had grown into the hundreds. On occasion their daughter's school friends, Nigerian and British, would come at weekends to play in the gardens of Government House.

Cecillie Swaisland says that they had to send their elder child home for schooling, but by the time their younger one was ready, she was able to go to school in Enugu and Nsukka. In Eastern Nigeria multi-racialism was taken for granted, as she states, 'And, of course, the children all grew up together; they all went, black, white and mixed, all went to the same schools and play groups and so on, so they all played together' (Ms., p. 27). At the time of Independence, she remembers the children taking part in the parade, 'black and white children marched in glorious disarray, not one in step with the other, waving madly at all the parents' (p. 48).

But multi-racialism was not achieved everywhere without some battles. As headmistress of St Saviour's School in Ikoyi, a suburb of Lagos, Anne Macdonald threatened to resign after she had accepted two Hausa girls, daughters of the Minister of Education, and the secretary told her the trustees had never envisaged the inclusion of Nigerians. She told them she found it strange they had forgotten the furore and threats in the local papers when the idea of the school was first mooted – and heard no more about this. Soon quite a number of Nigerian children were attending (Ms.[a], pp. 20–1).

THE SHIFTING SOCIAL SCENE

Although the formal social patterns established during the high imperial culture remained the basis for reference throughout the colonial period, particularly in the Northern Region, the rapidly changing political scene now required new modes of social life to mark the transition in power relations between the colonial rulers and those who were soon to take their place. This new phase was perhaps more clearly perceived and enacted by officers of the younger generation, though some senior ones took the lead. Wives continued their accepted role in official entertaining according to the obligations of their husbands' rank. Some took further initiatives in reaching out to Nigerian women.

The domestication of colonial life sometimes inspired the use of traditional British forms for new ways of entertaining. During the war in Minna, where her husband was Resident and their small son was with them for the first time, Joan Sharwood Smith tells about their idea of holding a children's Christmas party. The sons and daughters of such local African notables as the station master, the postmaster and the senior government clerks were invited along with their parents. She writes about the response, 'This idea was quite new to the Africans in Minna and they were perplexed and even a little affronted. However, after a little coaxing, they agreed to lend themselves to this curious experiment' (Ms., p. 118). A festive tea of cakes and jellies, complete with Christmas crackers, was followed by games for the children; and, feted with lemonade and beer, the adults joined in the excitement. The general merriment in the garden of the Residency proved the success of this innovation.

Sir Bryan Sharwood Smith writes about the criticism of a young Northern Nigerian editor in 1943 that white officers had little sympathy for the rising generation of educated Northerners and did not invite them to their houses.[1] Whereas educated Southerners had adopted European social customs, he explains, Northerners of all classes still normally preferred their own way of life and, for this reason, entertainment had been limited to 'decorous tea parties and the drinking of fruit drinks'. He adds, 'But a beginning had to be made, and my wife, now fluent in Hausa, and I had already begun to include Northerners among our lunch and dinner guests, though many of them needed much persuasion' (1969, p. 155). Soon social arrangements reflected the new political scene. He writes of Sokoto:

> The Residency, too, was the ideal meeting place for Africans and Europeans. Gone were the days when the Sultan could only see privileged Europeans by special arrangement and only when accompanied by an Administrative Officer. Now, whenever we entertained on any scale, he and his councillors and visiting dignitaries from other emirates moved to and fro among our guests, perfectly at ease and radiating friendliness.   (pp. 176–7)

Ian Brook tells of changes in the Western Region, where the new Resident in Akure was young and efficient, with none of the 'irascible authoritarianism' of Residents he had known on his arrival. The Residency was now 'a centre for Europeans and Africans in the Province' (1966, p. 311).

When entertaining African guests, difficulties sometimes arose, as Noël Rowling comments on her experience in Lagos in 1950, because of difference in customs and backgrounds, the women's lack of education in comparison with the men, and different expectations involved. When her husband's appointment as Commissioner of Lands was confirmed, they gave a cocktail party in celebration. British guests left by 8.30 p.m., but Africans stayed on as they did for their own parties. The men followed her husband out to the veranda and she was left with the wives, as she describes, 'Their English was poor and my Ibo or Yoruba was non-existent, and they did not speak Hausa. We spoke of children, servants and schools. Dead silence. I racked my brain for subjects of conversation and talked of houses, cooking and children. Silence – while peals of laughter came from the veranda' (1982, p. 64). This continued until her little boy came down the stairs bringing her guests to a talkative mood and giving her the chance to excuse herself to put him to bed. She had found the evening exhausting and, she adds, her women guests must have been very bored.

In Eastern Nigeria after the war, the rigid protocol such as seating according to the 'Staff List' soon disappeared. As Cecillie Swaisland points out, 'the post-war generation was much less stuffy' (Ms., p. 23). Although club life continued, 'We had nothing to do with it in the early years when they were segregated'

(p. 15). The older generation of wives tried to stand by the previous patterns of social life, she says, 'But they were overwhelmed by the number of young wives who, quite honestly, were simply not interested in it. We'd got other things to do. We'd got our children with us' (p. 37). The Swaislands had African friends in government and the professions; there were quite a number of mixed marriages. They entertained one another, dining at each others' houses. She remembers Nigerian dishes being served, the hostess claiming she had put no pepper in at all: 'One mouthful and you had to send for the fire brigade' (p. 26). Despite the passage of over quarter of a century, they still keep in touch with many of these friends through letters and Christmas cards. Others as well tell of continuing friendships, as the next chapter relates.

9 Identity and Commitment

My daughter recently asked me if I had been content to lead the life of a bird shut up in a gilded cage. It was never like that . . . When I left university, I wanted a job because I wanted to be independent and to have a life of my own. But I was never a career woman. I taught in a school because there seemed to be no other jobs open to me. But when I married, marriage was my job. The 'gilded cage' was never gilded. A mud house, no proper sanitation, a vile climate and tropical heat were not much fun.

(Noël Rowling, 1982, p. 12)

'MARRIAGE WAS MY JOB'

In the conceptual system of the Colonial Service, as documented earlier, wives were considered to be instrumental: they were credited with the improvement of the health and well-being of male officers. Wives perceived no devaluation in this utilitarian, subsidiary ascription; rather, it gave them worth. Noël Rowling, for example, repeats the accepted view that the high death rate of officers in the early days decreased when wives were allowed to come to Nigeria. The reasons were simple:

> Men, after a hard day's work in the heat of a tropical day, can't as a rule, bother to inspect the kitchen or make sure that the water is properly filtered. And when a young man is posted to a lonely out-station with no compatriot near, he needs the companionship of a wife.

She concludes: 'Chas often told me that I earned his salary as much as he did, and although this was not true, I was proud to hear him say this' (1982, p. 12).

This argument originated as a defensive one, commending the presence of wives in Nigeria against the negative assessment so strongly held in the early years and persisting during the interwar years. As A. F. B. Bridges remarks of a station in Eastern Nigeria in 1930, 'There was still some antipathy to wives' (1980, p. 34). While the situation changed after the war, official resistance to the domestication of the Colonial Service was shown in the disregard for officers' families in such matters as poor housing, frequent change of postings, lack of medical facilities and schools.

When Noël Rowling went to Nigeria in 1933, most wives took for granted the asymmetrical marriage and their own dependent position. If wives were incorporated into the hierarchy of the Colonial Service, this coincided with the unwritten rules of gender relations within marriage; these cultural rules were implicit, submerged, hardly open to question. In the ideology of the 'good wife', one of the main rules was that a wife should follow her husband wherever his work took him, as Janet Finch perceptively observes: 'Being prepared to follow one's husband is a sign of the helpmeet wife, who ideally should not only follow, but should do so selflessly, loyally and cheerfully' (1983, p. 49).

At that time, moreover, the bonds of 'wifehood' were considered to have priority over those of 'motherhood'. Violet Bourdillon sets out the 'wife/mother' dilemma: 'But what I did hate was separation from my boys, and that nearly broke my heart. . . . But I had to do it and after all its pretty bad luck on a man who is serving abroad to have both his wife and his children away from him, so I stayed with my husband always' (Ms.[b], p. 25). Mercedes Mackay says she decided very early on that her place was with her husband because once when she had left him she came back to find him living in total squalor; he was ill for ages. She continues,

> And I lost one of my children. I'm never sure that it wasn't a result of this, although everybody assured me that it wasn't so, but it was a very very painful choice to make and in the end we left the Colonial Service because we weren't going to leave our last remaining child alone away from us.   (Ms., p. 32)

The war brought a break with the past in many ways, not least in directing women to jobs which brought forth their latent capacities. After it was over, many women arrived with high professional qualifications and experience, often in leadership positions in the women's services; they came as nurses, junior administrators, education and welfare officers, keen 'to do a good job' and help with the concerted push for development. A high proportion married male officers.

The post-war official attitude still regarded wives as a subsidiary category, but no longer with the earlier antipathy. Charles Jeffries praises them for the 'wifely support' (echoes of Ruskin) they give to their husbands, 'looking after their health and comfort, keeping house, dispensing hospitality, enduring when need be separation in order that the children may be brought up in the way that their fathers would wish' (1949, p. 157). He goes on to say that many have the opportunity of doing far more than this by providing 'an example which can be of great help to their colonial sisters' by enlisting the women's co-operation in a variety of socially beneficial activities. The 'instrumental' view of wives was thus restated in more positive terms, genially patronising to colonial wives and naïvely ethnocentric in relation to the women of the colonies.

When Anne Macdonald writes of the war as a 'kind of watershed between two experiences of Nigeria' (Ms.[a], p. 16), she gives two reasons for this marked change: the presence of children made family life possible, and wives could take on professional work. These new possibilities, however, were limited and contingent: children stayed in Nigeria only until the age of six or so when they went back to the homeland for schooling; and jobs for wives, as already noted, were restricted by the necessity for them to move when their husbands were reposted (a social rule apparently never questioned) and, often, by low pay.

As wives, they gave priority to babies and small children over jobs, but many took on professional work when opportunities came their way. Although few considered their work in terms of a 'career', they no longer took for granted the self-renunciation of earlier years. Husbands, on their side, were becoming more aware of wives' capacities outside the domestic sphere and their own role as parents. This was a period of two conflicting ideologies about women's roles: the desire to establish the stability of family life after the harrowing years of war with the wife at the domestic centre; while, at the same time, the recognition that marriage did not necessarily mean the end of women's professional work.

The post-war political change leading towards Nigerian Independence gave a particular urgency to the younger generation of colonial officers and their wives. They brought a fresh vision to the problems at hand, a less authoritarian approach, the desire to work with Nigerians to move ahead in all areas – agriculture, industry, communications, education and health. Yet, at a certain stage, they realised that their own colonial careers were coming to an end far sooner than had been generally expected. With families to support, they had to look ahead to relocation. In this situation, there were openings for wives in numerous directions to step in, help out, take temporary jobs; but this was not the climate for wives to consider their own professional development. While individual women no doubt had their aspirations, it was only later, with the resurgence of the women's movement in the 1960s, when the concept of 'marriage' was widely re-defined (among the educated middle class, at least) as symmetrical relations between two autonomous partners, that the unspoken difficulties of wives began to be made explicit: 'the problem that has no name' was probed (Friedan, 1963). Bureaucratic organisations remained relatively unchanged, but wives now began to register and articulate the dissonance from the demands placed on them by their husbands' occupations (for example, see Callan, 1975).

But this is to move ahead and anticipate a future which was then only dimly perceived. What identity did these wives create for themselves amid the living conditions of 'a mud hut' and 'a vile climate', the frequent displacements, the painful separations? Recalling the utter desolation of her small children at their partings, Noël Rowling writes, 'People to whom colonialism is a dirty word never seem to understand that it was only because we believed in what we were doing that we were able to cope with miseries like that' (1982, p. 77). For these officers and their wives, belief in the altruism of their work was its sustaining feature. This commitment to the men's work, and the wives' endorsement of the demands of the Colonial Service on their husbands' time and energy to the detriment of family life, set the boundaries of their world. Wives had to find the meanings of their lives within this context.

'WOMEN'S WORK' IN THE PRE-WAR YEARS

Wives took over the management of the household, provided the extra touches for more comfortable hospitality and more elegant entertaining, and played their assigned roles in the pageantry of imperial ceremonies. On occasion they acted as nurses for their husbands, and sometimes other officers, through bouts of illness and recovery. They also took on other self-assigned tasks such as helping their husbands with office chores, volunteer work among the African community, learning languages, sketching and painting, and ethnographic enquiry. If colonial life provided only confined spaces for wives, they enlarged these in individual ways.

Their first undertaking beyond the prescribed domestic sphere was usually helping their husbands in various ways. Burns, for example, credits his wife's help on the handbook of Nigeria he assembled privately in 1916: 'I worked at night, for many months, on the compilation, while my wife typed out the results' (1949, p. 41). Violet Cragg assisted her husband's official work. While touring with him in Bauchi Province in 1928, she writes, 'I have been copying Willie's 26-page report on the Dass District. The genealogical tables and wars were excessively boring, but the tribal burial, marriage and festival customs were interesting' (Ms., p. 51). When a clerk at Shendam was taken ill, Noël Rowling helped with office work, typing all the confidential reports and secret letters. At the end of 1938, she writes, there were numerous coded telegrams from government with instructions on what to do in case of war; she did most of the decoding (1982, pp. 32–4).

Sometimes the job undertaken to relieve a husband did not come within the conventional pattern of 'women's work'. Violet Cragg, for example, began redesigning the bush rest houses which were placed at intervals of about every fifteen miles:

> When we were at Jemaari recently Willie allowed me to rebuild the rest houses with prison labour, and I have now altered the rest house here. The great mistake in Katagum Division is that all the rest houses face west, getting the afternoon sun on the front veranda, when they should obviously face north and south. I have now closed up the west side of this one, where in any case there was nothing but a mud wall to look out on, and opened up the south, where there is a very pretty view of the town and palm trees. I found an old disused hut nearby full of sunburnt bricks which the prisoners brought up, and I laid them myself as a floor to the centre room.   (Ms., p. 80)

On one tour when her husband went off for the day, she was quite prepared to settle a 'palaver' between their twenty labourers and a chief who had driven them out of the village. She explains, 'I suppose they tried to play up as Willie was not there, but I soon showed them I was not to be sat upon' (p. 64).

Wives took on various types of voluntary work in relation to the African community.[1] All through these memoirs, men's as well as women's, are brief references to wives starting or helping at infant welfare clinics. Describing the devastating famine in Kano in 1914, Hastings notes, 'A crèche for small babies was started by the wife of the Director of Education, where tinned milk and other necessaries were provided' (1925, p. 112). This was Isabelle Vischer, who writes of the crèche and also of providing food each morning for the unfortunate famine victims who came from all directions, 'a miserable procession of skeletons' (1917, p. 130).

A. F. B. Bridges tells how his wife 'got roped in by the doctor from Akure' to help start a baby clinic in Ondo in the mid-1930s: 'Her first assignment was to go and see the Oshemowe's wives and win their support. Having done this the scheme flourished. Thereafter she went off regularly weighing babies and performing other rites unknown to me' (1980, p. 42). The annual Medical and Health Report for Nigeria of 1937 states, 'Infant welfare clinics have been run in many medical stations, often with the assistance of medical officers' wives and other volunteers' (1937, p. 25).

Sometimes impromptu medical work was called for, as when Lassie Fitz-Henry had to give first-aid to a fight victim with his throat cut. She writes, 'My medical knowledge in cases like this was pretty sketchy and the best I could do was to plug up the gaping wound with disinfected cotton wool, bandage it and pray that the doctor would be in the vicinity that night. He was' (1959, p. 24). Similarly, Elnor Russell tells of their being awakened in the middle of the night while on tour in Adamawa by a mother who feared her baby was dying. 'It obviously had fever. I knew nothing about medicine. We crushed up a little aspirin, deciding that that could not hurt it and might be good and forced it down the baby's throat' (1978, p. 77). When they returned a few days later they found a crowd of mothers waiting at their shelter; word had apparently gone round of her healing powers.

A number of these wives set themselves to learn one or more Nigerian languages. Constance Larymore tells how she and her husband had not understood complaints made in a particular village and found out only long afterwards that their interpreter and others in their party had seized every goat and fowl. She goes on, 'The lesson, however, went home to us both, and drove us to work ceaselessly at the Hausa language, knowing there could be no security for ourselves, or justice for the people, until we could be independent of dishonest interpretation' (1911, p. 16).

Sylvia Leith-Ross evidently spoke Hausa during her stay in Zungeru with her husband and, as a widow, took a professional interest in compiling a Fulani grammar and dictionary. Noël Rowling took up Hausa; while touring in the Shendam area where Hausa was not the principal language, she continued her lessons with a *mallam* (teacher) who travelled with them (1982, p. 28). When Joan Sharwood Smith arrived in Kontagora in 1939, she found very few people who spoke English. Her husband writes, 'So she determined to learn Hausa, and within three months, by a combination of hard work and a natural flair, she acquired a rough working knowledge of the language and, equally valuable, some understanding of the Hausa way of life' (B. Sharwood Smith, 1969, p. 125).

Some wives showed a strong interest in the material culture and social customs of the ethnic groups they encountered. In her account of her travels in Northern Nigeria and across the border into French territory, Olive MacLeod (1971, first published in 1912) gives vivid observations on the architecture, arts, musical instruments, tools, and ways of life of the peoples among whom she passed; her book also includes numerous drawings and photographs. After her marriage to C. L. Temple, she collated the intelligence records of administrative officers, giving her main attention to ethnographic data; this was published in Cape Town in 1919.

D. Amaury Talbot had been helping her husband with his ethnographic work by making clear copies of his rough notes and writing out information collected orally when she was requested to write a paper herself giving 'the woman's point of view'. She decided to carry out her own research among the Ibibio women of southeastern Nigeria. Beginning her study with the women's secret rituals of sacrifice to the female goddess, she describes the varied customs at each stage of women's lives. Published in 1915, this monograph – amateur in both senses of the word – must be one of the first fieldwork studies undertaken by a European woman on women in a pre-literate society.

Sylvia Leith-Ross was a widow, but maintained the status of wife of an administrative officer, when she carried out her research among Igbo women. In the wake of the 'women's war' in 1929 in the Eastern provinces of Nigeria, government reports called for sociological investigation as a basis for future administrative measures; Sylvia Leith-Ross and Margaret Green received research grants from the Leverhulme Trust. Leith-Ross set out a rather crude evolutionary framework for her study, with four locations ranging from 'primitive' to 'sophisticated' women. Her work was done through interpreters (as was that of the Talbots), lacking both the linguistic understanding and trained anthropological approach of Green's village study published in 1947. Despite these grave shortcomings (see Agbasiere, 1985), the monograph has its place in the social anthropology of women, as she modestly claims, 'The only originality of the book lies in the fact that practically all the information is obtained from women and that throughout, customs, laws, circumstances and happenings are described from the woman's point of view' (1965, p. 20).

WIVES' POST-WAR PROFESSIONAL WORK

Although the urgent demand for wives' labour ceased after the war, wives continued to take up work in a piecemeal fashion outside the domestic scene. Education proved to be the most accommodating profession for colonial wives. Although many single women officers were brought out from Britain after the war, the high marriage rate of these teachers at a time of rapid expansion in all areas of education meant that numerous jobs were open for qualified wives. They came up against the gap between the salary for 'permanent' or 'contract' officers and those 'locally engaged', but most wives at that time accepted the argument that their income was only supplementary to that of their husbands. The call for dedication masked the issue of poor pay and many wives were pleased to be doing 'useful' professional work.

Evelyn Clark, for example, arrived in 1949 with the mandate to restart teacher training in Sokoto (Chapter 6). She married in 1951; since her husband had a permanent commercial job in Sokoto, she considered herself even more 'permanent' than before. The Chief Woman Education Officer begged her to stay. She writes, 'I, of course, wanted to carry on with this job I had come to do, and though the salary was a shock I was always much too busy to give it further thought' (letter, 16 April 1984). She explains:

> Contract terms were not available to married women, we were designated as 'locally engaged' and salary was reduced to the lowest point on the scale. The effect of this was that I was earning exactly the same as the youngest recruit on my staff who was straight from a University Dip. Ed. course and without any experience other than two months' teaching practice during that. One remained at that level, there were no increments.

The one concession granted to her was retaining her basic car allowance since she needed a vehicle for visiting village schools and for supervising their infant school two miles away. She stayed with this demanding job as head of the Women's Training Centre until the end of 1957, when her husband returned to government service in Kano. She continued teaching until they left Nigeria in 1966.

Many of the women who took up junior administrative positions married fellow officers or men with commercial firms in Nigeria; those who wanted to continue work were offered posts after marriage. Felicia Wand-Tetley, for example, writes, 'I was required to resign on marriage but on my return with my husband was recruited again as an Assistant Secretary practically as I stepped off the plane at Kaduna' (Ms., p. 4). These women administrators continued their work after marriage with no loss of pay (except the expatriation allowance).

Joan Allen (née Parkes) came to Nigeria in 1949 in the rare position of a librarian, first to assess the needs for library services by touring throughout the country and then becoming Regional Librarian in Kaduna. When she married an education officer, she was re-engaged on a contract basis without loss of pay except that she had been in line for a promotion which was not then granted. When she and her husband planned to go on tour together to visit schools and training centres, the head of the department sent out a circular which created much amusement. She tells that its purpose was 'to remove any ambiguity' and it was worded to the effect that 'the Finance Officer would be touring with Mrs. Allen, the former Miss Parkes, and this had been issued so that people would not think there was any irregularity' (Ms., p. 9). She continued her professional work – building up the regional library, setting up a book box system, advising secondary schools on necessary equipment and books, training teachers for library management – until 1958, when her husband was posted to Sokoto.

Cecillie Swaisland was offered a special post after coming to Nigeria as a wife. In late 1950, when her husband was transferred to the British Cameroons on a mission to resettle the Bakweri people dispossessed by the plantation system, she was also appointed as a social welfare officer, her qualifications being a degree from the London School of Economics and experience in this field. When the team found that the Bakweri did not want to be resettled, her husband worked with the team leader to establish an Outward Bound training course at Man o' War Bay, while she and a nursing sister set off into the bush in a Land Rover to do maternity and child welfare work. This work continued for just over a year until they went on leave and she had her first child (Ms., p. 4). Later she taught in secondary schools in Eastern Nigeria and also gave English courses for Nigerians coming into the administration.

With the post-war emphasis on expanding education and improving social welfare, the professional work of wives was not only accepted by Nigerians but usually warmly welcomed. Less qualified wives, however, were perceived as taking jobs from Nigerians or receiving higher pay for similar work; they were, understandably, resented. In June 1947, when a national delegation of Nigerians had their historical meeting with A. Creech Jones, the Secretary of State for the Colonies, to demand the radical revision of the Richards Constitution, the delegation also submitted a memorandum of thirty-three other grievances, including the employment of European wives (Coleman, 1958, p. 293).

In Northern Nigeria the 'temporary wives', as those were known who took on short-term secretarial work to add to their husbands' salaries or because they were bored at home, were considered a great help in the Secretariat and provincial offices, but complaints came from Africans because some of these wives were not fully trained secretary-typists and they received monthly rates of pay which worked out more per annum than that of a fully qualified African. Although these wives were engaged on monthly terms with no security of tenure, the antagonism lingered and after Nigerian self-government the decree went through that only those European wives with full secretarial qualifications would be paid the top monthly rates and the others a reduced rate. This, in turn, brought an angry reaction from the wives concerned (MacDermot, Ms., p. 56).

WIVES' ROLES IN VOLUNTARY WORK

Wives took up 'voluntary' work according to the roles allotted to them and the spaces available for initiatives. As a prime example, wives were ascribed roles in the traditional charities in a hierarchy parallel to their husbands' positions; this, of course, helped to strengthen the charities because the structure of support remained constant despite the frequent changes of persons. Many wives who found themselves heading charities because of their husbands' promotions, whatever their personal misgivings, gave their energies and ideas to these obligations. Joan Sharwood Smith, for example, as governor's wife in Kaduna was automatically expected to be the President of the Regional Branch of the Red Cross Society and also of the Regional Girl Guides Association. Fortunately, she notes, the regional Girl Guides movement was in the competent hands of Dr. Constance Geary, the Chief Woman Education Officer, and her own duties consisted merely of taking the chair at the annual meeting and appearing at their functions in festive clothes with a smile and a 'few words' for the girls (Ms., p. 176).

Red Cross duties, however, presented her with greater anxieties. She is disarming about her lack of confidence before chairing the first meeting of the Executive Committee, made up of prominent Nigerian Ministers and British civil servants. During this period the organisation carried out a considerable amount of welfare work for mission hospitals and leper settlements. Junior Red Cross units were started in the larger schools and, in Kaduna, a blood transfusion service. She tells of one new idea which opened the way for reaching many more people: this was the decision to teach Red Cross techniques in Hausa. The only available manuals were in English, illustrated with white people in a European environment; a translation was commissioned with drawings of Northern Nigerians in their familiar settings and including treatments for such local mishaps as snake bite and scorpion sting.

Throughout the country European wives were drawn into philanthropic networks. Mary King was not untypical: 'I did some voluntary work during these years as Secretary to the Women's Corona Society, member of the Management Committee of the Corona Schools Trust Council, history lecturing in the British Council and fund raising for the Society for the Blind' (Ms., pp. 14–15). Many gave their time to Red Cross and Girl Guides. Joan Cheverton, for example, tells of the occasion when she was wearing her white Girl Guides uniform after a meeting in Ibadan and, because her arm was in a sling, her host told her not to change for dinner. At the dinner party a Nigerian asked her about the uniform. She explained how she had started a Guide company in the palace of the Emir of Kano, how they had adapted the teaching to subjects related to cultural traditions. It turned out that her questioner was a treasurer visiting from the North and later when money was allocated, the Guides received more than they had asked for (Alexander, 1983, p. 90).

Wives also took up activities related to their husbands' specific careers. Writing about the wives of education officers, for example, A. R. Allen states that some worked in school dispensaries or offices; others gave active support in the role of the headmaster's or housemaster's wife; the great majority participated in such school activities as dramatic productions and Sports Day (Ms., p. 23). As a Resident's wife, Elizabeth Purdy typed confidential reports for her husband in Yola and Sokoto. Wives received no pay for this: 'It just never occurred to me to think about it. We were glad to be able to help' (Ms.[b], p. 9). This desire to be of help was a key phrase in my interviews with these wives and recurs in their memoirs.

While working as a full-time medical officer after her marriage, Dr. Kathleen Abraham also ran first aid courses for the students in her husband's college and for senior girls at the Katsina Provincial Girls' School. Later when her husband became Principal of the newly-formed Bornu Training College in Maiduguri, she was not working because their daughter was still under a year old, but she agreed to make a regular evening visit to the college. For several periods a week, her husband brought his administrative work home to look after the baby while she went to the college to teach classes in simple health, hygiene and first aid. Then, every evening she drove over again to do her 'surgery' with a few supplies obtained from the hospital where she had previously worked. This innovative project proved so successful that the next year, in 1961, the principals of other government educational institutions asked her to set up a school medical service to save the students' time lost in trekking to the hospital and waiting for treatment. The result was that she went back to full-time work as a medical officer to establish a comprehensive school medical service for the schools and colleges within Maiduguri and even a skeleton service for nearby bush schools. This included regular routine medical examinations as well as diagnostic and treatment sessions (Ms., pp. 16–19).

With her experience as a librarian, Joan Allen volunteered to develop the library for Sokoto Provincial Secondary School, where her husband was posted. She ordered new books, catalogued them, and trained some of the prefects to take over library duties when she was not there. She took up another voluntary project when staff members of the school were asked to assist in making up the register of electors for the forthcoming Federal elections in late 1959. They were given a specific constituency and, in company with an official from the Native Authority central office, went to every compound to get the names and occupations of adult males. She remembers leaving home at dawn in order to ride horseback to an area about twenty miles outside Sokoto; this was in the hottest weather of April and May, when the temperature soon climbed to 110 degrees in the shade. Although she had studied Hausa, this was the first time she was able to make full use of her language skills. Later she helped with arrangements for the election, training young men to be in charge of polling stations, and on the day of the election touring 'our constituency' to make sure all was going well, and then counting the votes (Ms., pp. 16–21).

Elnor Russell (later Lady Maddocks), wife of the Civil Secretary in Kaduna, edited the first English-language magazine specially written for Northern school-leavers, gave lessons to the wives of ministers and other wives in purdah on household management and cooking, and took part in Red Cross activities (1978, p. 132). Masry MacGregor, an education officer who married a DO, writes of helping women in purdah, 'Later in Kaduna, I found myself visiting women in their compounds to help them acquire the social and linguistic skills to mix with European women' (Ms., p. 55).

During the post-war years mother and child welfare clinics

became more institutionalised and staffed with trained Nigerians, but a few European wives volunteered their services where clinics did not yet have government or mission backing. Eleanor Stephenson, formerly an education officer, started a clinic in Oturkpo in 1955, her husband relates. Although there was no encouragement from the medical department, the chief gave strong support to the project. With the help of another wife, she operated the clinic once a week with an average attendance of over a hundred women – some mothers walking as far as sixty miles and back. Two Idoma trained midwives acted as interpreters and proved to be natural teachers in basic hygiene, practical first-aid and mothercraft; cases needing professional attention were sent to the local mission hospital. This clinic, in the view of G. L. Stephenson, was the first of its kind in Northern Nigeria: 'Here the clinic was run by the people for the people' (Ms., pp. 124–5).

During the post-war period, the Women's Corona Society became a significant means for colonial wives to join with other women in a multi-racial association carrying out beneficial projects in the main cities of Nigeria. Started in London as an adjunct to the men's dining club of that name, the Women's Corona suspended its meetings during the war years and, in the post-war climate of ideas, transformed itself into a new organisation with its membership open to all women in sympathy with its work (Macdonald, Ms.[b]). In Lagos, the Society started with a government-loaned office; when members discovered a small derelict house and were granted its use by government, they were able to expand their activities. By 1953, with generous help from commercial firms, a Corona School and Day Nursery opened. With its paid, trained staff, the school occupied the premises during the mornings and for afternoons voluntary workers arranged lectures, exhibitions and teas for members. Very soon the schedule filled: Thursday afternoons for baby weighing, Tuesday evenings with Scottish dancing, and Sunday mornings a church service. As Anne Macdonald writes, the Corona House became a 'centre for friendship' (1959, p. 349).

The School Committee raised money for new equipment and recruited more teachers to meet the rapid expansion of the school and crèche as increasing numbers of Nigerian and Asian children joined the European ones from families in commerce and government. She describes the scene:

A visitor going round during break time might hear excited chatter from a French, Nigerian and a British girl about what they would do at an American birthday party to which they had just been invited . . . In the crêche, forty tiny camp beds would just have been put out for 'first rest' and several heads would bob up to see who was coming, Scandinavian flaxen plaits next to tight African curls.   (p. 349)

The demand became so great that two more schools were set up in suburbs of Lagos and, later, one each in Kano and Jos. These schools, made possible by the voluntary efforts of women in the multinational Corona Society, continued for many years after Independence.

RESOURCES AND REWARDS

Some wives talk about their experience in Nigeria – whether seen in terms of an active social life and meeting interesting people or in relation to service to the community through their work in paid or unpaid positions – as exciting and rewarding. Others, however, endured rather than enjoyed their years as colonial wives. Their voices have remained largely unregistered, not because of any external suppression, but rather because of self-imposed silence: the idea of dissent, even relatively mild and in the past tense, is 'unspeakable'. The Colonial Service operated within a discourse of altruism; its officers were widely seen as committed to a public service higher than any personal rewards. As Hilary Callan points out in her probing analysis of how wives' marital status links them to their husbands' bureaucracy, the wives resolve the ambiguities of their position by the 'premiss of dedication' (1975, pp. 87–104). Janet Finch (1983, p. 28) notes the special moral obligations imposed on wives of men engaged in 'noble endeavours' such as clergymen; this is precisely relevant to wives of colonial officers. Such a situation appears to inhibit wives' complaints at the extraordinary demands placed on them. A 'good wife' does not complain: this is a strong injunction, stronger for being internally accepted rather than externally dictated, held by these wives not only during their colonial experience but also, apparently, in perpetuity.

The logic of the system so pervades their self-awareness that they consider a confession of unhappiness during those years in Nigeria to be a symptom of their own inadequacy. If this typical pattern of women has been labelled by psychological theory as their 'inherent masochism', the distinguished psychoanalyst Jean Baker Miller counters by explaining that women think in terms of the dominant culture and when this dominant culture does not attend to their experiences, they may be left with a 'global, undefined sense' of being wrong (1976, p. 57). The Colonial Service, as has been amply documented, had no space in its ideological structures or its bureaucratic practice for women's experience.

Several wives agreed to talk with me about their experience only reluctantly and with the promise of anonymity. 'I didn't enjoy Nigeria, I put up with it,' one said. In her view, wives would say how marvellous it was but these were not their real feelings, only what they felt they were expected to say. She remembers the anxieties and unhappiness of an isolated station, being left with a small child while her husband went on tour, with no car or telephone, the doctor some eighty miles away and the only Europeans anywhere near two Catholic priests. Had there been an emergency, she says, they would have helped her, but she missed the company of other Europeans, especially women. Yet she did not find satisfying what she considered to be the artificiality of social life in larger stations. She set out tentatively the central issue as she perceives it, that women might feel a greater need for a home and continuity than men do; she yearned for 'permanence' and was glad when her husband retired. She concluded by considering herself inadequate in comparison with some other 'successful' wives – for not having more intellectual interests and not learning a Nigerian language. Interestingly, this woman was described to me by a male officer as an 'excellent hostess' and a great help to her husband as a senior officer. Clearly she was able in Nigeria (as well as later) to conceal her private misgivings.

Another had worked in an interesting and demanding job before her marriage and did not find any comparable opportunity in Nigeria. She did not like the competition by bored European wives to serve the best cakes at morning coffee or delicacies at lunch or whatever. Although she did some volunteer work, she had reservations about the hierarchical organisations, especially when Nigerians replicated the patterns of committees and the meetings became longer without actually getting anything done. She felt out of place, the ambiguities became more evident when Independence came, and she was glad to return with her husband and take up new work in the UK.

Although Rosemary Hollis writes of her decade as a DO's wife in Northern Nigeria with a certain wry humour, the details suggest a good deal of misery tinged with self-guilt. She had worked with Naval Intelligence during the war and later held a job with the British Council relating to music and the arts. Finding herself in Bauchi, she 'missed the human company, the busy rush of working life, and felt a hopeless sense of imprisonment, of clipped wings' (1981, p. 45). With strong determination she achieved certain goals: mastery of Hausa to be able to talk with local people (she was one of the few wives to pass the official language exam), teaching herself to type, learning to drive on the hazardous bush roads, and, perhaps most difficult of all, continuing her drawing and painting in isolation despite the problem of white ants consuming her limited supply of materials.

During a happy tour of Kaduna, she tells of designing costumes and painting sets for productions by the Kaduna Players as well as contributing the drawing for the cover of the official durbar programme at the time of the Queen's visit. But, as she explains, 'Michael was not really a "Kaduna" type. He begged to be allowed to return to bush for his next tour of duty and his wish was granted' (p. 82). When after nine years, she found herself in yet another bush station with no telephone, no electricity, no public transport, no doctor and no other European women, she tells of 'a feeling that can only be described as anguish, of being uprooted, severed, raw at the edges, stranded' (p. 146). Writing of the numerous times when her husband returned much later than expected (on one occasion coming back from a day's duty 48 hours late because of a broken bridge), she states, 'I tried very hard not to complain or show that I was in any way unhappy – so anxious was I to make a success of bush life. I did so want to be of help' (p. 47). These lines might well be taken as the refrain of colonial wives.

Although it must have crossed her mind, she never blamed the series of miscarriages she had over ten years on the rough conditions of living or lack of medical care. Only with special medical attention at the end of their stay in Nigeria was she able to

complete a pregnancy; she returned to England four months early
to have this child, and another was born later. The male-derived
colonial ideology remained oblivious to the experiences of women.
Even the central requirement of physical reproduction for a
society came outside its boundaries; this ideally happened back in
the homeland, in the insignificant and obscured private sphere.

In the view of one informant, there were two types of wives:
'those who could stick it, and those who couldn't'. In her terms,
the second category marked the weaklings, those who returned
home on grounds of health or caring for children, those without
the inner resources to give full support to their husbands. Other
wives were disapproved of for not maintaining moral standards:
those at the centre of sexual gossip. With the high ratio of men in
relation to women, 'temptations' were only to be expected. While
the unwritten code among male officers was clear – 'Do not seduce
a fellow officer's wife', it is hardly surprising that the traditional
double standard of sexual morality prevailed, with the blame
pointing to the woman. Again, some wives had mental
breakdowns requiring psychiatric treatment (as did some men),
though the statistical evidence is lacking to determine whether the
proportion was higher among colonial wives in Nigeria than in a
similar group of middle-class wives remaining in Britain.

Among those who took a positive view of their life in Nigeria, a
Resident's wife regretted that it was not possible to stay for the
completion of her husband's career there; in her view,
Independence came earlier than it should have done because of
American pressure on the international scene. She feels they were
not just existing and making a living in Nigeria, but achieving a
purpose; it was a tremendously satisfying life, she says in
retrospect, although much of what they worked for has now
disintegrated. Despite the forcible criticisms over the last thirty
years, she retains in effect the paternalistic and ethnocentric
world-view of the colonial period.

Another wife who has since done a degree in West African
Studies looks back on the attitudes which they developed as
members of the colonial group in Nigeria – and have since had to
'unlearn'. Cecillie Swaisland says, 'You did tend to imbibe the
idea that the Empire was a very good thing and it was a tutelage'
(Ms., p. 34). And again: 'There is no doubt that we regarded the
colonial period as an educative period . . . I can remember using
the analogy of children growing up – you know, which now makes

me sort of shudder' (p. 46). Her questionings have left her convinced that there was a great deal of benefit in the system; she does not go along with those who think that everything with the label 'colonial' on it must have been wrong. She remembers nationalism being in the air when they first arrived in Eastern Nigeria, but even so they did not realise how rapidly everything would change. She explains, 'And we were partly regretful, and still are, you know, it's a whole period that disappeared and left you sort of stranded in time. But partly also, recognising the inevitability of it – and the rightness of it, too, whatever happened' (p. 35).

If many of these wives gained self-realisation through helping their husbands' careers, their public rewards were similarly derived: the status of 'senior lady', the power accorded the few who became 'Resident's wife', the title gained with the husband's knighthood. Niven writes, 'The awarding of a title makes an enormous difference to a wife and in the Service we always thought it was the ideal way for us to repay our wives, if it lay within our power, for all they had done and been through in the long hard years in the Tropics' (1982, p. 269). From a feminist perspective, this has an unacceptably patronising tone, extending his own achieved glory in compensation to his wife. But within the world-view of this vanished colonial group, this can be read at face value. The officer had received high recognition for his service; his wife had given invisible support for his career. 'Marriage' was her job; his title, if not officially acknowledging her individual personal role, at least gave her visible reward. Yet in cases of early death or divorce, the wife who shared 'the long hard years in the Tropics' might not have been the one to enjoy the status of the derived title.

A few wives gained independent recognition. Anne Macdonald was one who received an MBE award for her educational services to the international community in Lagos. Appreciation from Nigerians afforded rewards for many wives. In Constance Larymore's case, she was named *Uwamu* by the people of Katagum, a Hausa word meaning 'Our Mother'; for her, this was 'the highest expression of respect and affection that the African man can offer to a woman' (1911, p. 85). The name followed her on her travels. At a later period, the Sardauna of Sokoto, Sir Ahmadu Bello, gave fulsome praise to some of the wives of senior officers for their personal achievements. Of Lady Sharwood Smith (wife of the Governor of Northern Nigeria, 1952–7), he said, 'Of her we shall always retain the most affectionate memories. Her knowledge of the country, her understanding of the people, and her proficiency in the Hausa language entitle her to a position of her own in our hearts' (Sharwood Smith, 1969, p. 385). And of Lady Maddocks (wife of the Deputy Governor, 1957–8): 'K. P. has been lucky enough to have as a wife one who enjoyed the confidence of all European and African women wherever they have worked. Mrs. Maddocks has been the cement between our wives and the wives of Europeans and has helped in improving child welfare in this town' (Russell, 1978, p. 135).

In Ibadan, Mercedes Mackay ran the radio station and made friends with many Yoruba women: 'Of course they never write to you but I know I could go back any time and be welcomed and embraced with open arms' (Ms., p. 38). They honoured her with a special ceremony, at which the police band played, by dressing her in Yoruba robes and awarding her a title.

Perhaps the most unusual ovation for a European wife came from Nnamdi Azikiwe, the nationalist leader later to become President of Nigeria, who usually reserved the columns of the *West African Pilot* for the most critical comments on Europeans. On the day of the departure of Governor Bourdillon, he printed a prose poem in honour of Lady Bourdillon entitled 'She Stands Unique':

> Eight years ago she came here . . . She rose above the people's wildest imaginations, she was a friend to all who would be friendly, she was every inch as charming with the highest as with the lowest in the community . . . Never had Government House seen such scenes as she caused to be created there, nor was Government House ever visited by so many members of the community . . . Such a lady could excite nothing but the love and affection of all who came in contact with her . . . (15 May 1943, quoted in Pearce, 1983, p. 275)

This and other examples suggest the need for an alternative interpretation to the negative one usually accorded wives of colonial officers; my concluding chapter takes up this theme.

Part Four

Women of the Empire
Revalued

10　Another Meaning

*Power, then, returns to our centre in social anthropology. But it is
not simply the power which rests on the acquisition of land, myth,
and material objects, but rather that which comes from unequal
access to semantic creativity, including the capacity to nominate
others as equal or unequal, animate or inanimate, memorable or
abject, discussor or discussed.*

(Parkin, 1982, p. xlvi)

THE IMPERIAL CONTRADICTION

This study began with certain observations: the strong resistance
of the Colonial Service in the early years to the presence of
European women in Nigeria; their negligible place in the memoirs
of male officers and in the colonial record itself; the negative
stereotypes of 'colonial women' in novels, films and the 'oral
tradition'; and their problematic position in successive accounts
by social scientists. The preceding chapters have shown, in
contrast, professional women engaged in health care, education
and administration – their work widely seen by Nigerians as
beneficial – and wives of colonial officers actively involved in
backing their husbands' careers and in welfare for the wider
Nigerian community. Their work, of course, was subsidiary to
that of men; for quite obvious reasons, these women do not often
feature in the 'history of the greats'. Yet the question has not been
fully answered: why should these European women in the colonies
remain all but invisible or else be represented in pejorative
stereotypes?

The Historian G. A. Pocock points out that all stereotypes, however obsolete or otherwise inadequate, are elements
in the models of itself a society uses for its political thinking (1964, p. 199). This insight, however, does not probe the
question of unequal power among sectors of the society in the
construction of social meanings. Here Edwin Ardener's incisive
analysis of dominant and 'muted' groups (1972, 1975) and Shirley
Ardener's elaboration of this theory (1975) are relevant. The

dominant group in a society imposes the communication system defining the society's total reality or 'world structure' (see also E. Ardener, 1978), impeding the free expression of subdominant or 'muted' groups, perhaps even inhibiting the generation of other models.

In citing the return of power to the centre of social anthropology, David Parkin gives emphasis to its cognitive dimensions revealed in the capacity to nominate others as 'equal or unequal, animate or inanimate, memorable or abject' (1982, p. xlvi). When the dominant culture (during the imperial era and in our own day) fashions stereotypes in creating and re-creating its models of society, these are components in its definitions of self and other, its structures of authority and hierarchy, its nostalgia for lost power and glory.

A key suggestion comes through in the work of the well-known psychoanalyst, Jean Baker Miller, who writes that when women step beyond the bounds of the realms assigned to them, they confront and challenge men. She adds, 'But even in their traditional roles, women, by *their very existence*, confront and challenge men because they have been made *the embodiment of the dominant culture's unsolved problems* (1976, p. 56, her emphasis). What women are and have been, their attributes and capacities, their strengths and failings – these 'facts' about women – appear to be shaped by the dominant group according to the needs of its current political thinking. The 'unsolved problems' in relation to European women in the colonies point to the dilemma of imperialism itself. Placed under scrutiny, this ethnocentric and crudely expansive phase in European history has proved itself not only morally questionable (as probed in the novels of E. M. Forster and George Orwell) but built on illusions (for example, Howard, 1981). Yet with its sudden demise something central to European men's imaginative space would seem to have disappeared: the territories of the Empire represent a lost, and seemingly unrecoverable, masculine world. The specific burden of 'unsolved problems' might then be located: the dominant culture's perception of the contradiction between the celebration of men's 'masculinity' in a noble cause and the painful recognition of exposed illusions. Here the source of myth-making is revealed, as Lévi-Strauss informs us in his early structuralist essay, 'The purpose of myth is to provide a logical model capable of overcoming a contradiction' (1968, p. 229).

The negative images of colonial women embody the worst side
of imperialism – its trivial social competitiveness, snobbishness,
racism – while, at the same time, they can be seen to represent
'femininity' as the encoded contrast to 'masculinity'. The
question is not whether these stereotypes actually did exist; it
might well be argued that they are based on 'real' women.
Certainly the colonial enclaves of the interwar period provided the
setting for such women with closed-in horizons; examples can be
found in Nigeria. But by what processes do these negative female
images become pervading symbols of European women in the
colonies?

This might be designated a case of 'symbolic appropriation',
the term used by Malcolm Chapman in his perceptive study of the
way Gaelic culture had its shape imposed from without by the
dominant English literary discourse in the process by which the
latter defined its own cultural identity (1978, p. 28). Just as
Matthew Arnold was not primarily concerned to belittle the Celt
in using such words as 'nervous, unsteady, emotional, fanciful,
unreliable, moody, and the like' – a potent vocabulary for female
belittlement as well, Chapman notes (p. 107) – so the dominant
culture does not necessarily intend to depreciate women in this
case; yet the political climate requires the colonial female
stereotypes to carry a heavy load, both the imposed 'feminine/
other' and the negative weight of the high imperialist era.
'Symbolic appropriation' thus provides the means to repress the
imperial contradiction.

To a certain extent, in their acceptance of the dominant
reality-defining discourse and in the self-denying prescriptions of
their own code (cf. Kanter, 1977, p. 123), women have complied
with, even helped to validate, this model-building. As in the
Gaelic example shown in Chapman's fine analysis, the problem
remains 'more than one of simple political disequilibrium' (1978,
p. 231).

THE MASCULINE WORLD THAT WAS LOST

Much has been written about the way literary tradition both
pointed the way to imperialist enterprise and made use of its
settings for heroic fiction. Historians, literary critics and
psychoanalysts have, in turn, examined the complex

interrelations between – to cite Martin Green's work (1980) – 'dreams of adventure, deeds of empire'. The literary critic, Alan Sandison, for example, argues against the traditional assumption that action in the novels of Kipling, Conrad and Buchan was directed primarily to promulgating an imperial ideal. He takes an opposing view, that these novels portray noble action as a means for overcoming individual alienation and giving meaning to a world in chaos. He writes, 'Achievement and reality lie in the *process* of action itself since it alone can secure man his identity and integrity. Thus the imperial idea becomes not an end in itself but a major expression of the problems of self-consciousness' (1967, p. viii). His cogent interpretation reveals how these writers, in their separate ways, present their characters in a moral struggle; service and duty to the Empire provide the symbolism of self-salvation. This pattern of the imperial male quest for self-realisation through separation and daunting personal achievement might be cited as a prime example of the male model of moral development traced through Western civilisation in Carol Gilligan's seminal study (1982). Sandison analyses how the physical reality, the concrete details of colonial settings, became transmuted to a moral plane: 'Authority, discipline, fidelity, devotion, fortitude and self-sacrifice constitute the ideal imperial servant whether he is making his soul in the fiction of Kipling, Buchan or Conrad, or in the ranks of the pro-consuls' (p. 199).

Examining more popular adventure literature, A. H. M. Kirk-Greene (1977) shows how the hero in the widely-read novel *Sanders of the River* and other stories by Edgar Wallace projects the archetypal image of 'district commissioners of bush and boma'. Here was the 'slim and dapper figure in spotless white', asserting his authority when required with 'cold and prohibitive' eyes and a voice of 'steely timbre'. If the secret of his administration lay in its 'simplicity and strength', his rule was also heavily paternalistic and his execution of justice stern and swift (in contrast, Kirk-Greene notes, to interminable delays of British justice in practice). His knowledge of his district was thorough and far-reaching, matched only by his scorn of officials and 'the artificial life' at headquarters. While this image of the colonial officer in Africa is a stereotype, Kirk-Greene points out, it had its roots in fact as well as in fiction and, although the British commissioner no longer exists, 'Sanders of the River is alive and well'. Fiction thus sustains the world that was lost.

These writers do not bring into their analyses – perhaps because the point is so obvious – that this imaginative world, to an even greater extent than imperial 'reality', is entirely male. No systematic study has yet been carried out, to my knowledge, of the role of female characters in imperial fiction; but it appears that in the imaginative celebration of masculine ethos at the 'frontier', women had little part. This symbolic struggle for the salvation of the soul was a male exercise of power and self-discipline; indeed, women were perceived, mainly at the unconscious level, as a threat to men's redemptive enterprise. Wurgaft observes, 'The primordial image of the castrating female preoccupied Kipling during his years in India' (p. 135); and Molly Mahood notes, 'A rather trying obsessive fear of what Blake called female domination runs in fact through all Cary's work' (1964, p. 117).

In his study of 'the imperial imagination' of Kipling's India the psychoanalyst Lewis Wurgaft argues that British rulers at the turn of the century, in order to ward off the pressures of Indian nationalism, became increasingly dependent on authoritarian institutions bolstered by notions of moral and racial superiority. For inspiration, they turned away from the complexities of contemporary India to the simpler reality of an earlier period as projected in the exploits of such renowned officers as Henry and John Lawrence, who conquered the important northern province of the Punjab at mid-century and then went on to crush the Indian Mutiny of 1857. Wurgaft observes, 'The earmarks of the "Punjab Style" were heroic action, the exercise of unlimited power, and evangelical zeal' (1983, p. 35). He analyses the British preoccupation with the stoic ideal of self-denial and self-control, the readiness to take on a staggering burden of work, the dawning sense of personal power, the celebration of self-sacrifice to empire as a political ideal. In Wurgaft's account, Lord Curzon 'saw himself and the Raj as the incarnation of righteousness and moral order in India' (p. 159). The Viceroy expounded imperial ideas on the formation of character by pointing to the north-west frontier of India (particularly in an earlier era). Comparing this with the American frontier at the beginning of the nineteenth century, Curzon saw a parallel discipline: 'an ennobling and invigorating stimulus for our youth, saving them alike from the corroding ease and the morbid excitements of Western civilization' (1907, pp. 55–7; quoted in Wurgaft, 1983, p. 164).

This glorification of the 'frontier' in a past era appears in the memoirs of administrative officers in Nigeria, in their adverse comparisons of the red-tape of contemporary bureaucracy with the self-sacrificing military action of earlier officers. Stanhope White, for example, pauses in his description of the everyday affairs in Birnin Kebbi in 1947 to trace from entries in an old station diary the exploits of an officer in January 1906:

> To me, the absence of heroics and the matter of fact way in which McAllister made what might well have been his last entry in this or any other diary, is notable in the extreme; moreover, his leaving at once with his pitifully small body of men to go to the aid of the stricken garrison in Sokoto, is to me a matter of intense pride, and is a small part of the story of the Colonial Administrative Service which surely deserves to be widely known.   (1966, p. 212)

With her sharp powers of observation, Margery Perham in 1932 identifies the metaphorical qualities of men's 'frontier' with its exclusion of white women. Noting the ban that had only recently been lifted for one or two wives, she describes Bornu as 'not only physically rather a formidable province; it has also a formidable political reputation as the furthest from the capital, the preserve of tough polo-playing British officials, hard men ruling a hard dry frontier land' (1983, p. 115).

Despite sharing with their husbands the arduous living conditions and undertaking rugged treks in the bush, women were expected to show 'feminine' qualities, as Mary Oake describes. An Oxford graduate and the only woman in the station at Buea, she writes, 'I was used to men having known them at university, but I didn't feel quite at home with these; they always gave me the feeling that they expected me to be ultra-feminine – fluffy' (1933, p. 11). The dominant culture thus defined women in logical opposition to men's self-definitions: the 'ultra-masculine' required the 'ultra-feminine'.

THE COLONIAL ENCLAVE

In the discourse of the dominant culture the symbolic world of the 'frontier' ('the wilds') was created in opposition to the 'artificial life' ('civilisation') of the colonial headquarters with an underlying parallel relation of 'masculine' to 'feminine'. The stereotypes of colonial women were thus generated from the powerful interplay of what in another context has been so aptly termed 'historical metaphors and mythical realities' (Sahlins, 1981). In Nigeria, following the reforms of Sir Hugh Clifford in 1919, more wives joined their husbands for at least part of their tours. Living conditions improved with the laying out of European reservations and the construction of housing for married officers. This period marks the formation of the enclave, in its social as well as physical dimensions. The descriptions given by Sylvia Leith-Ross of Lagos and Erick Berry of Zaria during the interwar years show the accelerated social pace resulting when women were placed in a confined location within an alien culture, deprived of their usual responsibilities (childcare, domestic duties, volunteer work) and expected only to fill their time and, implicitly, to foster their husband's careers. The game of 'entertaining' was set in motion according to rules already becoming outmoded in the homeland; any individual wife joining for the first time would find the board already in a state of play. Those who might have turned their energies to learning a Nigerian language or exploring the local scene were discouraged in subtle ways and expected to conform. As Erick Berry found to her dismay, there was little time after late nights and tired mornings for her to get on with her painting.

It is important to note that many wives throughout the colonial period in Nigeria accompanied their husbands to remote stations and lived in pioneer conditions. Of central significance, the colonial enclave was at its height during the interwar period when European children were not allowed in the country and wives were not able to take up professional work. When the war came, necessity required women to take on work previously done by men; after the war, wives became occupied with their families and with paid and volunteer work. Then, as the transfer of power took place, in Eastern and Western Nigeria at least, the social rules changed rapidly and what had formerly been called the 'European reservation' was now 'the GRA' – the Government Reservation Area, no longer reserved for whites.

The analysis of the interwar enclave shows that its physical dimensions were not created by women nor were its social rules of hierarchy, precedence, formality and exclusion (derived from military organisation and the general social practice of the late Victorian and Edwardian period), although some women accepted these as sacrosanct and applied them to the letter. Other women who took part, however, cast a critical eye on the social process, certainly in retrospect; some women at the time broke through its boundaries to take on projects of their own. Social competitiveness, then, cannot be attributed to colonial wives as individuals, but rather to their position as 'the incorporated wife' (Callan and Ardener, 1984) in their husbands' institution.

In her discussion of the 'two-person career', in which the wife is actively engaged in supporting her husband's career, Hannah Papanek notes, 'It is the wives who are most closely involved with the institutionalised perquisites of rank outside the office – housing, level of consumption, friendship circles, clothes, sociability, manners, club memberships, and so on' (1973, p. 859). She analyses how women are expected to undertake a wide range of unrecognised work to maintain and enhance family social status (1979). Rather than attributing certain psychological flaws to women, this analysis of assigned social roles suggests a more suitable explanation of why these wives of colonial officers were seen to be specially involved in the rivalry of 'entertaining' and the concentrated competition at particular moments for the limited social rewards of colonial life (invitations during the Governor's visit, for the 'Captain's Table', and the like).

WOMEN AND RACE RELATIONS

While providing the political complexities of a specific context, historians and sociologists of the colonial period tend to repeat the widespread generalisation that the presence of European women in a colonial territory can be seen as a cause for the worsening of race relations, or at least a widening of social distance between the rulers and the subject peoples (for example, Ballhatchet, 1980; Banton, 1971; Henriques, 1974). In his excellent study of race, sex and class in imperial India, Ballhatchet analyses the effect on race relations of the arrival of Englishwomen: 'As wives they hastened the disappearance of the Indian mistress. As hostesses they fostered the development of exclusive social groups in every civil station. As women they were thought by Englishmen to be in need of protection from lascivious Indians' (1980, p. 5).

It is quite obvious, as others have pointed out (for example, Kuklick, 1979, p. 129; Mason, 1970, pp. 88–9), that sexual relations between colonial officers and women of the colonised group does not mean egalitarian race relations; however generous the individual officer might have been, the association was unequal and open to exploitation. Nor did this lead to harmonious relations with the colonised society as a whole. Whether the officer lost his impartiality was not so much at question as whether he was seen to have lost it; and in some countries (not in Nigeria, apparently) bitter anger and resentment resulted from white men using their privileged position to take African women, as shown in evidence from Northern Rhodesia (Mason, 1970, p. 88).

On the second count, as already discussed, the exclusive social groups developed more because of the confined physical domains set out according to the imperial spatial model and the limited roles assigned to women than from women's autonomous action. Women's need for 'protection', however strongly women themselves concurred in perceiving this need, also arose from the politics of imperialism, as will be discussed. Clearly, it was not women as active agents who *caused* the rift in race relations, but the new structural alignment of the society brought about by official decisions not of their making. As Ballhatchet emphasises, the preservation of social distance remained a central concept in the exercise of imperial power and authority.

In her study based on research in Uganda, Gartrell (1984) writes of the role of colonial wives in 'policing' the sexual boundaries between the races and of their own 'sexual fear' of African men which restricted women's activities beyond the European enclave. In Nigeria, the evidence suggests that colonial officers used considerable discretion in their relations with African women whether or not European women were present in the station (discussed in Chapter 2). Since part of the oral tradition of colonial life in Nigeria was the existence of 'Secret Circular B' (whatever its contents), it is likely that for self-preservation in a competitive career service officers having affairs with African women exercised caution so that their activities would not come to the attention of superior officers. The Colonial Service itself served as the 'policing agent' by the threat posed by its confidential reports and, in the case of the post-war nursing sisters seeking friendships with Nigerians in the suggestive setting of a moonlight picnic, through instant transfer.

On the question of European women fearing the 'sexually threatening African male', all the evidence from Nigeria throughout the colonial period points in the other direction, that women felt confident in remaining in an isolated camp for the day without any European male protection and in travelling freely on their own to remote parts of the interior. In 1913, for example, Sylvia Leith-Ross (1983, p. 70) travelled for several weeks up the Benue in a canoe with an African crew; when she happened to meet a German forestry officer, he was amazed that she should travel 'alone' without any escort. As shown in their accounts, women education officers from the time between the wars toured long distances on horseback, by lorry or car, often accompanied by African male servants to make wood fires and carry water at bush rest houses. The concerns of these women had to do with tropical storms, bad roads, flooded rivers and washed-out bridges rather than any anxiety about possible male assault. They tell of sympathetic Nigerians stopping on the road to help repair tyre punctures and of friendly receptions from ordinary people wherever they went.

The only account of 'sexual fear' in the many records I have examined arises from a different source. In a letter to her women colleagues at home about her journey on the boat train from Lagos to Kano, Dr. Greta Lowe-Jellicoe tells of the difficult position she found herself in during the middle of the night when a drunken British army man boarded the train and attempted to force his way into her compartment. She concludes, 'Candidly I'm scared of drunken white men' (letter, 29 May 1933).

In none of the memoirs or letters, female or male, during the entire colonial period in Nigeria is there even the slightest apprehension of any Nigerian male aggression towards a British woman. Pat Walters, a rural education officer who spent fourteen years in Western Nigeria, writes,

> Never once in my many years of travel through such lonely bush outposts did I meet with anything but respect and kindness. The lovely courtesy and kindness of the villagers – how absolutely safe one always was in those isolated little resthouses ... What one feared were snakes, scorpions, and stray leopards.   (letter, 14 January 1984)

Nor were the cities seen as dangerous. Mary King writes of the teeming backstreets of Lagos:

> I have a vivid recollection of going alone to a Nigerian party one

night in the old town. To reach my host's home, I had to leave the car and walk through the market, past the stalls lit by tiny oil lamps, with the woman calling friendly greetings. I felt welcome and wondered if I could have felt so safe in the streets of London or New York.   (Ms., p. 13)

It was not only in Nigeria that women journeyed without fear. Margery Perham writes,

I travelled much in Africa between the wars, trekking widely, sometimes on horse, sometimes on foot or Model T lorry, far away from centres and main roads. And yet I never saw any overt signs of discontent or antagonism; everywhere I met friendliness and eager curiosity. Colonial officers often accompanied me, but they never hesitated for a moment to let me trek and camp alone.   (1961, p. 34)

The question of European women's 'sexual fear' appears to arise in special circumstances of unequal power structures at times of particular political pressure, when the dominant group perceives itself threatened and vulnerable, as in the cases analysed by Inglis on Papua New Guinea (1974) and Ballhatchet on India (1980). In India, of course, the Mutiny of 1857 provided a powerful and enduring reference for the imagery of violence against European women and children by the subordinated group.

In situations of imperial domination (as well as of military occupation), men of the ruling group often assume the privilege of sexual relations with women of the subordinate group, while jealously placing their own women under the 'protection' of a prohibited boundary. The concept of 'protection of women' conceals further dimensions: not only the ruling group maintaining control over the subordinate society, but also reinforcing control over its own women. In situations of political dominance, women's sexuality becomes a symbol for the body of the ruling group; a woman sexually penetrated by an outsider (even at her own invitation, in which case she is ostracised) represents the violation of that group's integrity. At specific junctures, violence against its women becomes a potent symbol of political revenge against the ruling group. Here again the question of women's 'sexual fear' (real enough in certain situations) need not be blamed on the lasciviousness of the men in the colonised situation nor on women's peculiar fastidiousness or fantasies, but interpreted within the context of the political tensions and ideological structures of imperial power.

In Nigeria, the nationalist movement was waged at a different level and with a negotiated response. Compared to other regions of Africa where white settlers pressed for their own economic and political interests and often maintained a rigid colour bar, race relations in Nigeria appear to have been relatively congenial. As the administrative officer John Smith writes, 'The colonial situation is not, of course, conducive to easy social relationships between master and subject, and independence makes an enormous psychological difference' (1968, p. 62); but he goes on to tell of the trust and confidence which had been built up over the years in Northern Nigeria. Even that severe Australian critic of British administration, W. R. Crocker, adds in a footnote, 'An interesting and admirable feature of British imperialism in West Africa is that there is virtually no race prejudice of the kind that prevails in Asia' (1936, p. 207).

Educated Nigerians during certain stages of colonial rule, however, may well have expressed an opposing view when their hopes for appropriate jobs and promotions were not met by the British bureaucracy. When the nationalist movement for self-government became active after the Second World War, the feeling against European racial exclusiveness came to a head in Lagos in the 'Bristol Hotel Incident' in February, 1947 (Coleman, 1958, pp. 292–3; Flint, 1983). A senior Colonial Office official, British-born and black, was refused accommodation in this privately-owned hotel, on grounds of race, even though the government had reserved a room. As an immediate result of the scandal, opposition to racialist practice became a common focus for the nationalist campaign. Competing nationalist groups formed a united front. In response to the Nigerian outcry as well as Colonial Office indignation, Governor Richards (later Lord Milverton) was forced to concede to a deputation of influential Nigerians that government policy now opposed racial discrimination in all its forms and that measures would be introduced to prohibit discrimination in all public institutions (including hospitals, cinemas and bars) and in government residential areas. This decisive victory for the nationalists marked the beginning of a long series of government concessions.

Clubs all over the country, however, were still considered

private. A Nigerian serving at that time in the Colonial Legal Service as Crown Counsel, later becoming Chief Justice of Nigeria, writes, 'Another thorny point was the fact that we were not allowed to join the Ikoyi Club which was then still regarded as a European club and a bastion of expatriate superiority' (Fatayi-Williams, 1983, p. 30). This came to an end in 1953 when the succeeding Governor-General, Sir John Macpherson, ordered that European clubs should open their membership to Nigerians or risk being closed.

In his analysis of racial discrimination in West Africa, Flint shows that during the war years both Governors, Burns of the Gold Coast and Bourdillon of Nigeria, worked to break the white monopoly not only in the administrative service, but also in the executive councils. After the war when the Colonial Office attempted to form inter-racial clubs in the colonies to counter 'the apparent contradiction between our political liberalism and our social exclusiveness', Bourdillon criticised the model of the all-male club by saying that 'in Nigeria the women are much more important than the men. They are far more go-ahead and anxious to improve relations. My wife has got a first class club going here', with 120 members equally European and African (quoted in Flint, 1983, p. 83). In this case, women were actively taking the lead in creating better understanding between the races. But Bourdillon was followed in 1943 by Richards, whose political position was far less liberal and who soon dissipated the good relations with Nigerians in Lagos that the Bourdillons had fostered. His reactionary leadership proved disastrous when he tried to force through an unpopular constitution, and it was only when Macpherson arrived as replacement (soon after the Bristol Hotel episode) that the momentum of colonial reform was restored. By the time of the 1954 constitution, the nationalist struggle with Britain came to an end as Nigerian leaders became pre-occupied with the rapid advance towards Independence.

Just before Independence, a New Zealand psychologist concluded his inquiry on race relations in Nigeria with the view that in acceding to the general wish for political change, 'the British have fostered a climate of good will towards Europeans which has few parallels in Africa' (Rogers, 1959, p. 63). The evidence from Nigeria (and for Malaya, see Brownfoot, 1984) suggests that – far from widening the distance between the two races – European women played a considerable part, through their professional and volunteer work and in their daily encounters, in helping to build a reservoir of mutual understanding.

THE DEMAND FOR 'WOMEN'S WORK'

In the early years, officers of the Colonial Service in Nigeria carried out their work in situations of hardship and considerable risk to health and life. Nurses, carrying out 'women's work', were tentatively accepted and their professional skills proved beneficial in saving European men's lives. After the First World War, official attention turned to problems of African health and education. Nursing sisters and a few women doctors were recruited to work in the new 'Native' hospitals and to set up training courses for African nurses, male as well as female. While their letters reveal typical European racial attitudes of the time, they also show awareness of mistaken communication and their own lack of cultural understanding. The work these women carried out – often in difficult circumstances, including surgical operations by 'hurricane lamp' – clearly benefited ordinary people, particularly women and children. Few Nigerians today would fail to appreciate the value of such medical work, though they might criticise it on grounds of 'too little and too late'.

After the Second World War, with the rapid expansion of health and medical services supported by Colonial Development and Welfare funds, new opportunities arose for European nurses. As health visitors, they helped to set up and maintain networks of urban and rural clinics (now considered 'primary health care') with their supervision, in some cases travelling many miles by horseback. As sister tutors in specialised areas, they were committed to better training for nurses in the classroom and in practical work. As matrons, many of them helped to organise hospitals to higher standards, despite such difficulties as no electricity in the station and goats wandering through the operating theatre. They brought more egalitarian attitudes. Some now worked under Nigerian doctors with Nigerian nursing colleagues. Many served for a decade or more, at least one for more than a quarter century.

In education, the few women recruited as 'Lady Superintendent of Education' or 'Mistress' during the interwar years were assigned the special task of educating girls and women. Since their work again supplemented that of missionaries, they were required mainly in the Muslim regions of the North. As the melancholy account of Sylvia Leith-Ross reveals, they received little support. The case of the outspoken Miss Booker in Sokoto shows the teacher dedicated to 'her girls', but ethnocentric in attempting to impose alien cultural values. Her efforts to improve the conditions of Muslim women met with obstruction by the administration, who rightly sensed the difficulties that could arise if such indigenous customs as child marriage were directly challenged.

Only in the Southern Provinces where Gladys Plummer began her touring to encourage girls' education and to set up 'non-formal' classes for women, did the work prosper. This experience placed her in a position after the Second World War, now as the Deputy Director of Education, to launch an 'all-out attack' on women's education. As related in Chapter 5, this resulted in a significant decade for establishing the foundations of education for girls and women in Northern Nigeria and in improving and expanding it in the Western and Eastern Regions. Although today colonial education is often criticised for its cultural imperialism, these women were acutely aware of this problem in their attempts to provide a sound academic education relevant to the Nigerian environment. They did not, however, question the gender roles transmitted through the curriculum of domestic science for girls and agriculture for boys in a country where much of the food production is carried out by women. Many of these women education officers worked for as long as ten years; a few served for over twenty. Their retrospective reports show their drive and commitment, as well as self-criticism of faults and shortcomings. Personal ties meant a great deal; many kept in touch with pupils and Nigerian friends. Their achievements can be more clearly seen a generation later with the outstanding success of so many Nigerian women who were their pupils. These links were marked, in several cases, by the gratitude and generosity of students in inviting their founding principals back for twenty-fifth year celebrations.

WOMEN TAKING ON 'MEN'S WORK'

Besides the work traditionally considered appropriate for them, women moved into positions previously reserved for men. This began during the Second World War when qualified wives took on jobs in administration formerly carried out by DOs and ADOs. When the war was over, many of these women continued to assist their husbands' work in various ways, although no longer in any official capacity. A decade later, as the recruitment for men on a permanent basis was coming to an end, single women were engaged on temporary contracts for junior administrative work. In the implicit policy of the Colonial Service, women in their professional capacities were clearly seen as secondary, to be deployed when required as a reserve labour force. These women administrators proved successful in their jobs, as shown by the renewal of their contracts; some of them served beyond Independence and were promoted to higher grades.

For many male officers, administrative work in the Secretariats in any case represented 'that half-sexed desk-bound life' (White, 1966, p. 248). 'Men's work' was out in the districts in the midst of African life, 'among real people' (Smith, 1968, p. 106), touring the villages to settle disputes and collect taxes, building roads and bridges, charting agricultural development, and keeping a sceptical watch on native administration. No woman could take on such strenuous touring and exertion in physical terms, nor would she be accepted in any commanding official position by African men; these limitations that women were purported to have were strongly stated by the Colonial Office during the interwar years, affirmed by most women as well as men. Yet many women carried out extensive touring: from the earliest times accompanying their husbands, as shown by the intrepid Constance Larymore, and later in their professional duties as health visitors, social welfare and education officers.

In the Colonial Office minutes from the interwar years defending itself against the phalanx of women's organisations urging the removal of the ban on women's employment, the recurring argument was that African and Asian men would not accept European women in superior official positions. This argument again proved tenuous. Matrons and nursing sisters were often in charge of hospitals with male nurses and attendants under them. Women education officers inspected schools, taught in men's training colleges, took charge of literacy programmes. Women in junior administrative posts held places of superiority over some Nigerian male administrators and over male clerks and messengers. The salient examples of women in executive roles were Pat Walters and Jeanne Keene (née Batchelor), both appointed as Principals of Rural Education Colleges with male Nigerian staffs. The conclusion must be drawn that African men were amenable to the authority of professional European women who proved their worth; it was European men, it would seem, who had some difficulty on this score.

Not many women at that time had the qualifications or the aspirations to take on the work reserved for men in the Colonial Service, but such positions were blocked to the few who might have made significant contributions in their own way. Margery Perham has been referred to by an anonymous DO as 'someone who should have been a Colonial Governor' (quoted in Kirk-Greene, 1982, p. 131); clearly she had physical courage, an undaunted spirit, political astuteness and authority, a formidable understanding of colonial administration. It is interesting to speculate on the role of a woman as colonial governor and to consider the effects this might have had, particularly for the women, in a country such as Nigeria.

THE POST-WAR TRANSFORMATION

In Chapter 8 I examined the domestication of colonial life which came about after medical advances made it possible for children to be with their parents in Nigeria and thus for more wives to stay with their husbands for the complete length of their tours. This marked a distinct change from the pre-war period. But, on a much deeper plane, something akin to 'feminisation' occurred within the official colonial world-view itself. The imperial vision at the turn of the century, which had seen Nigeria as 'the wilds' where a superior breed of men (defined in gender terms as representing the height of 'masculinity') took control in order to direct its progress to a more advanced 'civilised' state, now gave way to a post-war concept of a nation ready for 'development', social welfare, and – eventually – self-government and Independence. The original imperial model involving conquest, power, authority, hierarchy and control was superseded by a new one revealed in the semantic field of cooperation, 'partners for progress' and the 'transfer of power' (Jeffries, 1949). In symbolic terms, men's duties in 'the wilds' had turned into tame administration at desks, the 'masculine' virtues into a 'de-sexed' existence (even 'feminine' in the overtones of caring in social welfare).

From the period immediately before and during the war, when the Bourdillons in Government House set an example of more egalitarian racial and social relations, to 1960 when Princess Alexandra presided over Independence celebrations, the pace of political and social change accelerated – with Nigerians taking a progressively greater part in shaping the destiny of the new nation. This was the time when European women came into their own, as single women and wives, in both professional and voluntary work; the preceding chapters have documented their commitment and their contributions.

While these women were critical of specific aspects of colonial rule, they did not, it is true, shape any strong critique of imperialism. Most of them, however, arrived at the time when Nigerian Independence was forecast and their main efforts went towards providing the better health care and education demanded by Nigerians, the 'development and welfare' that at its last stages represents the enlightened side of empire.

The well-known saying, that 'the women lost us the Empire' might then be seen in a more positive way than its conventional use: that the women contributed to the loss of the Empire by helping to gain the Commonwealth. The 'masculine' ethos of the imperial era – characterised by hierarchy, authority, control and paternalism – had to be replaced by what might be seen as more 'feminine' modes required for 'the family of nations' – sympathetic understanding, egalitarian rather than authoritarian relations, diplomacy and flexibility. In relation to the European women who took part, the study of colonial Nigeria thus reveals 'another meaning', a meaning and a history that have been hidden.

Notes

1 WOMEN IN 'A MAN'S COUNTRY'

1. Reported in 'Sayings of the Week', *Observer*, 24 February 1985. The context is not revealed, unfortunately, nor Sir David's tone of voice.
2. This follows the lead of feminist historians who for more than a decade have been discovering women's documents and, in their analyses, bringing forth new conceptual frameworks. On colonial women, see Brownfoot (1984), Gartrell (1984), Kirkwood (1984).
3. British administration in Nigeria began in a piecemeal fashion, but it is convenient to set the date as 1 January 1900, when the word 'Nigeria' first came into official use to name the new Protectorates of Southern and Northern Nigeria. Before that date, the colony of Lagos had an established administrative service, including Africans, and both the Niger Coast Protectorate at Calabar and the Royal Niger Company in its stations on the river had rudimentary forms of administration. Only in 1914, with the amalgamation of the two protectorates under Sir Frederick Lugard, did the present form of Nigeria come into being. Through a series of constitutional changes after the Second World War, three regions – Western, Eastern and Northern – emerged, and by the time of Independence in 1960 the foreign administration had been transformed into a federal, parliamentary government with Nigerian Ministers and 'Nigerianised' public services. Nicholson (1969) gives a provocative and controversial analysis of British administration in Nigeria; Kirk-Greene (1965) provides a valuable introduction with his collection of the main administrative documents. The best overall history of Nigeria is still the very readable account by Crowder (1978, 1st edn, 1962) while Hodgkin's introduction to his historical anthology of pre-colonial Nigeria (1975; 1st edn, 1960) remains an inspiring classic.
4. Official statistics in Northern Nigeria according to Leith-Ross (1983, p. 37). In Lagos, including the town and adjacent islands, the annual death rate of Europeans in 1899 was 71.12 per thousand; in 1900, 87.64 per thousand (Joyce, 1971, p. 225).
5. These letters are being edited for publication by Alan Bishop, who kindly gave me access to those relevant to my research.
6. Although Margery Perham was an eminent figure in relation to the Colonial Service in Nigeria, she was neither an officer nor a wife and thus does not belong within the group selected for this study. Her journals of her travels in Nigeria and other writings provide important insights, of course, not only on the wider questions of colonial rule but on the position of European women.
7. In her review of Joan Alexander's *Voices and Echoes* (1983), Deborah Birkett states that the visibility of Alexander's colonial women was achieved at a price: 'the invisibility of the largest, most oppressed, and constantly least visible group in colonial history – the Africans and Asians whose homes were the colonised lands . . .' (1983, p. 2). Since my study risks similar criticism,

it may be necessary to point out that Nigerian history by Nigerians has flourished during the last three decades and gives a full view of the colonial period from Nigerian perspectives. While Nigerian women's history has come later, a beginning has been made in this field (for example, Awe, 1977; Mba, 1982; Okonjo, 1976). In social anthropology, Nigerian women have been studied since early times (for example, Bowen, 1954; Green, 1964 [1947]; Leith-Ross, 1965 [1939]; Talbot, 1968 [1st edn, 1915]).

8. Lugard defines this: 'The cardinal principle upon which the administration of N. Nigeria was based was what has been commonly called Indirect Rule, viz. rule through the Native Chiefs, who are regarded as an integral part of the machinery of Government, with well-defined powers and functions recognised by Government and by law, and not dependent on the caprice of an Executive officer' (1970, p. 296; quoted in Kirk-Greene, 1982, p. 124).

9. Although Erving Goffman's explorative and suggestive ideas on 'total institutions' (1968, pp. 13–116) do not take gender differences into account, they provide insights which are applicable to the way an institution structures gender relations.

10. Leonore Davidoff (1973) gives a perceptive sociological analysis of the patterns of etiquette used to confer and consolidate status by the upper-middle class in Victorian and Edwardian Britain. These provide the basis for the hierarchical social processes elaborated in 'imperial culture'.

11. The begrudging attitude of the Colonial service to wives in Nigeria contrasts sharply with that of missionary organisations who, from the beginning of their work in the mid-nineteenth century, sent both single women missionaries and wives to work alongside their husbands. They established mission stations and often continued their efforts for many years in one place with infrequent home leave (as, for example, the seventeen years David and Anna Hinderer spent in Ibadan from 1853). Pregnant wives often stayed for their confinements and kept their children with them; because of the high infant mortality, they were strongly criticised by colonial officials. J. F. A. Ajayi (1965) and Ayandele (1966) provide comprehensive histories of Christian missions and their work in Nigeria. A more popular version of pioneer missionaries, conventional in its view of imperialism as altruistic, is Ellen Thorp's study (1956).

2   IMPERIAL REPRESENTATIONS OF GENDER

1. In this study I am following the distinction established by Ann Oakley (1972) between 'sex' as the biological categories of male and female and 'gender' as the socially constructed categories of masculine and feminine.

2. Sources include Bolt (1971), Lorimer (1978), Stepan (1982) and Stocking (1982).

3. The term 'complementary' has been used with various meanings in anthropology. In itself, 'complementary' applies to parts forming a complete whole, with no designation of the relations between parts, whether equal or hierarchical, static or dynamic. The Victorian view of the complementary roles of men and women clearly posits hierarchical relations of dominance

and subordinance. The authors in the collection edited by Etienne and Leacock (1980) use the term to imply equality between women and men (with different roles) in pre-class societies. Gregory Bateson in *Naven* (1958 [1936]) uses 'complementary' as a category for the dynamic processes of group interaction within a society, in the case of the Iatmul one group (male) showing assertion or exhibitionism and the other group (female) responding with submission or audience appreciation, and so on.

4. It is beyond the scope of this study to trace how the model of the 'angel in the house' was constituted as social reality for women in the upper classes during the Victorian and Edwardian periods. Collections edited by Vicinus (1973, 1977), Hartman and Banner (1974), Delamont and Duffin (1978), and Newton, Ryan, and Walkowitz (1983) provide insights on the various constraints set during this period by science, medical concepts, education and law. Rosenberg (1975–6, 1982) and Alaya (1977) review scientific writings on the 'nature' of women. Dyhouse (1976, 1981) and Purvis (1981) analyse the social forces directing the development of girls' education. The studies of schooling by Okely (1978) and Kirkwood (1984 [a]) show how the patterns of middle-class girls' education have persisted in Britain and been reproduced in the colonies.

5. Brian Harrison cogently analyses the relation of imperialism and the anti-suffrage movement:

> Nowhere was the forming of *ad hoc* clubs more common than in early twentieth-century imperialist circles: Milner's kindergarten seems itself to have constituted one big club, four of whose eleven members were fellows of All Souls and all but two of whom had been educated at New College. A large section of the anti-suffrage leadership flourished in this milieu. (1978, p. 104)

6. The term 'gone native' appears in colonial usage in several different ways: (a) a shorthand expression for sexual relations with an African woman; (b) as in Hastings' novel, a European who lives among Africans, takes their point of view and defends their interests; (c) a European who does not conform and is therefore excluded from the colonial group and considered to belong to 'the other'.

7. For sources on the code of gentlemanly behaviour in Victorian poetry and novels, see Gilmour (1981), Letwin (1982) and Mason (1982) and on its dramatisation in popular boys' fiction, Howarth (1973) and Quigley (1982).

8. Sources include Papanek (1973, 1979), Callan (1975), Kanter (1977), Finch (1983) and Callan and Ardener (eds; 1984).

9. While Emily Bradley shows genuine openness for friendship with individual Africans, she is unashamedly ethnocentric in her lack of recognition of African cultures and history. Her book is full of generalisations presented as self-evident truths and supported by anecdotes, as for example, her offensive dismissal of the Muslim religion (1950, p. 209).

10. In her journal, Margery Perham comments that her experience in Northern Nigeria confirmed the warning of critical southern officers that their northern colleagues were sometimes more Islamic in official matters than the Africans themselves (1983, p. 56). When she visited the Emir of Katsina, he greeted her with warmth breaking through the conventional dignity of his

office. She notes: 'Strange how these Muslim potentates accept my sex and so belie the fears of the British political officers' (p. 106).

11. Sources include Van Allen (1972), Ifeka-Moller (1975), Mba (1982), Agbasiere (1985).

3 POWER AND RANK MADE VISIBLE

1. To anthropologists this needs no identification; for others, it refers to the title of the anthropological classic on the Indian caste system by Louis Dumont (1980, 1st edition in French, 1966).

4 WOMEN IN HEALTH CARE

1. Sir George Taubman-Goldie was called the 'founder of Nigeria' by his first biographer, Dorothy Wellesley, Duchess of Wellington (Flint, 1960, p. vii). In 1879 he brought together all the major companies trading on the Niger in order to meet the competition from the French and the Germans; this became the Royal Niger Company which held treaties with numerous local rulers and provided the basis for Britain's claims to the lands later proclaimed as the Protectorates of Northern and Southern Nigeria.

2. In the development of modern medical services in Nigeria, it should be emphasised that it was the Christian missionaries who led the way in the building of hospitals for indigenous people, the opening of rural clinics, the spread of maternity and child welfare services, and the training of Nigerian nurses and dispensary attendants (Schram, 1971). Missionary doctors (women as well as men) and nurses arrived sooner in Nigeria and worked for lower pay and poorer service conditions than did their counterparts with the Colonial Service. The Voluntary Agencies (as they became known) continued to provide an important component of medical care to the time of Independence and beyond.

3. As well as references cited in the text, this chapter draws on the extensive records of the Overseas Nursing Association deposited in Rhodes House and from the reports that nurses presented to the ODRP on 'Medicine and Public Health in Africa during the Period of Decolonisation'.

4. Further clues might be found in the biography of Sir William MacGregor (Joyce, 1971), one of the few colonial governors to rise from the working class and an unusually progressive one for his time. When he came to Lagos, he had a distinguished record as a doctor in the Colonial Medical Service and a strong interest in all aspects of public health. He supported the views, for example, of Dr. Ronald Ross on malaria prevention and launched a forceful anti-malaria campaign in Lagos. He supplied quinine not only to officials but to Lagos women and children through the Lagos Ladies League, a group of African and European women volunteers who have been called the first health visitors in Nigeria (Schram, 1971, p. 120). MacGregor also stood out far in advance of his time for his strong support of Africans. He objected

strongly when the West African Medical Service was reorganised in 1902 with separate service conditions for African doctors on a lower pay scale and with a junior status preventing them from seniority over even the most newly-trained Europeans (p. 130). It is perhaps not surprising that such a crusading leader would find European 'lady' nurses who led an active social life less than dedicated to their work, as well as providing a diversion to the concentration to his officers.

5. Defending this difference in pay, Dr. Lowe-Jellicoe writes:

> However qualified in England, the African doctor went HOME to his wife or wives and family. The white doctor had to leave his wife and family. White wives were not expected to stay more than 4 months in each tour and children were not permitted. The black doctors lived in a country where they were immune or partially immune to local disease whereas the white doctor was not, and in these days smallpox vaccine was the only immunisation available . . . Black doctors could do private practice – not so white Civil Servants.   (letter, 13 September 1986)

5   WOMEN EDUCATION OFFICERS

1. In the long historical development of Nigerian education along Western lines, these government women education officers clearly played only a brief part. When Christian missions began their work in 1841, schools were opened as part of the evangelical enterprise to spread Christianity and 'civilisation'; soon African catechist-teachers were helping this effort. While in Southern Nigeria the missions carried out the main educational work, with the benefit of government grants-in-aid for schools meeting required standards, in Northern Nigeria at the time of the conquest Lugard promised Muslim rulers that their religion would not be interfered with; thus Christian missions were to be restricted to the 'pagan' or non-Muslim areas. Education along Western lines had to be established by government.

2. This section makes use of the contributions to the ODRP on 'The Development of Education in Pre-independent Africa' from education officers who served in Northern Nigeria. Since this project did not include Eastern and Western Nigeria, I undertook myself to collect reports from women education officers who had worked in those areas.

3. This type of toilet known as the 'thunder-box' or the 'BG' (initials of the Hausa words *bayan gida*, meaning 'behind the house') consisted of a wooden seat in a frame above a large bucket of sand, which was removed by a night watchman through a hole in the side of the house or out-house behind the bucket.

6   WOMEN AS COLONIAL ADMINISTRATORS

1. For this section, Kenneth Robinson was most helpful in providing sources of files in the Public Records Office on the employment of women in the

Colonial Office and in loaning me a copy of his unpublished Callander Lectures given in 1979 at Aberdeen University on 'The Colonial Office in the Thirties: Headquarters of Colonialism'. He also made useful comments on a draft version.

2. The main documentation for this chapter comes from the ODRP on 'The Role of Women Administrative Officers in Colonial Africa'.

3. Ortner and Whitehead (1981) give an interesting analysis of the social organisation of prestige in relation to gender.

4. A Nigerian view of Lagos during this time is found in Cyprian Ekwenski's *People of the City* (1954).

5. Janet Longden's perception of women being more intellectually able than the average male ADO might be contested, but John Smith writes of the group recruited in 1950, the last year of large-scale intake by the CO into West Africa: 'The thirty of us who assembled at Oxford destined for Northern Nigeria were all ex-servicemen but not all ex-officers, and by no means all graduates' (1968, p. 4).

6. *Sabon gari* is the Hausa term for 'new town'. In Kaduna this refers to the area where those from Southern Nigeria lived – technicians, clerks and traders. This town grew in its own crowded way and showed the vibrant activity of the cities of the coast.

7 PART-TIME WIVES: BEFORE 1940

1. Here Constance Larymore uses typical imagery of the time related to Africa (for example, H. M. Stanley's book of 1890, *In Darkest Africa*), with its ambiguous connotations of black-skinned peoples, a 'dark' continent in terms of being unexplored by Europeans and therefore unknown, and 'dark' suggesting a note of the sinister and evil.

2. With her French sister-in-law, Genevieve Ruxton, she assembled *Practical West African Cookery*, published locally and praised for its emphasis on local foods. Her research among Igbo women after the 'women's war' of 1929 was published in *African Women* (1939); she also wrote a more intimate account of her fieldwork in *African Conversation Piece* (1956) and compiled her memoirs, *Stepping Stones* (edited by Michael Crowder and published posthumously in 1983), sources with sharp observations on both Europeans and Africans.

3. *Gida* is Hausa for house. *Dan Hausa* means son of a Hausaman, referring to Hanns Vischer's fluency in Hausa and knowledge of their customs. John Smith (1968, p. 8) writes of this house, 'It stands today, an ancient monument, and a memorial to the first British officers in Kano.'

4. *Doki* means 'horse', thus *doki*-boy designating the servant in charge of the horses and stables.

5. *Bayan gida* in Hausa means literally 'behind the house'. (See ch. 5 n. 3 above.)

8 THE DOMESTICATION OF COLONIAL LIFE: AFTER 1940

1. An account of the correspondence between this editor, Abubakar Imam, and Lord Lugard on this topic and other problems of Northern Nigeria in 1943 was published in the *New Nigerian* special supplement, 17 January 1979.

9 IDENTITY AND COMMITMENT

1. Janice N. Brownfoot (1984, p. 200) provides an interesting analysis of the voluntary work of European women in Malaya with the suggestion that rather than impeding Malayan nationalism, as is generally considered, these women helped to advance it.

Bibliography

This study draws on interviews, unpublished documents and published works. In addition to the interviews of colonial officers conducted by the Oxford Development Records Project (ODRP) and deposited in Rhodes House, I undertook a number of formal and informal interviews. Those relevant to its work and completed before its closure were transcribed by the ODRP and placed in Rhodes House (listed below); the remaining tapes have also been offered for its collection. Some of those interviewed requested that the session not be recorded; others wished to remain anonymous. In relation to his BBC programmes and his book, *Tales from the Dark Continent*, Charles Allen carried out interviews with colonial officers and wives in Nigeria; these tapes and transcripts were deposited and made available at the Imperial War Museum (IWM).

Unpublished documents include government documents in the Public Records Office (PRO) and in Rhodes House (RH), as well as numerous private papers and reports in Rhodes House. The collections of the ODRP have been specially valuable, particularly its projects on 'The Development of Education in Pre-independent Africa', 'Medicine and Public Health in Africa during the period of decolonization' and 'The Role of Women Administrative Officers in Colonial Africa'. Since its education project included only Northern Nigeria, the Director, A. H. M. Kirk-Greene, generously suggested that I undertake the collection of reports from women education officers in Western and Eastern Nigeria under its auspices; this was carried out from June to December 1983 and deposited with the main collection in Rhodes House.

UNPUBLISHED DOCUMENTS

Abraham, Dr. Kathleen (née Burn): Medical Officer, Northern Nigeria; wife of Education Officer, 1957–64. RH MSS. Afr. s. 1755 (31).

Agbasiere, Mary Joseph Thérèse (1985), 'The Image of Womanhood in Igbo Traditional Society', unpublished D. Phil thesis, University of Oxford.

Akinyemi, Barbara: Health Visitor – Lagos, Kano, Katsina and Makurdi, 1947–51. RH MSS. Afr. s. 1872 (1).

Alexander, Lady, Dr. Constance (née Geary): Chief Woman Education Officer, Northern Nigeria, 1948–52; Assistant Director of Education (Women), 1952–7. RH MSS. Afr. s. 1755 (33).

Allen, A. R., 'Conferring Benefits on the Land – The Colonial Education Service in Northern Nigeria 1945–60'.

Allen, Joan (née Parkes): Travelling Librarian, Nigeria Regional Librarian, Northern Nigeria; wife of Education Officer; 1949–77. Interview with H. Callaway, July 1983. RH MSS. Afr. s. 1851.

Allison, Philip: Officer, Nigerian Forest Department 1931–60. Interview BBC. IWM Acc. no. 4703/04.

Atkinson, M. C., 'The Bush out of my Soul: Two Decades in Western Nigeria (1939–59)', RH MSS. Afr. s. 1836.

Beswick, Barbara (née Beeston): Woman Education Officer, Kano and Maiduguri, 1949–54. RH MSS. Afr. s. 1755 (38).

Bourdillon, Joy: Wife of Harry Bourdillon, Assistant District Officer, Northern Nigeria, 1936–43 and Palestine; Manager, Colonial Service Club, Oxford, 1950–6. Interview with H. Callaway, November 1983. RH MSS. Afr. s. 1853.

Bourdillon, Lady Violet: wife of Governor of Nigeria, 1935–43. Interview by Andrew Wright, 1972–3. RH Brit. Emp. s. 475[a].

——, Interview, BBC. IWM Acc. no. 4706/03[b].

Bozman, Ursula M.: Provincial Woman Education Officer, Bornu, 1950–9; Assistant Lecturer, Teacher Training College, Bornu, 1959–60. RH MSS. Afr. s. 1755 (40).

Bridges, D., 'Black and White Notes. Life in Nigeria by the Wife of a Colonial Officer, 1927–49', RH MSS. Afr. s. 1634.

Burness, Helen Margaret: Establishment Officer, Lagos, 1949–50; Principal, Provincial Girls' School, Birnin Kebbi, 1950–3; Provincial Woman Education Officer, Katsina and Ilorin Provinces, 1953–6; Woman Education Officer, later Senior Woman Education Officer, Northern Nigeria, 1956–63. RH MSS. Afr. s. 1755 (79*).

Chamberlain, Margaret (née Buckerfield): Provincial Woman Education Officer, Kabba and Ilorin Provinces, 1950–2; Principal, Women's Training Centre, Kabba, 1952–7; Inspector of Education (Women), 1957–9; Assistant Director of Education (Women), Uganda, 1959–62). RH MSS. Afr. s. 1755 (43).

Clark, Evelyn (née Hyde): Principal, Women's Training Centre, Sokoto, 1949–57; Education Officer, Kano, 1958; Senior Education Tutor, Sacred Heart Training College, Kaduna, 1959–63; Senior Education Tutor, Women's Training Centre, Kano, 1963–6. RH MSS. Afr. s. 1755 (44).

Clayton, Aileen (née Morris), MBE: Woman Assistant Secretary, Government of Northern Nigeria, Kaduna, and Federal Government, Lagos, 1953–9; Senior Assistant Secretary, Lagos, 1960. RH MSS. Afr. s. 1799 (4).

Congleton, Florence Iris: Woman Education Officer, Women's Training Centre, Sokoto, 1952–3; Provincial Girls' School, Kontagora, 1953–6; Queen Elizabeth School, Ilorin, 1956–7; Women's Training Centre, Kabba, 1957–8. RH MSS. Afr. s. 1755 (46).

Cooper, Annie (née McGregor): Woman Education Officer, Girls' Training Centre, Kano and Sokoto, 1948–52; Principal, Women's Training Centre, Maiduguri, 1952–7. RH MSS. Afr. s. 1755 (47).

Corrie, Morag: Woman Assistant Secretary, Government of Northern Nigeria, Kaduna, 1956–7; Assistant District Officer, Ilorin, 1958–9. RH MSS. Afr. s. 1799 (6).

Cragg, Violet, 'Violet in Nigeria, by herself and Margaret Kerrich', typescript copies of letters from Nigeria, 1924–30, as the wife of Major William G. Cragg, Political Officer, Northern Nigeria. RH MSS. Afr. s. 1588.

Daniels, Margery (née Bell): Woman Assistant Secretary, Federal Government of Nigeria, Lagos, 1954–6. RH MSS. Afr. s. 1799 (8).

Davies, Carol (née Allen): Woman Assistant Secretary, Government of Northern Nigeria, Kaduna, 1957–8. RH MSS. Afr. s. 1799 (9).

Davies, Henrietta (née Roy): Provincial Woman Education Officer, Adamawa

Province, 1953–7; Acting Inspector of Education (Women), 1957. RH MSS. Afr. s. 1755 (50).

Davies, Marjorie (née Wilkinson): Woman Assistant Secretary, Government of Northern Nigeria, Kaduna, 1956–9. RH MSS. Afr. s. 1799 (10).

Davies, Mary, 'Reminiscences of a Police Officer's Wife, 1948–1962', RH MSS. Afr. s. 1784 (8).

Dinnick-Parr, Joyce 'Catherine': Woman Education Officer, Northern Nigeria 1947–52; Organiser, Domestic Science 1953–8; Chief Woman Education Officer, 1959–63. Interview, BBC. IWM Acc. 004710/03.

Evans, Jean (née Jacoby): Teacher, Boys' Secondary School, Ibadan, 1951–4; Principal, Provincial Girls' School, Yola, 1955–8. RH MSS. Afr. s. 1755 (52).

Everett, Florence Joan (née Way): Woman Education Officer, Girls' Training Centre, Sokoto, 1949–50. RH MSS. Afr. s. 1755 (54).

Fottrell, Zelma (née Wood): Woman Assistant Secretary, Government of Northern Nigeria, Kaduna, 1957–61. RH MSS. Afr. s. 1799 (12).

Goldsworthy, Mary (née Kinton): Woman Education Officer, Women's Training Centre, Kano, 1949–51; Middle School, Bauchi, 1951–3; Provincial Girls' School, Maiduguri, 1953; Women's Training Centre, Kabba, 1955–6. RH MSS. Afr. s. 1755 (55).

Gwilliam, Freda: Assistant Adviser, later Deputy Adviser to Education, Colonial Office, 1947–67. Interview with H. Callaway, February 1984. RH MSS. Afr. s. 1901.

Hargreave, Mary: Headmistress, Government Provincial School, The Gambia, 1945–9; Woman Education Officer, Women's Training Centre, Sokoto, 1950–1; Men's Elementary Training Centre, Bauchi, 1952–4; Women's Training Centre, Kano, 1955–8; Principal, Provincial Girls' School, Kontagora, 1959–60. RH MSS. Afr. s. 1755 (56).

Harwood, Margaret (née Gentle), CBE: Assistant History Mistress, Achimota, Gold Coast, 1951–4; Senior English Mistress, Queen's School, Ede, Western Nigeria, 1954–6; Principal, Queen's College, Lagos, 1956–63; Assistant, later Adviser on Secondary Education, Federal Government of Nigeria, 1963–8; Senior Education Officer, Government College, Sokoto, 1971–7; Government College, Kaduna, 1977–9. RH MSS. Afr. s. 1755 (57).

Hepplestone, Marian: Woman Education Officer, Calabar, Owerri, Onitsha, 1951–5; Provincial Education Officer, Okoja, 1956; Examinations Officer, Enugu, 1957; Chief Woman Education Officer, Eastern Nigeria, 1957; Chief Inspector, Teacher Training, 1958–61. RH MSS. Afr. s. 1755 (79*).

Holmes, Muriel: Nursing Sister, later Matron, Northern Nigeria, 1955–63; Assistant Matron, Queen Elizabeth Hospital, Eastern Nigeria, 1963–5. RH MSS. Afr. s. 1872 (80).

Hooley, Marion: Midwife Teacher, Maternity Hospital, Lagos, 1951–8, 1960–2. RH MSS. Afr. s. 1872 (81).

James, Phillis: Nursing Sister, later Matron, Northern Nigeria, 1952–61. RH MSS. Afr. s. 1872 (88).

Jenkins, Carolyn: Woman Assistant Secretary, Government of Northern Nigeria, Kaduna, 1957–60. RH MSS. Afr. s. 1799 (17).

Keene, Jeanne (née Batchelor): Rural Education Officer, Bauchi, 1956–9; Principal, Rural Education College, Minna, 1959–64. RH MSS. Afr. s. 1755 (62).

King, Mary (née Beaton): Woman Assistant Secretary, Federal Government of Nigeria, Lagos, 1953–6. RH MSS. Afr. s. 1799 (19).

Kirby, H. M., 'Reminiscences of the wife of a Director of Agriculture, A. H. Kirby, Nigeria, 1912–14, 1916–18; Tanganyika, 1921–9', RH MSS. Afr. r. 44.

Leak, Gladys M., Letters home of the wife of Oswald Leak, Public Works Department officer in the Sudan, 1924–6, and in Nigeria, 1928–44. RH MSS. Afr. s. 416.

Longden, Janet (née Lloyd): Woman Assistant Secretary, Government of Northern Nigeria, Kaduna, 1957–69. RH MSS. Afr. s. 1799 (21).

Lowe-Jellicoe, Dr. Greta (née Lowe): Medical Officer, Princess Christian Hospital, Freetown, Sierra Leone, 1926; Wesleyan Mission Hospital, Ilesha, Nigeria, 1927–8; Lady Medical Officer, Colonial Medical Service, Nigeria, 1928–35. RH MSS. Afr. s. 1872 (97).

Lugard, Lord: Papers. Inaugural dinner of the Protectorate, list of guests, 1 January 1900. RH MSS. s. 65.

MacDermot, Patricia: Woman Assistant Secretary, Government of Northern Nigeria, Kaduna, 1956–61. RH MSS. Afr. s. 1799 (22).

MacDonald, Anne, MBE, 'A Police Officer's wife in Nigeria, 1933–58', RH MSS. Afr. s. 1784 (12)[a].

——, 'A Brief History of the Women's Corona Society' (1968)[b].

MacGregor, Masry: see Prince, Mrs Masry.

Mackay, Mercedes: wife of Geologist with the Mines Department, Tanganyika and Nigeria. Interview, BBC. IWM Acc. No. 004723/04.

Maddocks, Lady, Elnor (née Russell): 'Diary of wife of Sir Kenneth Maddocks', RH MSS. Afr. s. 1663.

Moore, Lady, Daphne, Diaries and letters home as wife of the colonial administrator Sir Henry Monck-Mason Moore: Bermuda, 1922; Nigeria, 1924–8; Kenya, 1929–34, 1940–3; Sierra Leone, 1934–5; South Africa, 1943, 1947. RH MSS. Brit. Emp. s. 466.

Moresby-White, Betty: Resident's wife in Western and Eastern Nigeria. Interview, BBC. IWM Acc. No. 004727/01.

Morris, Mair (née Evans): Woman Assistant Secretary, The Gambia, 1944–5. Interview with H. Callaway, May 1983. RH MSS. Afr. s. 1799 (26).

Overseas Nursing Association: Papers, 1896–1966. 119 bound volumes, 32 boxes. RH MSS. Brit. Emp. s. 400.

Paterson, Elizabeth, MBE: Nursing Sister, Eastern and Western Nigeria, 1951–62; Principal Matron, Kaduna, then Maiduguri, 1962–70; contract work after formal retirement in Maiduguri and Bauchi, 1970–7. RH MSS. Afr. s. 1872 (120).

Pears, Marjorie: Adviser on Secretarial Education to the Government, Eastern Nigeria, 1958–62. RH MSS. Afr. s. 1755 (79*).

Pickering, Susan (née Stockford): Woman Education Officer, Women's Training Centre, Kabba, 1955–7. RH MSS. Afr. s. 1755 (69).

Pine-Coffin, Jane (formerly Sandiford, née Moss): Woman Education Officer, Bamenda, Cameroons, 1947–51. RH MSS. Afr. s. 1755 (79*).

Player, Kathleen: Woman Education Officer, King's College, Lagos, 1945–9; Cameroons, 1949–52; Principal, Queen Elizabeth School, Ilorin, 1954–62. RH MSS. Afr. s. 1755 (70).

Prince, Christine: Woman Assistant Secretary, Federal Government of Nigeria, Lagos, 1953–7. RH MSS. Afr. s. 1799 (30).

Prince, Masry (née MacGregor): Woman Education Officer, Provincial Girls' School, Kontagora, 1954–6. RH MSS. Afr. s. 1755 (71).

Purdy, Elizabeth (née Sharp): Woman Assistant Secretary, Government of Northern Nigeria, Kaduna, 1955–6. RH MSS. Afr. s. 1799 (31)[a].

——, Wife of Resident in Yola, Jos and Sokoto. Interview with H. Callaway, July 1983. RH MSS. Afr. s. 1854[b].

Robinson, Kenneth, Unpublished Callander Lectures, Aberdeen University, 1979.

Russell, Joan (née Foster): Acting Principal, Queen's College, Lagos, 1946; Provincial Education Officer, Bida, 1946–8; Acting Principal, Girls' Training Centre, Sokoto, 1948–9; Provincial Woman Education Officer, Bida, Katsina, Bauchi, 1950–4; Inspector of Education, 1955–6; Chief Woman Education Officer, Northern Nigeria, 1956–9. RH MSS. Afr. s. 1755 (73).

Schofield, Barbara, OBE, MBE: Nursing Sister, later Senior Nursing Sister, Nigeria, 1936–50; Matron, Tanganyika, 1950–1; RH MSS. Afr. s. 1872 (133).

Sharland, Jane-Ann (née Stockford): Woman Education Officer, Provincial Girls School, Niger Province, 1953–6; Women's Training Centre, Kano, 1956; Art and English teacher, St. Louis Convent, Kano, 1960–72. RH MSS. Afr. s. 1755 (75).

Sharwood Smith, Lady, Winifred Joan, 'Uwargida', unpublished autobiography as wife of DO and Governor, Northern Nigeria, 1939–57. RH MSS. Afr. r. 108.

Spence, Annette: Principal, Ovim Girls' School, 1940–5; Education Officer, Cameroons 1945–7; Acting Chief Woman Education Officer, Eastern Nigeria, 1947–8; Adult Education Officer 1947–8. RH MSS. Afr s. 1755 (79*).

Stephenson, G. L., 'Nigerian and Other Days, 1936–72', RH MSS. Afr. s. 1833.

Swaisland, Cecillie: Social Welfare Officer, Cameroons, 1949–50; wife of administrative officer, Eastern Nigeria, 1949–63. Interview with H. Callaway, August 1983. RH MSS. Afr. s. 1855.

Swire, Pamela (née Godley): Woman Education Officer, Girls' Training Centre, Sokoto, 1950; Girls' Training Centre, Birnin Kebbi, 1950–2. RH MSS. Afr. s. 1755 (77).

Tattersall, Eunice: Deputy Principal, School of Nursing, UCH, Ibadan, 1952–62; Principal, School of Nursing, Lagos University, 1962–8; Director of Nursing Education, ABU School of Nursing, Zaria, 1968–79. RH MSS. Afr. s. 1872 (140).

Treitel, Phyllis (née Cook): Woman Assistant Secretary, Federal Government of Nigeria, Lagos, 1953–4; Assistant District Officer, Buea, Cameroons, 1954. RH MSS. Afr. s. 1799 (35).

Trevor, Jean: Woman Education Officer, Women's Training Centre, Sokoto, 1953–5. Papers relating to study of 'Education of Moslem Hausa Women of Sokoto, Northwestern Nigeria'. RH MSS. Afr. s. 1755 (79).

Walters, Eleanor 'Pat': Rural Education Officer, Moor Plantation, 1953–8; Senior Inspector, W. Nigeria, 1958–60; Principal, Rural Education College, Akure, 1960–4. RH MSS. Afr. s. 1755 (79*).

Wand-Tetley, Felicia (née Bloxham): Woman Assistant Secretary, Government of Northern Nigeria, Kaduna, 1957–63. RH MSS. Afr. s. 1799 (38).

Watt, Margaret J.: Typed extracts from letters from Nigeria to her father, 1951–60. RH MSS. Afr. 1413.

Weatherhead, Sir Arthur Trenham, 'But always as friends' (a personal account of administration in Northern Nigeria, 1927–60). RH MSS. Afr. s. 232.

Whitfield, Jill (née Forrest): Woman Assistant Secretary, Government of Northern Nigeria, Kaduna, 1955–7. RH MSS. Afr. s. 1799 (42).

Wilkinson, Clare: Woman Education Officer, Lagos, 1952–7; Assistant Federal Adviser on Teacher Training, 1957–61. RH MSS. Afr. s. 1755 (79*).

Wren, Anne (née Maltman): Woman Assistant Secretary, Government of Northern Nigeria, Kaduna, 1957–8. RH MSS. Afr. s. 1799 (45).

Wrench, Sheelagh: Woman Assistant Secretary, Government of Northern Nigeria, Kaduna, 1953–5. RH MSS. Afr. s. 1799 (46).

PUBLISHED WORKS

Abel-Smith, B. (1975), *A History of the Nursing Profession* (London: Heinemann, 1st edn, 1960).

Adam, R. (1975), *Woman's Place 1910–1975* (London: Chatto & Windus).

Ajayi, J. F. A. (1965), *Christian Missions in Nigeria 1841–1891. The Making of an Educated Elite* (London: Longman).

Alaya, F. (1977), 'Victorian Science and the "Genius" of Woman', *Journal of the History of Ideas*, 38, pp. 162–280.

Alexander, J. (1977), *Whom the Gods Love* (London: Heinemann).

—— (1983), *Voices and Echoes. Tales from Colonial Women* (London: Quartet).

Allen, C. (1977), *Raj: a Scrapbook of British India 1877–1947* (London: André Deutsch).

—— (1979), *Tales from the Dark Continent* (London: André Deutsch).

Annan, N. G. (1951), *Leslie Stephen. His Thought and Character in Relation to his Time* (London: MacGibbon & Kee).

Ardener, E. (1972), 'Belief and the Problem of Women', in La Fontaine (ed.), *The Interpretation of Ritual* (London: Tavistock). Reprinted in S. Ardener (ed.), *Perceiving Women*, 1975.

—— (1975), 'The "Problem" Revisited', in S. Ardener (ed.), *Perceiving Women* (London: Malaby).

—— (1978), 'Some Outstanding Problems in the Analysis of Events', in E. Schwimmer (ed.), *The Yearbook of Symbolic Anthropology* (London: C. Hurst).

Ardener, S. (ed.) (1975), *Perceiving Women* (London: Malaby).

—— (1984), 'Incorporation and Exclusion: Oxford Academics' Wives', in H. Callan and S. Ardener (eds), *The Incorporated Wife* (Beckenham: Croom Helm).

Awe, B. (1977), 'The Iyalode in the Traditional Yoruba Political System', in A. Schlegel (ed.), *Sexual Stratification* (New York: Columbia University Press).

Ayandele, E. A. (1966), *The Missionary Impact on Modern Nigeria, 1842–1914* (London: Longman).

Ballhatchet, K. (1980), *Race, Sex and Class under the Raj* (London: Weidenfeld & Nicolson).

Banton, M. (1971), 'Urbanization and the Colour Line in Africa', in V. Turner (ed.), *African Society and Colonial Rule* (Cambridge University Press).

Basch, F. (1974), *Relative Creatures. Victorian Women in Society and the Novel 1837–67* (London: Allen Lane).

Bateson, G. (1958), *Naven* (Palo Alto, California: Stanford University Press; 1st edition, 1936).

Beidelman, T. O. (1982), *Colonial Evangelism* (Bloomington: Indiana University Press).

Bell, E. M. (1947), *Flora Shaw (Lady Lugard DBE)* (London: Constable).

Bell, H. (1946), *Glimpses of a Governor's Life* (London: Sampson Low, Marston).

Beresford-Stooke, G. (1959), Foreword to L. Fitz-Henry, *African Dust* (London: Macmillan).

Berry, E. (1941), *Mad Dogs and Englishmen* (London: Michael Joseph).

Birkett, D. (1983), Review of *Voices and Echoes* by Joan Alexander, Women's Research and Resources Centre *Newsletter*, no. 6.

Blackburne, K. (1976), *Lasting Legacy. A Story of British Colonialism* (London: Johnson).

Bolt, C. (1971), *Victorian Attitudes to Race* (London: Routledge & Kegan Paul).

Boserup, E. (1970), *Woman's Role in Economic Development* (London: George Allen & Unwin).

Bourdieu, P. (1977), *Outline of a Theory of Practice* (Cambridge University Press; 1st edn in French, 1972).

Bowen, E. S. (1954), *Return to Laughter* (London: Victor Gollancz).

Bradley, E. (1950), *Dearest Priscilla. Letters to the Wife of a Colonial Civil Servant* (London: Max Parrish).

Bradley, K. (1966), *Once a District Officer* (London: Macmillan).

Bridges, A. F. B. (1980), 'In the Service of Nigeria', *The Nigerian Field*. Monograph no. 2 (supplement to vol. 45).

Brook, I. (Brinkworth) (1966), *The One-Eyed Man is King* (London: Cassell).

Brownfoot, J. N. (1984), 'Memsahibs in Colonial Malaya: A Study of European Wives in a British Colony and Protectorate, 1900–40', in H. Callan and S. Ardener (eds), *The Incorporated Wife* (Beckenham: Croom Helm).

Bryant, K. J. (1959), 'Thirty Years On', in *Advancing in Good Order. Northern Nigeria Attains Self-Government* (Kaduna: Government Press).

Bryne, E. M. (1978), *Women and Education* (London: Tavistock).

Burns, Sir A. (1949), *Colonial Civil Servant* (London: George Allen & Unwin).

Callan, H. (1975), 'The Premiss of Dedication: Notes towards an Ethnography of Diplomats' Wives', in S. Ardener (ed.), *Perceiving Women* (London: Malaby).

—— (1984), 'Introduction', in H. Callan and S. Ardener (eds), *The Incorporated Wife* (Beckenham: Croom Helm).

Callan, H. and S. Ardener (eds) (1984), *The Incorporated Wife* (Beckenham, Croom Helm).

Cary, J. (1933), *An American Visitor* (London: Michael Joseph).

—— (1939), *Mister Johnson* (London: Michael Joseph).

Chapman, M. (1978), *The Gaelic Vision in Scottish Culture* (London: Croom Helm).

Cohn, B. S. (1983), 'Representing Authority in Victorian India', in E. Hobsbawm and T. Ranger (eds), *The Invention of Tradition* (Cambridge University Press).

Coleman, J. S. (1958), *Nigeria. Background to Nationalism* (Berkeley and Los Angeles: University of California Press).

Coomassie, A. (1957), 'Adult Education Campaign in The Northern Region of Nigeria', *Fundamental and Adult Education UNESCO* 9(1), pp. 39–45.

Crocker, W. R. (1936), *Nigeria: a Critique of British Colonial Administration* (London: George Allen & Unwin).

Crowder, M. (1978), *The Story of Nigeria* (London: Faber & Faber; 1st edn, 1962).

—— (1983), Introduction to S. Leith-Ross, *Stepping Stones* (London and Boston: Peter Owen).

Curzon, G. (1907), *Frontiers* (Oxford University Press).

Davidoff, L. (1973), *The Best Circles. Society, Etiquette and the Season* (London: Croom Helm).

Davies, C. (ed.) (1980), *Rewriting Nursing History* (London: Croom Helm).

De Beauvoir, S. (1972), *The Second Sex* (Harmondsworth: Penguin; 1st edn in French, 1949).

Delamont, S. and L. Duffin (1978), *The Nineteenth-Century Woman* (London: Croom Helm).

Douglas, M. (1966), *Purity and Danger* (London: Routledge & Kegan Paul).

—— (ed.) (1973), *Rules and Meanings* (Harmondsworth: Penguin).

Dumont, L. (1980), *Homo Hierarchicus. The Caste System and its Implications* (Chicago and London: The University of Chicago Press; 1st edn in French, 1966).

Dyhouse, C. (1981),*Girls Growing Up in Late Victorian and Edwardian England* (London, Boston and Henley: Routledge & Kegan Paul).

Ekwensi, C. (1954), *People of the City* (London: Heinemann).

Etienne, M. and E. Leacock (eds) (1980), *Women and Colonization, Anthropological Perspectives* (New York: J. F. Bergin).

Fatayi-Williams, A. (1983), *Faces, Cases & Places* (London: Butterworths).

Finch, J. (1983), *Married to the Job. Wives' Incorporation in Men's Work* (London: George Allen & Unwin).

Fitz-Henry, L. (1959), *African Dust* (London: Macmillan).

Flint, J. E. (1960), *Sir George Goldie and the Making of Nigeria* (London, Ibadan, Accra: Oxford University Press).

—— (1963), 'Mary Kingsley, a Reassessment', *Journal of African History* 4(1), pp. 95–104.

—— (1983), 'Scandal at the Bristol Hotel: Some Thoughts on Racial Discrimination in Britain and West Africa and Its Relationship to the Planning of Decolonisation, 1939–47', *The Journal of Imperial and Commonwealth History*, 12(1), pp. 74–93.

Forster, E. M. (1979), *A Passage to India* (Harmondsworth: Penguin Books; 1st edn, 1924).

Friedan, B. (1963), *The Feminine Mystique* (New York: W. W. Norton).

Furse, R. (1962), *Aucuparius. Recollections of a Recruiting Officer* (London: Oxford University Press).

Gailey, H. A. (1982), *Clifford: Imperial Proconsul* (London: Rex Collings).

Gamarnikov, E. (1978), 'Sexual Division of Labour: the Case of Nursing', in A. Kuhn and A. Wolpe (eds), *Feminism and Materialism* (London: Routledge & Kegan Paul).

Gann, L. H. and P. Duignan (1978), *The Rulers of British Africa, 1870–1914* (London: Croom Helm).

Gann, L. H. and P. Duignan (eds) (1978), *African Proconsuls, European Governors in Africa* (New York: The Free Press; London: Collier Macmillan).

Gartrell, B. (1984), 'Colonial Wives: Villains or Victims?', in H. Callan and S. Ardener (eds), *The Incorporated Wife* (Beckenham: Croom Helm).

Gilligan, C. (1982), *In a Different Voice* (Cambridge, Mass. and London: Harvard University Press).

Gilmour, R. (1981), *The Idea of the Gentleman in the Victorian Novel* (London: George Allen & Unwin).

Girouard, M. (1981), *The Return to Camelot. Chivalry and the English Gentleman* (New Haven and London: Yale University Press).

Goffman, E. (1968), *Asylums* (Harmondsworth: Penguin; 1st edn, 1961).

Green, M. M. (1964), *Igbo Village Affairs* (London: Frank Cass; 1st edn, 1947).

Green, M. (1980), *Dreams of Adventure, Deeds of Empire* (London and Henley: Routledge & Kegan Paul).

Gwynn, S. (1932), *The Life of Mary Kingsley* (London: Macmillan).

Harrison, B. (1978), *Separate Spheres: The Opposition to Women's Suffrage in Britain* (London: Croom Helm).

Hartman, M. W. and L. Banner (eds) (1974), *Clio's Consciousness Raised* (New York: Harper & Row).

Hastings, A. C. G. (1925), *Nigerian Days* (London: John Lane, The Bodley Head).

——— (1928), *Gone Native* (London and New York: G. P. Putnam's Sons).

Hastrup, K. (1982), 'Establishing an Ethnicity: The emergence of "Icelanders" in the Early Middle Ages', in D. Parkin (ed.), *Semantic Anthropology* (London, New York: Academic Press).

Henriques, F. (1974), *Children of Caliban. Miscegenation* (London: Secker & Warburg).

Hertz, R. (1973), 'The Pre-eminence of the Right Hand: A Study in Religious Polarity', in Needham (ed.), *Right and Left: Essays on Dual Symbolic Classification* (Chicago and London: University of Chicago Press; first published in French, 1909).

Heussler, R. (1961), 'Why Study the Colonial Service?', *Corona*, 13(5), pp. 165–8.

——— (1963), *Yesterday's Rulers. The Making of the British Colonial Service* (London: Oxford University Press).

——— (1968), *The British in Northern Nigeria* (London: Oxford University Press).

Hilliard, F. H. (1957), *A Short History of Education in British West Africa* (London: Thomas Nelson & Sons).

Hobsbawm, E. (1975), *The Age of Capital* (London: Weidenfeld & Nicolson).

Hobsbawm, E. and T. Ranger (eds) (1983), *The Invention of Tradition* (Cambridge University Press).

Hodgkin, T. (1975), *Nigerian Perspectives. An Historical Anthology* (London: Oxford University Press; 1st edn, 1960).

Hollis, R. (1981), *A Scorpion for Tea or to Attempt the Impossible* (Ilfracombe, Devon: Arthur H. Stockwell).

Howard, M. (1981), 'Empire, Race and War in pre-1914 Britain', in H. Lloyd-Jones, V. Pearl and B. Worden (eds), *History and Imagination. Essays in Honour of H. R. Trevor-Roper* (London: Duckworth).

Howarth, P. (1973), *Play Up and Play the Game. The Heroes of Popular Fiction* (London: Eyre Methuen).

Huxley, E. (1948), *The Walled City* (London: Chatto & Windus).

Hyam, R. (1986), 'Empire and Sexual Opportunity', *The Journal of Imperial and Commonwealth History*, 1(2), pp. 34–90.

Ifeka-Moller, C. (1975), 'Female Militancy and Colonial Revolt: The Women's War of 1929, Eastern Nigeria', in S. Ardener (ed.), *Perceiving Women* (London: Malaby).

Inglis, A. (1974), *The White Women's Protection Ordinance. Sexual Anxiety and Politics in Papua* (London: Sussex University Press).

Jacobus, M. (1979), 'The Difference of View', in M. Jacobus (ed.), *Women Writing and Writing about Women* (London: Croom Helm).

Jeffries, C. (1938), *The Colonial Empire and its Civil Service* (Cambridge University Press).

—— (1949), *Partners for Progress: The Men and Women of the Colonial Service* (London: George G. Harrap).

Jones, G. I. (1974), 'Social Anthropology in Nigeria during the Colonial Period', *Africa*, 44(3), pp. 280–9.

Joyce, R. B. (1971), *Sir William MacGregor* (Melbourne: Oxford University Press).

Kanter, R. M. (1977), *Men and Women of the Corporation* (New York: Basic Books).

King, A. D. (1976), *Colonial Urban Development* (London, Henley and Boston: Routledge & Kegan Paul).

Kirk-Greene, A. H. M. (1955), 'Those were the Days', *Corona*, 7(3), pp. 108–11.

—— (1956), 'Who Coined the Name "Nigeria"?', *West Africa*, 22 December 1956, p. 1035.

—— (1959), 'Breath-taking Durbars', in *Advancing in Good Order. Northern Nigeria Attains Self-Government* (Kaduna: Government Press).

—— (1965), *The Principles of Native Administration in Nigeria: Selected Documents, 1900–1947* (London: Oxford University Press).

—— (1977), 'Sanders of the River', *New Society*, 42 (788), pp. 308–9.

—— (1978), 'On Governorship and Governors in British Africa', in L. H. Gann and P. Duignan (eds), *The Rulers of British Africa, 1870–1914* (London: Croom Helm).

—— (1980), 'The Thin White Line: The Size of the British Civil Service in Africa', *African Affairs*, 79(314), pp. 25–44.

—— (1982), 'Margery Perham and Colonial Administration: A Direct Influence on Indirect Rule', in F. Madden and D. K. Fieldhouse (eds), *Oxford and the Idea of Commonwealth. Essays presented to Sir Edgar Williams* (London and Canberra: Croom Helm).

—— (1983), 'Introduction', to M. Perham, *West African Passage* (London and Boston: Croom Helm).

—— (1985), 'Imperial Administration and the Athletic Imperative: The Case of the District Officer in Africa', in S. A. Mangan and W. Baker (eds), *Sports in Africa* (New York: Holmes & Meier).

Kirkwood, D. (1984a), 'The Suitable Wife: Preparation for Marriage in London and Rhodesia/Zimbabwe', in H. Callan and S. Ardener (eds), *The Incorporated Wife* (Beckenham: Croom Helm).

Kirkwood, D. (1984b), 'Settler Wives in Southern Rhodesia', in H. Callan and S. Ardener (eds), *The Incorporated Wife* (Beckenham: Croom Helm).

Kisch, M. S. (1910), *Letters and Sketches from Northern Nigeria* (London: Chatto & Windus).

Knowles, E. (1954), 'Jobs for the Girls', *Corona*, 6(9), pp. 336–8.

Kuklick, H. (1979), *The Imperial Bureaucrat: The Colonial Administrative Service in the Gold Coast, 1920–1939* (Stanford, California: Hoover Institution Press).

Langa Langa (The Hon. H. B. Hermon-Hodge) (1922), *Up Against It in Nigeria* (London: George Allen & Unwin).

Larymore, C. (1911), *A Resident's Wife in Nigeria* (London: George Routledge; 1st edn, 1908).

Laver, J. (1969), *Modesty in Dress. An Inquiry into the Fundamentals of Fashion* (London: Heinemann).

Leith-Ross, S. (1944), *African Conversation Piece* (London, New York, Melbourne: Hutchinson).

—— (1965), *African Woman. A Study of the Ibo of Nigeria* (London: Faber & Faber; 1st edn, 1939).

—— (1983), *Stepping-Stones. Memoirs of Colonial Nigeria, 1907–1960*, edited by M. Crowder (London and Boston: Peter Owen).

Leith-Ross, S. and G. Ruxton (1908), *Practical West African Cookery* (Zungeru: Government Press).

Letwin, S. (1982), *The Gentleman in Trollope: Individuality and Moral Conduct* (London: Macmillan).

Lévi-Strauss, C. (1968), *Structural Anthropology* (London: Allen Lane, The Penguin Press; 1st published in French, 1958).

Lorimer, D. A. (1978), *Colour, Class and the Victorians* (Leicester: Leicester University Press).

Lugard, Sir F. D. (1922), *The Dual Mandate in British Tropical Africa* (Edinburgh and London: William Blackwood & Sons).

—— (1970), *Political Memoranda* (London: Frank Cass; previous editions, 1906, 1919).

Lukes, S. (1977), *Essays in Social Theory* (London: Macmillan).

MacDonald, A. (1959), 'Centre for Friendship', *Corona*, 11(9), pp. 349–50.

Mackenzie, N. and J. Mackenzie (eds) (1982), *Glitter Around and Darkness Within The Diary of Beatrice Webb. Volume One 1873–1892* (London: Virago).

MacLeod, O. (1971), *Chiefs and Cities of Central Africa* (Freeport, New York: Books for Libraries Press; 1st edn, 1912).

Maggs, C. (1980), 'Nurse Recruitment to Four Provincial Hospitals, 1881–1921', in C. Davies (ed.), *Rewriting Nursing History* (London: Croom Helm).

Mahood, M. M. (1964), *Joyce Cary's Africa* (London: Methuen).

Mangan, J. A. (1981), *Athleticism in the Victorian and Edwardian Public School* (Cambridge University Press).

Marcus, S. (1966), *The Other Victorians. A Study of Sexuality and Pornography in Mid-19th Century England* (London: Weidenfeld & Nicolson).

Mason, P. (1970), *Patterns of Dominance* (London: Oxford University Press).

—— (1982), *The English Gentleman* (London: André Deutsch).

Mba, N. E. (1982), *Nigerian Women Mobilized* (Berkeley: University of California Press).

Mill, J. S. (1970), 'The Subjection of Women', in J. S. Mill and H. T. Mill, *Essays on Sex Equality*, ed. Rossi (Chicago and London: The University of Chicago Press; 1st edn, 1869).

Miller, J. B. (1976), *Toward a New Psychology of Women* (Boston: Beacon Press).

Millett, K. (1973), 'The Debate over Women: Ruskin vs. Mill', in M. Vicinus (ed.) *Suffer and Be Still* (Bloomington and London: Indiana University Press).

Morris, J. (1968), *Pax Britannica* (London: Faber & Faber).

Muffett, D. J. M. (1978), *Empire Builder Extraordinary Sir George Goldie* (Douglas, Isle of Man: Shearwater Press).

Nduka, O. (1964), *Western Education and the Nigerian Cultural Background* (Ibadan: Oxford University Press).

Newton, J. L., M. P. Ryan and J. R. Walkowitz (eds) (1983), *Sex and Class in Women's History* (London, Boston, Melbourne and Henley: Routledge & Kegan Paul).

Nicolson, I. F. (1969), *The Administration of Nigeria 1900–1960* (Oxford University Press).

Nicolson, N. (1977), *Mary Curzon* (London: Weidenfeld & Nicolson).

Nigerian Government (1937), *Medical and Health Report for Nigeria* (Lagos: Government Printer).

—— (1946), *A Ten-Year Plan for Development and Welfare for Nigeria* (Lagos: Government Printer).

Niven, Sir R. (1982), *Nigerian Kaleidoscope* (London: C. Hurst).

Oake, M. E. (1933), *No Place for a White Woman* (London: Lovat Dickson).

Oakley, A. (1972), *Sex, Gender and Society* (London: Temple Smith).

Oakley, R. (1938), *Treks and Palavers* (London: Seeley, Service).

Okely, J. (1978), 'Privileged, Schooled and Finished: Boarding Education for Girls', in S. Ardener (ed.), *Defining Females* (London: Croom Helm).

Okonjo, K. (1976), 'The Dual-Sex Political System in Operation: Igbo Women and Community Politics in Midwestern Nigeria', in N. J. Hafkin and E. G. Bay (eds), *Women in Africa* (Stanford, California: Stanford University Press).

Oliver, C. (1982), *Western Women in Colonial Africa* (Westport, Connecticut and London: Greenwood Press).

Ortner, S. B. and H. Whitehead (eds) (1981), *Sexual Meanings. The Cultural Construction of Gender and Sexuality* (Cambridge University Press).

Orwell, G. (1967), *Burmese Days* (Harmondsworth: Penguin; 1st edn, 1934).

Papanek, H. (1973), 'Men, women and work: reflections on the two-person career', *American Journal of Sociology*, 78(4), pp. 852–72.

—— (1979), 'Family Status Production: The "Work" and "Non-Work" of Women', *Signs*, 4(4), pp. 775–81.

Parkin, D. (ed.) (1982), *Semantic Anthropology* (London, New York: Academic Press).

Parkinson, Sir C. (1947), *The Colonial Office from Within* (London: Faber & Faber).

Pearce, R. D. (1983), 'Violet Bourdillon: Colonial Governor's Wife', *African Affairs*, 82(327), pp. 267–77.

Pembleton, E. and J. H. Boyes (1948), *Live on the Country* (Lagos: CMS Bookshop; 1st edn, 1940).

Perham, M. (1937), *Native Administration in Nigeria* (Oxford: Oxford University Press).

—— (1956), *Lugard. The Years of Adventure 1858–1898* (London: Collins).

Perham, M. (1960), *Lugard. The Years of Authority 1898–1945* (London: Collins).
—— (1961), *The Colonial Reckoning* (London: Collins).
—— (1974), Foreword to Sir J. Robertson, *Transition in Africa* (London: C. Hurst).
—— (1983), *West African Passage*, edited by A. H. M. Kirk-Greene (London and Boston: Peter Owen).
Pocock, G. A. (1964), 'The History of Political Thought: A Methodological Enquiry', in P. Laslett and W. C. Runciman (eds), *Philosophy, Politics and Society. Second Series* (Oxford: Blackwell).
Purvis, J. (1981), 'Towards a History of Women's Education in Nineteenth Century Britain: a Sociological Analysis', *Westminster Studies in Education*, 4, pp. 45–79.
Quigley, E. (1982), *The Heirs of Tom Brown: The English School Story* (London: Chatto).
Ranger, T. (1980), 'Making Northern Rhodesia Imperial: Variations on a Royal Theme, 1924–1938', *African Affairs*, 79(316), pp. 349–73.
Ricoeur, P. (1965), *History and Truth* (Evanston: Northwestern University Press; 1st edn in French, 1955).
Robertson, Sir J. (1974), *Transition in Africa. From Direct Rule to Independence* (London: C. Hurst).
Robinson, K. (1965), *The Dilemma of Trusteeship* (London: Oxford University Press).
Rogers, C. A. (1959), 'A Study of Race Attitudes in Nigeria', *Rhodes–Livingstone Institute Journal*, 26, pp. 51–64.
Rooney, D. (1982), *Sir Charles Arden-Clarke* (London: Rex Collins).
Rose, K. (1969), *Superior Person. A Portrait of Curzon and his Circle in Late Victorian England* (London: Weidenfeld & Nicolson).
Rosenberg, R. (1975–6), 'In Search of Woman's Nature, 1850–1920', *Feminist Studies*, 3, pp. 141–54.
—— (1982), *Beyond Separate Spheres. Intellectual Roots of Modern Feminism* (New Haven and London: Yale University Press).
Rowling, N. (1982), *Nigerian Memories* (Braunton, Devon: Merlin Books).
Ruskin, J. (1970), *Sesame and Lilies* (London, Melbourne and Toronto: Dent; New York: Dutton; 1st edn, 1865).
Russell, E. (1978), *Bush Life in Nigeria* (Privately published).
Sahlins, M. (1981), *Historical Metaphors and Mythical Realities* (Ann Arbor: The University of Michigan Press).
Sandison, A. (1967), *The Wheel of Empire* (London: Macmillan; New York: St. Martin's Press).
Schram, R. (1971), *A History of the Nigerian Health Service* (Ibadan: Ibadan University Press).
Sciama, L. (1984), 'Ambivalence and Dedication: Academic Wives in Cambridge University, 1870–1970', in H. Callan and S. Ardener (eds), *The Incorporated Wife* (Beckenham: Croom Helm).
Shadbolt, K. (1959), 'Wives in Perspective', *Corona*, 11(8), p. 305.
Sharwood Smith, Sir B. (1969), *'But Always as Friends'. Northern Nigeria and the Cameroons, 1921–1957* (London: George Allen & Unwin).
Shaw, F. L. (Lady Lugard) (1905), *A Tropical Dependency* (London: James Nisbet).

Smith, J. (1968), *Colonial Cadet in Nigeria* (Durham, N. C.: Duke University Press).

Smith, M. F. (1954), *Baba of Karo. A Woman of the Muslim Hausa* (London: Faber & Faber).

Stanley, H. M. (1890), *In Darkest Africa* (London: Sampson Low, Marston, Searle & Rivington).

Stanley, R. (1975), *King George's Keys* (London: Johnson).

Stepan, N. (1982), *The Idea of Race in Science* (London: Macmillan).

Stocking, G. W. Jr. (1982), *Race, Culture, and Evolution* (Chicago and London: University of Chicago Press; 1st edn, 1968).

Talbot, D. Amaury (1968), *Woman's Mysteries of a Primitive People. The Ibibios of Southern Nigeria* (London: Frank Cass; 1st edn, 1915).

Temple, O. (1922), *Notes on the Tribes, Provinces, Emirates and States of the Northern Provinces of Nigeria*, edited by C. L. Temple (Lagos: CMS Bookshop; 1st edn, 1919).

Thorburn, J. W. A. (1958), 'Some Memories of Western Nigeria in the Twenties and Thirties', *The Nigerian Field*, 23(2), pp. 85–8.

Thorp, E. (1956), *Ladder of Bones* (London: Jonathan Cape).

Tremlett, Mrs H. (1915), *With the Tin Gods* (London: John Lane, The Bodley Head).

Trevor, J. (1975), 'Western Education and Muslim Fulani/Hausa Women in Sokoto', in G. Brown and M. Hiskett (eds), *Conflict and Harmony in Education in Tropical Africa* (London: George Allen & Unwin).

Trollope, J. (1983), *Britannia's Daughters. Women of the British Empire* (London: Hutchison).

Trudgill, E. (1976), *Madonnas and Magdalenes: The Origin and Development of Victorian Sexual Attitudes* (London: Heinemann).

Udell, F. (1949), 'Queen Elizabeth's Colonial Nursing Service', *Corona*, 1(4), pp. 23–4.

Van Allen, J. (1972), ' "Sitting on a Man": Colonialism and the Lost Political Institutions of Igbo Women', *Canadian Journal of African Studies*, 6(2), pp. 165–82.

Vicinus, M. (ed.) (1973), *Suffer and Be Still. Women in the Victorian Age* (Bloomington and London: Indiana University Press).

—— (ed.) (1977), *A Widening Sphere. Changing Roles of Victorian Women* (Bloomington and London: Indiana University Press).

—— (1985), *Independent Women. Work and Community for Single Women, 1850–1920* (London: Virago).

Vischer, I. (1917), *Croquis et Souvenirs de la Nigérie du Nord* (Paris, Neuchatel: Attinger Frères).

White, S. (1966), *Dan Bana. The Memoirs of a Nigerian Official* (London: Cassell).

Wilkinson, R. H. (1964), *The Prefects. British Leadership and the Public School Tradition* (London: Oxford University Press).

—— (1970), 'The Gentleman Ideal and the Maintenance of a Political Elite', in P. W. Musgrave, *Sociology, History and Education* (London: Methuen).

Woolf, V. (1966), *Collected Essays. Volume One* (London: The Hogarth Press).

Wurgaft, L. (1983), *The Imperial Imagination. Magic and Myth in Kipling's India* (Middletown, Connecticut: Wesleyan University Press).

Young, M. (1984), 'Police Wives: A Reflection of Police Concepts of Order and Control', in H. Callan and S. Ardener (eds), *The Incorporated Wife* (Beckenham: Croom Helm).

Index

Pratt, Mrs E., 107
precedence, 17, 60, 69, 70, 71, 233
Preliminary Training School (student nurses), 101
prestige, 56, 74
  male prestige structures, 8, 144
'the primitives', 128
Prince, Christine, 147, 157, 161
Prince, Masry (*see* Masry MacGregor)
Privy Council, Nigeria, 147, 153
professional women in Colonial Service, 10, 84, 184, 206, 242
  statistics from 1922–43, 14
  as 'marked' category, 14
  relation with colonial wives, 47–8
  difficulties of, 46–8 (*see also* nurses, women administrative officers, women education officers)
'protection' of women, 40, 51, 234, 235, 237
protocol, 27, 70, 71, 75, 132, 203
public schools, 40, 41, 47
Punch, 71
purdah, 89, 95, 98, 217
  Muslim women in, 114, 137, 158
  school girls kept in, 122
  situation of European teachers compared, 135
Purdy, Elizabeth, 79, 150, 156, 157, 196, 200, 216
Purvis, Dorothy, 92–4

Queen Elizabeth School, Ilorin, 117, 124, 126
  Silver Jubilee celebration, 138
Queen Elizabeth's Overseas Nursing Service, 84, 101
Queen's College
  Ede, 126
  Lagos, 112, 117, 123, 126–7
Queen's Proclamation (1900), 58

rabies, 197
race, racial
  assumed superiority, 65
  class and gender, 30–2
  disloyalty, 50
  division within Colonial Medical Service, 99
  exclusiveness, 44, 238, 239
  women's multi-racial activities, 189, 218–19, 239
  multi-racial schools, 201
  race relations, 24, 27

women as cause of deteriorating relations, 3, 24–5, 234–40 (*see also* 'Bristol Hotel Incident')
Ranger, Terence, 55, 56, 57
Rathbone, Eleanor, MP, 140
Ransome-Kuti, Mrs Funmilayo, 53
Red Cross, 25, 126, 132, 215, 217
'relative creatures', 7, 11, 26
representations of colonial women, 26–9
  as worst side of ruling group, 3
  nameless figures in men's memoirs, 22–6
  negative images in fiction, 26–7
Resident's wife
  negative assessments of, 25
  perks of, 79
  power accorded, 223
A Resident's Wife in Nigeria, 166
rest houses, 95, 181–2, 209, 236
Richards, Dr. Audrey, 139
Richards, Sir Arthur (*see* Milverton, Lord)
Richards Constitution, 143, 214
rituals, official, 5, 10, 16, 55, 57, 59, 60, 68
Rhodes, Cecil, 34
Rhodes, Gloria, 158
Robertson, Lady Nancy, 75
Robinson, Kenneth, 141, 249
Roe, Dr. Daphne, 99
Roman Catholic Sacred Heart Hospital, Abeokuta, 95
Ross, Dr. Ronald, 248
Rowling, Noël, 5, 175, 184, 185, 190, 192, 194, 203, 205, 208, 209, 211
Royal Niger Company, 58, 245, 248
Royal Niger Constabulary, 58
Rural Education Centre, Ibadan, 130
Rural Education Colleges, Akure, Bauchi, 131–2
rural education officers, women, 130–2, 243
Rural Science College, Minna, 131
Ruskin, John, 32, 33, 34, 39, 44
Russell, Elnor (Lady Maddocks), 173, 176, 182, 192, 210, 217
Russell, Joan, 117–18, 137
Ruxton, Genevieve, 23, 250

sabon gari ('new town'), 158, 250
St. Saviour's School, Ikoyi, 188, 201
Sanders of the River, 230
Sandison, Alan, 230
'Sarah Gamp' stereotype, 86